Intersectional Listening

Gentrification and Black Sonic Life in Washington, DC

Allie Martin

Oxford University Press is a department of the University of Oxford.
It furthers the University's objective of excellence in research, scholarship,
and education by publishing worldwide. Oxford is a registered trade mark of
Oxford University Press in the UK and in certain other countries.

Published in the United States of America by Oxford University Press
198 Madison Avenue, New York, NY 10016, United States of America.

© Oxford University Press 2025

All rights reserved. No part of this publication may be reproduced, stored in a retrieval system, transmitted, used for text and data mining, or used for training artificial intelligence, in any form or by any means, without the prior permission in writing of Oxford University Press, or as expressly permitted by law, by license or under terms agreed with the appropriate reprographics rights organization. Inquiries concerning reproduction outside the scope of the above should be sent to the Rights Department, Oxford University Press, at the address above.

You must not circulate this work in any other form
and you must impose this same condition on any acquirer

CIP data is on file at the Library of Congress

ISBN 9780197671573 (pbk.)
ISBN 9780197671566 (hbk.)

DOI: 10.1093/9780197671603.001.0001

Paperback printed by Integrated Books International, United States of America
Hardback printed by Bridgeport National Bindery, Inc., United States of America

Intersectional Listening

Contents

Acknowledgments	*vii*
Introduction: Listening Intersectionally to the Chocolate City	1
1. "I'm On My Way to Atlanta"	32
Interlude: Notes on Soundwalking as Black Feminist Method	57
2. Smooth Jazz and Static	64
3. 7th and Florida	95
4. Life, Death, and Legacy in Go-Go Music	129
Interlude: Sounds of the City	168
5. "Plainly Audible"	176
Coda: Freedom Sounds in the Nation's Capital	197
Bibliography	*211*
Index	*221*

Acknowledgments

This book belongs to many, many people.

To the living:
First and foremost, I'm grateful to everyone who shared their stories with me. People invited me into their homes, their shows, their studios, and their lives, and helped me to hear the city in new, beautiful, and heartbreaking ways. I am appreciative of every interview, every passing conversation, and every invitation to hear more or listen further. This book would not exist without my conversation partners, many of whom I am happy to now call friends.

This work took place over the course of many years and was supported by many institutions. Thank you to the Ford Foundation, the Society for Ethnomusicology, Dartmouth College, the Hopkins Center for the Arts, the Society for American Music, the American Musicological Society, the Smithsonian Institution, the Bogliasco Foundation, and the Columbus Museum of Art.

My editors at Oxford University Press, Lauralee Yeary and Rachel Ruisard, have shepherded this project with curiosity, patience, and generosity. I have felt free to write and think in the ways that I want to and for that I'm grateful. Thank you to those who took the time to read the book and offer gracious and thoughtful feedback: Natalie Hopkinson, Samir Meghelli, Will Cheng, Kimberly Juanita Brown, and Deborah King.

Many people have read these ideas and helped me to think them through, but no one more than Dionte Harris, who has read every word of this book many times over. He has pushed, and pulled, and made me better. I am also grateful to Kate Mullen, my steadfast editor, for the froots and crunches along the way.

I am supported by friends and colleagues that make this work much lighter: Daniela, Richel, Nikko, Molly, Jenn, Sunaina, Naiima, Trica, Jorge, Cristina, Kennedi, Danielle, Shay, Chloe, Shontay, Ayanna, Asha, Patience, Shay, Kianna, Jane, Richard, Will, Ash, César, Jacque, Roopsi, and the entirety of Good Zoom. Thank you to my students Armond Dorsey, Lydia Davis, Shivangi Tandon, Arielle Isedenu, and everyone else who has come through the Black Sound Lab to make it a special and beautiful place.

Many people over the years have taken chances on me, and without them I would not be writing this book: Nancy Snider, Teri Lazar, Samir Meghelli, Ann Kang, Fernando Benadon, Fernando Orejuela, Alisha Lola Jones, Mellonee Burnim, Portia Maultsby, and Ruth Stone.

Because Black people believe in repetition: I sat in Fernando Orejuela's office very early one morning in 2016 and asked him if I could leave graduate school. He said no.

Repetition, again: Alisha Lola Jones, pastor, professor, mentor, and friend, told me over lunch that the mishearing of Black women is an ethnomusicological problem. This solved every disciplinary question I've ever had and freed me to work.

I became a digital humanist by accident. Despite my discomfort, many gracious and generous people have welcomed me into the field, principally Kalani Craig and Michelle Dalmau. I'm always due for a consult with IDAH. Thank you for helping me make maps, count car horns, and everything in between.

My Uncle David has been so unbelievably helpful through this process, hanging my recorders and being willing to problem solve and brainstorm with me as I try to make these sounds come to life.

The stories of my family are all over this book; they are an important part of me. I know DC first through my family. My great-grandmother used to live in a house on H Street NE. My family has been attending Calvary Episcopal Church for four generations. My father taught me how to drive the city. I watched Angie take street ways and cut throughs, 27 turns to avoid 395. I was born at Washington Hospital Center and raised in Prince George's County. There are roots that go beyond me in this city, and I am grateful to know them.

The gratitude I have for my mother and sister defies all words. With them I am never alone, never too much, never too lost. I wish everyone an earth-moving love like theirs.

To the dead:
Robert Martin taught me from a very early age that one goes to four and four goes to five. I am thankful for his ear, always. I did not have much time with Rotelia Green but we had our stories, our noontime news with JC Hayward, and our graham crackers.

I did not realize until well into the writing of this book how much my writing has been shaped by Black people dying at the hands of the police. I began graduate school in 2014, moved to Indiana just days after Mike Brown was killed in Ferguson, Missouri. I remember semesters where my cohort and I would write our final papers while livestreaming protests in Ferguson, or Baltimore, or Fort Worth. I attended a "die-in" at Indiana University in 2014 or 2015,

I don't remember which. We marched to the Indiana Memorial Union and laid down on the floor of the Starbucks in the building, for four minutes; one for every hour that Mike Brown's body was left in the street. White students stepped over my body to order their coffee. I didn't protest for a long time after that. The names of the dead are found throughout this text: Breonna Taylor, Sandra Bland, and Trayvon Martin in Chapter 2, Prince Jones in Chapter 5, George Floyd in the coda. Tony McDade, Philando Castile, Walter Scott. They are all here, because I have marked time with these deaths since the not guilty verdict was released for George Zimmerman the night before my twentieth birthday, contemplating with my best friend how we might keep our brothers safe from those who would wish us all dead. In listening to Black people, I am always listening to our dead as well as our living. This book is, in many ways, a means of grieving those who have been unjustly murdered at the hands of the state.

Introduction: Listening Intersectionally to the Chocolate City

Books like this usually start with an anecdote, a short story to introduce the problem or the question that the author is trying to interrogate. But this book is about multitudes, so we have to start with multiple stories:[1]

1) I once interviewed a preacher in the fellowship hall of her church, a church that she preached in and that I grew up in. As we sat in the hall together and talked, I remembered the sights and sounds of vacation bible school almost twenty years earlier, Easter Sundays and summer days spent with my grandmother, who ran the church office for what seemed like forever. During that conversation, the preacher talked about her transition from veteran police officer in the Metropolitan Police Department to full time Episcopalian priest, and how she had seen the city change over her lifetime. These kinds of conversations are about memory, stories moving in fits and starts as one memory sparks another. She talked about how the city used to sound like old school, like Chuck Brown, the godfather of go-go music in DC. She reminisced about working for Summer in the Parks, the National Park Service program that featured concerts and other outdoor events in public parks while kids were out of school. At these events, go-go bands that are now world famous would come at the drop of a hat to entertain their community in places like Malcolm X Park or Anacostia Park. There was a sense of familiarity, where "you could walk through the city and know where you are just by the sounds . . . now it's totally different."[2]

---

[1] As we begin with multiple stories in the body of the text so too do we begin with multiple stories in the footnotes as well. Inspired by Katherine McKittrick, whose footnotes are rich beyond measure, I use this space liberally to reference ideas, stories, and other constellations of thought. Footnotes are a way to continue the conversation, to have a side conversation, to offer an extra thought or two or three. This book is about multitudes and for as many stories and quotes as I have fit into these pages, please know that there are always more beyond the text.

[2] Gayle Fisher-Stewart, interview with the author, 2018.

Intersectional Listening. Allie Martin, Oxford University Press. © Oxford University Press 2025.
DOI: 10.1093/9780197671603.003.0001

2) In a newly built Starbucks nestled at the edge of a newly built shopping center in Prince George's County, Maryland, I interviewed a DJ that has spent her entire career amplifying local DMV (DC, Maryland, Virginia) artists, from radio shows to sporting events to open mic nights. About her Southeast DC neighborhood growing up, she told stories of hearing the ice cream truck, singing Bel Biv Devoe, hearing people getting whooped outside, all the sounds of what she described as a close-knit neighborhood. When I asked her later about what DC sounds like now, she said it sounded like a Whole Foods.[3]

3) Interviewing people is one of the best parts about being an ethnomusicologist, but perhaps even better is watching someone being interviewed, because you get to lose yourself more fully in a person's story. As an intern at the Smithsonian Institution I had the good fortune of sitting in on a number of interviews, one with a local organizer who had been fighting for land and equity in DC for decades. On the topic of gentrification he said, "I remind people that there are people like me that are alive that know that this whole city could have been for everybody. And the reason why this city isn't for everybody is because not just urban planners or architects or developers. Churches gave consent, the middle-class population gave consent, and definitely the government gave consent. So now we have a city where almost only rich people can live here."[4]

4) Not everything is an interview; some things are just life. Riding in the passenger seat of my father's car, we came across a new apartment complex in the Northeast Washington, DC, neighborhood where he was born. As we passed the building, my father said "I love change, but sometimes I look around and I'm like, 'Damn, where am I? I don't recognize this.'" What struck me about that moment was not *what* my father said but the sound of his voice when he said it. When he got to the emphasis on the "*Damn*, where am I?" a slight DC accent appeared where there had been none previously.[5] Looking around his old neighborhood and being struck by its drastic change made him *sound*, if only for a moment, like he was from there, despite years as a DJ on white radio stations diminishing the accent that would have marked him a Black Washingtonian.

All of these are stories about gentrification, a process of development and transformation that was originally coined by sociologist Ruth Glass to describe the

---

[3] Nicole Mosley, interview with the author, 2018.
[4] Dominic Moulden, interview by Samir Meghelli, Smithsonian Institution, Washington, DC, 2016.
[5] DC's accent, not quite a Southern drawl but not quite as thick as New York City, is typically associated with the Black working class that has lived in the city for generations alongside the transient population that comes and goes as federal administrations rise and fall.

"gentry" as they moved into London and displaced the working class.[6] These stories are also about sound, music, and how people use sound and language to observe gentrification and mark themselves as remaining when they would be otherwise forgotten or misremembered. This book begins with the question "what does gentrification sound like?" and immediately interrogates its own premise because sound does not exist in a vacuum, without a listener or a sound-maker. Sound exists as soundwaves and vibrations, yes, but in many ways only happens in the interpretation of sound.[7] "What does gentrification sound like?" Well, to whom? Thus, this book firmly asks: "What does gentrification sound like to Black people in Washington, DC?" The usefulness of such a question is not diminished by its specificity. Understanding how Black people in DC experience gentrification as a racialized, sonic process gives way to new conversations about studying gentrification, studying sound, and listening to Black life.[8] Furthermore, the work of theorizing gentrification sonically requires a reckoning with what it means to listen to Black people, who have been willfully silenced and misheard for centuries in Washington, DC, the seat of federal power in the United States. What would it mean to listen to Black people, intentionally, as their neighborhoods morph and shift around them?

Intentionally and thoughtfully listening to Black people requires a disavowal of historical and current American logics of listening, which dictate that Black people be heard as violent noisemakers, unintelligible nonbeings, or silent altogether. These logics are upheld throughout the United States, but stem from white supremacist quests to sonically "other" Black people. Early depictions of the music of enslaved Black people seemed to swing on a pendulum between distaste and confusion: "What makes it all the harder to unravel a thread of melody out of this strange network is that, like birds, they [Negroes] seem not infrequently to strike sounds that cannot precisely be represented by the gamut."[9] This description, recorded by William Francis Allen in 1867, depicts Black music-making as strange and alien because it is undepictable on a European staff. Western classical music has historically

---

[6] Ruth Lazarus Glass, *London: Aspects of Change* (London, MacGibbon & Kee, 1964).
[7] Nina Eidsheim suggests that "voice's source is not the singer; it is the listener," that "the voices heard are ultimately identified, recognized, and named by listeners at large." I would say the same for the sounds of gentrification, that they are ultimately named and articulated by those that experience them. Nina Sun Eidsheim, *The Race of Sound: Listening, Timbre, and Vocality in African American Music* (Durham, NC: Duke University Press, 2019), 9.
[8] The ethnographic work conducted for this book was done primarily with African American people in DC, but the city is home to a much larger African diaspora, including the largest population of Ethiopian people outside of Ethiopia. I use "Black" here throughout the book to speak to the diaspora, not in a gesture of conflation but rather in solidarity with the global nature of Black struggle.
[9] Eileen Southern, *The Music of Black Americans: A History*, 3rd ed. (New York: Norton, [1972], 1997).

relied in large part on the musical notes that can be found on a piano: 12 notes repeated over 7 octaves, resulting in 88 keys, since the 1880s. Black people were making sounds that did not exist in the European imagination, sounds that were thus interpreted as unmelodic, strange, or unnecessary.

This confusion has continued. Almost a century later music business executive Syd Nathan advocated against funding James Brown's album *Live at the Apollo* in 1963 because he did not want the sounds of the crowd screaming and yelling in affirmation to be captured on record. Many necessary elements of Black musical practice are considered extramusical: handclaps, foot stomps and other body percussion, audience participation, call and response, and even screaming in musical ecstasy. These sounds seemed extraneous to Nathan, rather than an integral part of Black sonic life. Many Black musical practices such as the spirituals Allen was listening to in 1867 or the funk that Brown was producing in the 1960s are communal and participatory, built to be performed and shared with an audience that, rather than operating as static observers, participate and shape performances. The importance of these sounds and interactions has been used to contribute to characterizations of Black musical and sonic life as informal or unserious.

These listening logics are detrimental to Black life, because they make Black people eligible for violence for engaging in the breadth of sonic practices that are essential to Black life. Authorities that seek to control Black people draw on difference in sonic practice in order to mark Black life as aberrational. Jennifer Stoever articulates these logics as the "sonic color line," an audible contour of racialization and race that is subsequently upheld by the white "listening ear."[10] The sonic color line is derived from DuBois's famous declaration that the problem of the twentieth century was the "color line," particularly the inevitability of racialization and racism in the United States. Musicologist Will Cheng has offered the language of "white misimaginations of Black skin, Black ears, and Black voices," which have in turn "abetted racist ideologies that dehumanize, discredit, or outright destroy Black life."[11] These violent aural misimaginations have indeed destroyed Black lives, from the fabricated whistle that ended Emmitt Till's life in 1965 to the 2012 murder of teenager Jordan Davis, killed by Michael Dunn over loud rap music and perceived disrespect.

The American listening practices that authorize white men to murder Black children also exist in gentrifying cities, where Black residents are denied the

---

[10] Jennifer Lynn Stoever, *The Sonic Color Line: Race and the Cultural Politics of Listening* (New York: NYU Press, 2016).

[11] William Cheng, "Black Noise, White Ears: Resilience, Rap, and the Killing of Jordan Davis," *Current Musicology* no. 102 (2018): 119.

same services and funding opportunities that are extended and overextended to their white counterparts. As long-time Maryland resident James recalled:

> My office used to be over on R Street—16th and R. Now, when I was over there, with our church office, services that we tried to get the city to put in, we got nowhere. When the neighborhood started changing up there, all these services started coming. So the change was good in a way, for people who still wanted to stay in the area, because they could benefit from some of the changes.

The connection here is one of humanity. Michael Dunn considered Jordan Davis—and by extension the loud rap music he enjoyed—a reason to categorize him as less than human and kill him. Cities like Washington, DC, drawing on a similar inability to hear Black people as human, do not respond to the requests and pleas of Black and poor residents at the same rate that they do wealthy residents, who are often but not always white. Unequal responses to requests for city services is a sonic and racialized issue. It is an issue about who is listened to, who is heard, and whose voice prompts action. Increased noise complaints that lead to arrest, carceral noise legislation, pay to play clubs, elderly jazz musicians not being able to age in place—all of these are sonic concerns. *Intersectional Listening* attends to these issues in order to make audible the harms of gentrification and complicate the stories of neighborhood change and development in DC through attention to the sonic.

Gentrification and Sound in Washington, DC

It's important at this time to make clear what I mean by gentrification, because the word has been theorized and stretched in a number of ways since Glass coined the term in 1964. Neil Smith's "rent gap" theory has been one of the prevailing explanations for gentrification, detailing the differences between current and potential rental incomes of a given property. Gentrification has also been formulated in waves, from first wave to fifth wave, from the 1960s to the present, measured primarily by principal actors, locations, and speed.[12]

---

[12] The first three waves of gentrification were chronicled by Smith and Hackworth in 2001. First wave gentrification is described as "sporadic and state led," whereas second wave expands on initial transformation and inspires resistance to change. Second wave is when neighborhoods that were previously experiencing disinvested begin to experience gentrification and displacement. Third wave gentrification, beginning in the 1990s, entails some neighborhoods and cities experiencing further gentrification while some further from the center city experience gentrification for the first time. In 2019, Aalbers expanded on this work to consider the scope of fourth and fifth wave gentrification, the latter of which involves a process led by finance rather than the state. Manuel B. Aalbers, "Introduction to the Forum: From Third to Fifth-Wave Gentrification," *Journal of Economic and Human Geography* 110, no. 1 (2019): 1–11; Jason Hackworth and

Ananya Roy has recently used the term "racial banishment" to focus on the role of the state and the centrality of race that traditional understandings of gentrification and displacement do not emphasize.[13] Michelle Boyd's work on "defensive development" works through Black gentrification, where members of the Black middle class act as the gentrifying parties.[14] Loretta Lees et al. explore "planetary gentrification" as a way of understanding these processes and consequences on a global scale.[15] All of these approaches are an attempt to describe, understand, and in some instances predict the transformations that come with processes of gentrification. Beyond the academy, gentrification has ballooned into a catchall term for the combination of violent dispossession and appropriation. For example, white people have "gentrified" the Black Lives Matter Movement, natural hair care, and sneaker culture. Refraining from this reframing of gentrification as appropriation, I understand gentrification to be the transformation of residential and commercial spaces that is deeply rooted in racialized and classed ideas of desirability, development, and progress.

My intervention in gentrification studies is to allow sound to lead the conversation, from the way city space is produced sonically to the way that gentrification changes how sound is consumed in public and private spaces. There are obvious examples that I draw on throughout the book, such as the Amplified Noise Act, a proposed DC law that directly criminalizes musicians, or the Don't Mute DC Movement, which was a response to the shutdown of a beloved neighborhood musical space. More than legal and punitive structures, though, sound permeates every facet of gentrification and the theorization of these processes. Gentrification is not (just) an ocular phenomenon. Displacement, eviction, and development are all explicitly sonic apparatuses. They take place over conversation, screaming, pleading, and the sounds of demolition. The work of *Intersectional Listening* is to engage with gentrification through listening critically to the everyday and extraordinary sounds of gentrifying space.

For some people in DC, gentrification was not a surprise. Many cite "The Plan," a piece of urban lore circulated in the 1970s that detailed how white people were eventually going to tire of the suburbs and move to resettle the city

---

Neil Smith, "The Changing State of Gentrification," *Journal of Economic and Human Geography* 92, no. 4 (2001): 464–77.

[13] Ananya Roy, "Racial Banishment," *Keywords in Radical Geography: Antipode at 50* (2019): 227–30.
[14] Michelle Boyd, "Defensive Development: The Role of Racial Conflict in Gentrification," *Urban Affairs Review* 43, no. 6 (2008): 751–76.
[15] Loretta Lees, Hyun Bang Shin, and Ernesto López-Morales, *Planetary Gentrification* (New York: Wiley, 2016).

in the decades to come. The Plan predicted that "the decline of low-income Black residents and their replacement by wealthier white people from outside of Washington, D.C. is intentional through the calculated use of gentrification and urban renewal."[16] While processes of gentrification are more complex than white people moving in and Black people moving out, the predictions of The Plan have come to pass in terms of both demographic shifts and how expensive the city has become. The Plan foregrounds a kind of sinister intentionality of the changes in the city, rather than the more innocent argument of many city officials, which is that DC is growing and open for business, and that the new residents need somewhere to live. The city growing more expensive and uninhabitable for the working class in the meantime is considered merely a consequence of positive growth for the District.

Disappointment in DC's demographic shifts are in part a response to the city's history as a prominent majority Black city. A planned city designed by Pierre L'Enfant in 1791, the capital city supported and participated in the slave trade and federal buildings such as the White House and the Capitol were built by the labor of enslaved Black people. After the Civil War, DC became home to a large free Black population, many of whom resided in alley dwellings as the city struggled to accommodate its residents. This population continued to grow into the twentieth century as Black people continued to flock to the city during the Great Migration (my own grandparents came from Georgia and North Carolina in the 1950s). Many were unable to achieve the "American dream" of home ownership because of racist mortgage practices, from redlining to racial covenants. The Black population of DC swelled to 71% in the 1970, solidifying the city's position as a "Chocolate City." Amidst this history of racism the city has also long been home to a Black elite, which has facilitated infra-racial tensions as the city as gentrified as well. These tensions are well documented in urban sociology, with Elijah Anderson detailing that many "members of the black middle class . . . seek to be as far as possible from the black underclass, believing that the closer to the ghetto they live, the more likely they are to receive the same treatment as their poorer counterparts."[17] This social stratification has existed in DC for centuries, built and maintained through social clubs, churches, educational institutions, colorism, and legislation. Black communities in DC have not always thought of one another as one singular unit, but rather differently classed neighborhoods with varying statuses. Despite their differences, all of these groups have been affected by

---

[16] Ruben Casteneda, "What's the Plan?," *Washington City Paper*, March 5, 2020.
[17] Elijah Anderson, *Streetwise: Race, Class, and Change in an Urban Community* (Chicago: University of Chicago Press, 1990, 248.

gentrification, from public housing being demolished to property taxes going up for homeowners.

Traditional markers of gentrification have revolved around movement, money, and people, specifically the movement of money and people. The statistics around DC are particularly striking, leading to its status as the most intensely gentrified city in the country as of 2019.[18] DC's Black population was 71% of its overall population in the 1970s, and as of 2020 is approximately 44%. In 1990, the city's median income was $52,000 and now is over $90,000. Even considering inflation, the wealth of white households in Washington, DC is an astonishing 81 times that of Black households.[19] Rent prices and tax rates in DC have skyrocketed as well, making it home to the most gentrifying neighborhoods in the country.[20] These demographic changes are combined with shifts in amenities: Starbucks on every corner, fusion restaurants, dog parks. Furthermore, the combination of DC's small size and particular racial politics have exacerbated the racialized tensions of gentrification. The city earned its nickname, "Chocolate City," because of its high population of African American residents and concentration of Black political power.[21] Chocolate cities are also characterized by rich Black expressive cultural practices, such as specific vernacular expressions, fashions, music scenes, and dance movements. Natalie Hopkinson describes the notion of the chocolate city as a type of utopia for Black people. She observes that "when you happen to be born Black in a world designed for white people, to live in a Chocolate City is to taste an unquantifiable richness. It gives a unique angle of vision, an alternate lens to see world power. In a Chocolate City, Black is normal."[22] Gentrification has disrupted the normalcy of Blackness in DC, prompting organizers like Ron Moten to create t-shirts with pointed slogans like "I'm not a gentrifier, I've been here." The label of "gentrifier" is often assigned to those that are considered new, disrespectful to local cultures, or otherwise disruptive toward Black quotidian life.

---

[18] Katherine Shaver, "D.C. Has the Highest 'Intensity' of Gentrification of Any U.S. City, Study Says," *Washington Post*, March 3, 2019, https://www.washingtonpost.com/transportation/2019/03/19/study-dc-has-had-highest-intensity-gentrification-any-us-city.

[19] Perry Stein, "Net Worth of White Households in D.C. Region Is 81 Times That of Black Households," *Washington Post*, November 2, 2016, https://www.washingtonpost.com/news/local/wp/2016/11/02/net-worth-of-white-households-in-d-c-region-is-81-times-greater-than-black-households/.

[20] Cordilia James, "D.C. Has Had the Most Gentrifying Neighborhoods in the Country, Study Finds," *DCist* (blog), March 19, 2019, https://dcist.com/story/19/03/19/d-c-has-had-the-most-gentrifying-neighborhoods-in-the-country-study-finds/.

[21] This nickname was solidified by "Chocolate City," the 1975 song and album by Parliament Funkadelic, which was a musical tribute to the nation's capital.

[22] Natalie Hopkinson, *Go-Go Live: The Musical Life and Death of a Chocolate City* (Durham, NC: Duke University Press, 2012), 10.

What we now call gentrification has had many iterations in DC, from "slum clearance" as a part of urban renewal projects in the Southwest quadrant in the 1950s to redevelopment programs in Shaw in the 1960s and 1970s.[23] Thus, this latest combination of development and transformation is not new in principle, but new in scale and in the technologies that both facilitate and document it, especially social media.[24] In its current iteration, gentrification in DC began in the 1990s with an influx of development in the center of the city and quickly moved outward into more residential neighborhoods.[25] The city center became home to a revamped Chinatown-Gallery Place neighborhood, anchored by what was originally called the MCI Center, home of the Washington Wizards basketball team, the Washington Capitals hockey team, and a host of other major events and concerts. The presence of the MCI Center and Gallery Place shifted the direction of the neighborhood, making it a more bustling tourist attraction. Other neighborhoods moved in similar directions in the years that followed, such as the 1986 construction of the Reeves Center in the U Street Corridor. The Reeves Center is a government building (and former nightclub) spearheaded by Mayor Marion Barry, one of DC's most beloved and controversial political figures, as an attempt to revitalize the neighborhood after decades of disinvestment following the riots of 1968. Developments such as these, combined with the advent of the Metro System, particularly the Green Line, all contributed to the eventual gentrification of Washington, DC.

These processes and their effects have been well documented by anthropologists, sociologists, and journalists such as Brett Williams, Sabiyha Prince, Natalie Hopkinson, Derek Hyra, Ashanté Reese, and Brandi Thompson Summers, as well as the historians George Derek Musgrove and Chris Meyers Asch.[26] *Intersectional Listening* continues along in the tradition of "DC Studies" that these capable scholars have carved out, drawing from ethnomusicology, sound studies, and Black Studies in order to explore

---

[23] Chris Myers Asch and George Derek Musgrove, *Chocolate City: A History of Race and Democracy in the Nation's Capital* (Chapel Hill: University of North Carolina Press, 2017).

[24] Sociologist Tanya Bolash-Goza expertly details the periods of rising mass incarceration and disinvestment preceding gentrification's beginnings in the 1990s in *Before Gentrification: The Creation of DC's Racial Wealth Gap* (Berkeley: University of California Press, 2023).

[25] Derek S. Hyra, *Race, Class, and Politics in the Cappuccino City* (Chicago: University of Chicago Press, 2017).

[26] See Brett Williams, *Upscaling Downtown: Stalled Gentrification in Washington, D.C.* (Ithaca, NY: Cornell University Press, 1988); Hopkinson, *Go-Go Live*; Sabiyha Prince, *African Americans and Gentrification in Washington, D.C.: Race, Class and Social Justice in the Nation's Capital* (Farnham, UK: Ashgate Publishing, 2014); Asch and Musgrove, *Chocolate City*; Ashanté M. Reese, *Black Food Geographies: Race, Self-Reliance, and Food Access in Washington, D.C.* (Chapel Hill: University of North Carolina Press, 2019); Brandi Thompson Summers, *Black in Place: The Spatial Aesthetics of Race in a Post-Chocolate City* (Chapel Hill: University of North Carolina Press, 2019); Hyra, *Race, Class, and Politics in the Cappuccino City*.

the relationships between Blackness and sound in the face of rapid change. In addition to these more recent DC studies, I also draw from the deep well of ethnographers that have documented Black life, from Elijah Anderson to DuBois to Zora Neale Hurston. With its tall glass apartment buildings and "gentrification font," the city *looks* shinier.[27] When Ruth Glass coined the term she noted the changes in the city visually, describing "a gleam of affluence in most of Central London . . . at least so it seems at first sight. It shows itself in an abundance of goods and gadgets, of cars and new buildings—in an apparently mounting flow of consumption."[28] Here, the connection between the economic and the visual is located most clearly: consumption is seen. *Intersectional Listening* argues that the gleam of the city is also sonic, that gentrified DC also *sounds* shinier, whiter, and more expensive.

Throughout the book I argue that gentrification in DC is indicated by two interwoven sonic markers: first, gentrification facilitates the rupture of local music scenes, particularly those performed primarily by people of color. Go-go music, DC's local subgenre of funk, has been the genre most displaced, which has had ripple effects on the rest of the city's music scene(s), from hip-hop to house. Go-go venues around the city have closed, and musicians that play the music frequently cannot afford to live in the city either, which pushes shows further into the suburbs of Maryland and Virginia. The rupture of local music therefore operates as a sonic marker of gentrification, racialized because of the tactics that align with long histories of policing Black sound that have been used to remove go-go from the city. More than just the go-go music scene, processes of gentrification also disrupt other scenes such as R&B, hip-hop, and house. In the midst of this disruption new scenes and bands are formed, giving way to performances that likely would not have occurred in a less gentrified city. Within rupture, processes of gentrification make space for new music, bands, and performance venues in the city.

The second sonic marker of gentrification is an increased tension surrounding sound, music, and noise in public space. This involves groups of people being punished for ever-changing definitions of loudness, as well as people imposing their sonic expectations onto a neighborhood, neglecting the local sonic histories and geographies of that place. This tension leads to an increase in surveillance and carcerality in Washington, DC. Black people come into contact with the police more often during processes of gentrification, in part because residents and homeowners of all races demand that the

---

[27] Gentrification font is described as "sleek sans serif" address numbers. See Bettina Makalintal, "A Deep Dive Into the 'Gentrification Font,'" *Vice*, September 9, 2020, https://www.vice.com/en/article/ep499w/gentrification-font-meme-neutraface.

[28] Glass, *London*, xiv.

city address the crime rate (particularly violent crime, property theft, and carjacking) through an increase in police officers and visible policing. The understanding of police and their function differs vastly across categories of identity. Whereas some imagine the police to be harassers and to be avoided lest they be accused of criminal activity, others consider the police to be public servants that work for them, the citizens and homeowners of Washington, DC. I attended many a neighborhood association meeting during which police officers promised to place more units on various blocks in an attempt to keep an eye on things and prevent theft, burglary, and assault. Within these varied expectations of policing and its function, I argue that the disruption of local music scenes and the increase in tensions around sound in public space operate in tandem, producing a city that forcefully silences some and amplifies others, which has dire consequences for those who make their livelihoods through music as well as those who have been deemed sonically unruly.

Sonic Intersections, Intersectional Listening

To upend a listening system that deems Blackness as both sonically excessive and simultaneously lacking requires an experimental approach to the sonic, one that operates with the goal of interpreting the constellations of Black sound and Black being on their own terms. To that end, this project is necessarily interdisciplinary and multimodal, engaging a wide array of sound sources that range from the human voice to the hiss of a Metro bus brake. Throughout this book, I use an extended meditation on the concept of the intersection as a thread to trace through these sound sources. My use of intersection here is inspired by anthropologist Vanessa Agard-Jones's use of sand as a point of entry for same-sex desire and gender transgression in the Caribbean. Unlike the (sometimes) smoother metaphor of water, she considers sand as that ubiquitous but messy grain that we find all over ourselves and throughout the earth containing its own history as it spills and sticks.[29] Intersections, similarly, are everywhere and yet often go unnoticed as we move through them. Be it the intersection at the crossing of two streets or two categories of identity, the point at which ideas and people and vibrations meet is a critical position for listening. It is at this point, this crossing, that we can begin to hear the frictions of a changing city. Like sand, sound is messy, and does not travel in straight lines or intersect neatly at one point or another. Sonic intersections,

[29] Vanessa Agard-Jones, "What the Sands Remember," *GLQ: A Journal of Lesbian and Gay Studies* 18, no. 2–3 (2012): 325–46.

then, offer a seemingly endless quantity of crossings and points of interaction in which to interrogate the racialized auralities of gentrification in DC.

Intersections have multiple meanings here: there are specific places, such as the intersection in DC where I initially set out to do fieldwork, at 7th Street and Florida Avenue Northwest. I chose this intersection because it is an iconic place to hear go-go music, DC's local genre of funk music and one of the best musical representations of Black Washingtonians.[30] I employ place rather than space intentionally here, drawing on Murray Forman's assertion that "place is structured along more narrowly circumscribed parameters than is space; it is defined by its closeness and proximity to individuals and groups and by its localized character, distinguished by its contrast with the distant and external character of abstracted space."[31] Place is known in a way that space cannot be, and part of hearing gentrification is listening to *how* people know places. An example: every time (because our elders ensure that we know what they want us to know through repetition) I pass through the intersection of East Capitol Street and Benning Road in Northeast DC with my grandmother, she mentions having worked there as a teenager in the 1950s at a restaurant called the Shrimp Boat. This restaurant, an iconic site on Benning Road, has been renovated several times and looks drastically different than it did when my grandmother worked there in the 1950s, but I imagine I will continue to make that connection and tell that story even after both the Shrimp Boat and my grandmother are gone. This is how I know the intersection of Benning and East Capitol, and the work of listening to gentrification is to listen to how people know places: through the music that's played there, or the sounds they heard growing up.

In addition to specific places, I also locate intersections within a more abstract space, operating as interstice between objects, places, people, ideas, and goals. Following Lefebvre's assertion that space is socially produced, these spatial (rather than placed) intersections in DC are produced through understandings of race, the morality of sound, and beliefs about who has the right to the city.[32] The riots of 1968, home rule's passing in 1973, the opening of the city's Metro system in 1976—all of these events act as interstices through which people have shaped understandings of DC and how the city is made and remade every day.[33] So where the intersection of 7th and

---

[30] I also credit author Natalie Hopkinson for influencing this choice, who suggested it when I told her that I wanted to listen to gentrification in the city.
[31] Murray Forman, *The 'Hood Comes First: Race, Space, and Place in Rap and Hip-Hop* (Middletown, CT: Wesleyan University Press, 2002), 25.
[32] David Harvey, "The Right to the City," *New Left Review* no. 53 (2008): 23–40.
[33] In 1973 the Home Rule Act was passed in Washington, DC, which gave the city the right to govern itself, up to a certain point. The city government shifted from the previous chief executive and board of

Florida is a place known to many, it is also a space heard and understood by different people in different ways. For some, it is a space of transition, only a point between one destination and another, from work or home or school. For others it is more deeply rooted space, open for lingering, conversation, or sleeping. Geographer Rashad Shabazz utilizes a similar idea of the intersection as a kind of liminal space as he theorizes the connections between home and prison in Chicago, which he refers to as the "carceral interstice."[34] The carceral interstice is but one part of a larger notion of "spatialized Blackness," which calls attention to how constraint is built into systems of everyday life, creating a prison-like environment for Black people in Chicago. This structure of constraint is also built into Washington, DC, and thinking through intersections as liminal space allows for an exploration of the city as operating at the intersection between development and displacement, where one seemingly requires the other in a gentrifying neighborhood.

Finally, I am holding intersections as a part of intersectionality, as I craft a theoretical framework called "intersectional listening" to frame the sonorities of gentrification. Intersectionality has gone from legal terminology to pop culture buzzword to scapegoat for ahistorical policymaking, but fundamentally remains a commitment to both/and rather than the either/or when considering relationships between identity and systems of oppression. The terminology of intersectionality is often attributed to Crenshaw alone, but the analysis of connected aspects of oppression and identity was occurring long before Crenshaw's work. For example, in *A Voice from the South*, Anna Julia Cooper penned the now famous declaration of black women's agency: "Only the Black woman can say when and where I enter, with the quiet undisputed dignity of my womanhood, without violence and without suing or special patronage, then and there the whole negro race enters with me."[35] Almost a century before Crenshaw, Cooper outlined the basic tenets of intersectionality and disrupted the hierarchy of Black freedom movements that presumed to place Black men above Black women. She made clear that there would be no freedom if Black women were not included. This assertion of agency centers Black women in a struggle against interwoven racial and gendered oppressions. This work has continued, from the work of the Combahee River Collective to sociologist Deborah King's theorization of "multiple jeopardy,"

---

commissioners model that it used in the early to mid-twentieth century to the mayor and council system that is still in place today. The first home rule mayor of Washington, DC was Walter Washington.

[34] Rashad Shabazz, *Spatializing Blackness: Architectures of Confinement and Black Masculinity in Chicago* (Champaign: University of Illinois Press, 2015), 68.

[35] Anna Julia Cooper, *A Voice from the South* (Oxford: Oxford University Press, [1892] 1988), 31.

where "the modifier 'multiple' refers not only to several, simultaneous oppressions but to multiplicative relationships among them as well."[36]

As intersectionality has challenged us to consider the legal premise of occupying more than one perilous category of identification, intersectional listening challenges us to hear multitudes. The commitment to multitudes has grounded my ethnographic exploration of gentrification in DC in the refusal of simple stories. Gentrification is not just a decrease in the Black population percentage of the city or an increase in rents, but rather the fundamental transformation of a space into something more exclusionary for marginalized people. In reflecting on the fraught role that intersectionality has had in academic and public discourses, I am cautious of operating in the "defensiveness" that Jennifer Nash articulates as a feature of many discussions of intersectionality.[37] To that end, this book does not operate as though intersectionality is "mine" as a Black woman to have and to hold exclusively; nor do I conflate intersectionality with a broader Black feminist politics, because these theorizations are varied and not always in harmony with each other. Rather, I employ intersectionality and thus intersectional listening because they are conceptually useful, prescient, and accessible to the imagined readers of this book. Committing to the both/and while excavating the knowledge of the margins is worthy work, and as gentrification is collapsed into the twin categories of "neighborhood change" and "white appropriation" it remains important to go further, to listen beyond. Where Sumi Cho et al. argue that "single-axis thinking undermines legal thinking, disciplinary knowledge production, and struggles for social justice," I contend that single-axis listening undermines ethnomusicological thinking.[38] We are unable to understand how people build their worlds through music and sound if we are unable to listen to their multitudes, to the ways that they impose and are imposed onto in different forms. More than imposition, though, listening intersectionally is about hearing the ways that people relate to one another and to themselves. Listening intersectionally calls for the analysis of multiple

---

[36] Deborah K. King, "Multiple Jeopardy, Multiple Consciousness: The Context of a Black Feminist Ideology," *Signs* 14, no. 1 (1988): 42–72.

[37] In her institutional history of intersectionality, Nash identifies the defensive position that Black feminists take up regarding questions of intersectionality, where the concept must be protected rather than stolen by outsiders. Nash suggests that "despite evidence that the attachment to the defensive position is toxic, the attachment persists because it offers the sense of collective world-making, and because it is the exertion of a certain form of agency." Given the temptation of the defensive posture, I strive to utilize intersectionality solely in service of the work, pinpointing both specific uses throughout the literature but also as a mode of listening that is experimental and operating in possibility. Jennifer C. Nash, *Black Feminism Reimagined: After Intersectionality* (Durham, NC: Duke University Press, 2019), 27.

[38] Sumi Cho, Kimberlé Williams Crenshaw, and Leslie McCall, "Toward a Field of Intersectionality Studies: Theory, Applications, and Praxis," *Signs: Journal of Women in Culture and Society* 38, no. 4 (2013): 787.

systems of oppression, for a type of hearing that is not centered on maleness or heteronormativity or whiteness.

Intersectional listening draws most from women and gender studies scholar Vivian May's four strategies to approaching intersectional thought: to take up intersectionality's insubordinate orientation, to set aside norm emulation as a research or political strategy, to follow opacities/read against the grain, and to embrace a matrix approach to analysis.[39] Intersectional listening seeks to hear those opacities, those situations or scenarios that are cloudy or not easily understood with current dominant means of knowledge production. It pushes us to hear the unknowns, things that slip through, and that complicate an otherwise easy analysis. This framework is not additive; categories of identification are not playing cards to be stacked for the purposes of articulating who is more oppressed than whom. While I indeed seek to approach the sonic from multiple axes, including race, class, gender, and sexuality, this is but the beginning of the work. The heart of intersectional listening in this context is an engagement with the possibilities of Black sound: what it is, has been, and can be.

This engagement with sound and possibility is what makes intersectional listening such a compelling method for listening to gentrification. Gentrification is a process that routinely dismisses and silences Black possibility through a host of interrelated state-sanctioned tactics, from legislative maneuvering to the demolition of public housing. To listen intersectionally to gentrification is a commitment to interrogating those facets of spatial and sonic transformation that are typically overlooked and underrepresented, providing a more useful critique of the process itself. In Washington, DC, this means listening to Black people who blame gentrification primarily on other Black people, particularly the Black middle and upper class; it means listening to and centering histories of Black women's activism in DC even as Black men are constructed as the primary victims of racist lawmaking; it also means listening to young Black men construct their musical identities as both noisy and nonviolent, which disrupts more mainstream activist messaging toward Blackness as not "noise." All of these instances demand a multidimensional aurality, one that is centered on hearing Blackness as expansive rather than reductive.

Taking an intersectional approach to listening fosters a way to analyze the lives and experiences of Black people and to audibly gauge pasts, presents, and the speculative sonic future. Additionally, intersectional listening allows us

---

[39] Vivian M. May, *Pursuing Intersectionality, Unsettling Dominant Imaginaries* (New York: Routledge, 2015).

to interrogate music, sound, and noise, as well as what lies in between these distinctions in their relation to broader understandings of space and place. I am working toward an embrace of the speculative ephemerality of sound, attempting not to draw hard and fast conclusions but rather to "tarry" with the relationship between sound and gentrification.[40] I draw here on the work of Deborah Kapchan, who considers listening to be a speculative method, and calls on scholars to "release our hold on intellective knowledge (with its drives to categorize, objectify, and subjugate."[41] I seek, then, a mode of knowledge production that speculates without being ahistorical, and listens with the intent of amplification rather than categorization. This intention toward speculation leads to very interesting conversations regarding gentrification and sound, in part because the academy encourages and rewards singular, decisive, expertise. When people ask me "what does gentrification sound like?" they expect an answer. I tell them that gentrification sounds like what my conversation partners tell me it sounds like: like complaint, like cream cheese, like smooth jazz, like Whole Foods, like exploitation, like the city being a lighter and brighter place to live. My work in *Intersectional Listening* is to tarry with these responses and situate them within larger histories of sound and Black life in Washington, DC.

In foregrounding the sonic, *Intersectional Listening* also engages deeply embedded cultural expectations of sound that consider acts of listening and sonic work to be subordinate to visualization. As described by ethnomusicologist Ana María Ochoa Gautier, "in the audiovisual complex of modernity, sound appears as the interior, immersive, and affective other of vision's prominent exteriorization, in modern formations of power such acousticity often appears as 'hidden' behind the visual."[42] Sound is treated as subjective and emotional, where the visual is external and objective. Jonathan Sterne describes these assumptions as the audiovisual litany, where "hearing is spherical, vision is directional ... hearing tends toward subjectivity, vision tends toward objectivity, hearing is about affect, vision is about intellect."[43] This litany, commonly practiced across institutions, devalues the sonic as a purveyor of information, instead considering sound as the sense of emotionality and

---

[40] Ashon Crawley describes tarrying as a kind of "stilled intensity and waiting," a time to "wait with fervent prayer and song." In this case, I am thinking with the intense waiting and sounding of tarrying work, rather than imposing sonic conclusions on to how Black people hear their own lives, as I listen and sound alongside them. Ashon T. Crawley, *Blackpentecostal Breath: The Aesthetics of Possibility* (New York: Fordham University Press, 2016).

[41] Deborah Kapchan, *Theorizing Sound Writing* (Middletown, CT: Wesleyan University Press, 2017), 15.

[42] Ana María Ochoa Gautier, *Aurality: Listening and Knowledge in Nineteenth-Century Colombia* (Durham, NC: Duke University Press, 2015), 14.

[43] Jonathan Sterne, *The Sound Studies Reader* (New York: Routledge, 2012), 9.

affect. In challenging the supposed inferiority of sound as a way of knowing, *Intersectional Listening* utilizes sound as a primary means of exploring Black experiences of gentrification, which is essential because Afro-diasporic ways of knowing often prioritize the sonic, which is both a mechanism of cultural retentions as well as a response to histories of enslavement and oppression.[44] Taken together as placed, spaced, and as a framework, these sonic intersections trouble the audiovisual litany and gesture toward an understanding of how race and sound operate during processes of gentrification. Geographer Yi-Fu Tuan's conceptualization is helpful here: space is that which allows movement and place therefore generates a pause in that movement.[45] The engagement of sonic intersections allows for the expansive movement of space but also the operation of the pause or stasis, as places and their meanings are ever shifting as gentrification continues to throw the city into flux.

Emancipatory Soundscapes

As the nation's capital, Washington, DC is brimming with (often contradictory) gestures toward freedom, from the architectural to the celebration of local and national holidays. One such holiday, DC's Emancipation Day, offers a rich space in which to listen intersectionally. Emancipation Day is a particularly apt case study because one of the calls of intersectional listening is to listen toward freedom, toward soundscapes in which Black people can live and sound in their neighborhoods without being subjected to violence. However, Black sonic freedom, in all of its multitudes, is uncomfortable for a gentrifying city, because the influx of development capital is contingent on the endurance of racial capitalism. While DC's lack of statehood taints the freedoms of everyday life granted to others in the United States, the city boasts the title of being the first jurisdiction in the United States to effectively abolish slavery, having emancipated enslaved people in April of 1862, eight months before the signing of the Emancipation Proclamation by President Abraham Lincoln. April 16, 2018 marked the 156th anniversary of emancipation in

---

[44] Inaccessibility to formal, Western education has led people of African descent to have a different relationship to text and textuality than others residing in the Western world. Rather, the sonic is the "principle modality in which Afro-diasporic cultures have been articulated"; see *Phonographies: Grooves in Sonic Afro-Modernity* (Durham, NC: Duke University Press, 2005), 5. Likewise, Stuart Hall reminds us that "displaced from a logocentric world—where the direct mastery of cultural modes meant the mastery of writing . . . the people of the diaspora have, in opposition to all that, found the deep form, the deep structure of their cultural life in music"; see "What Is This 'Black' in Black Popular Culture?," *Social Justice* 20, no. 1/2 (1993): 109. Black people, then, know genuinely and intensely through musical and sonic media.
[45] Yi-Fu Tuan, *Space and Place: The Perspective of Experience* (Minneapolis: University of Minnesota Press, 1977), 6.

Washington, DC, and as they have done annually since 2000, the city hosted a celebration that offers a resonant opportunity to practice intersectional listening.[46] In 2018 the parade marched down Constitution Avenue toward the aptly named Freedom Plaza, where a concert and firework celebration took place in front of the Wilson Building, the administrative home of the City Council. That year I stood along the parade route, watching as school bands, community groups, and Mayor Muriel Bowser herself marched along and waved to the crowd. Behind me, two seemingly middle-aged white men were attempting to guess the purpose of the parade. They suggested several potential scenarios before ultimately moving on to another topic of conversation. Possible reasons they considered for the parade: former Mayor Marion Barry's birthday, the Cherry Blossom parade (which coincidentally was held the same day), or other national holidays.

Their exchange embodies a key point of contention surrounding gentrification: many white residents of DC, either newcomers or long-term residents, are exercising great influence over a city with whose racialized histories they are not familiar. Furthermore, the city administration is more interested in moving forward with a new vision that includes the "entire" city rather than focusing on the specific needs and histories of the Black population. A parade intended to celebrate emancipation from slavery but not featuring prominent signage that reflects that message is indicative of the city's unwillingness to dwell on its racialized past and present.

After the parade ended and hundreds of mostly Black attendees gathered at Freedom Plaza, twelve-year-old African American singer Drew Tillman was introduced to sing the national anthem and begin the festivities. Considering that the day is intended to recognize and celebrate African American emancipation from chattel slavery, I expected Tillman to sing "Lift Every Voice and Sing," composed by brothers James Weldon Johnson and John Rosamond Johnson in 1900 and later adopted as the Black national anthem in the United States. "Lift Every Voice and Sing" is an integral part of Black social life, with a history of being sung at prominent Black church and school functions, a part of what Imani Perry describes as "Black formalism."[47] The song's lyrics, while

---

[46] The 2000 declaration of Emancipation Day as a holiday in the city was spearheaded by former council member Vincent Orange, who noted the local importance of the holiday. Furthermore, his intention to eventually host a parade (which the city now does annually) was drawn from late nineteenth-century celebrations of emancipation, then called Jubilee Day. Jubilee day festivities unfortunately ended in 1900, but Orange revived the spirit of the day when introducing legislation into the DC Council, which passed and has given employees in DC April 16 off ever since. Linda Wheeler, "D.C. Slave Emancipation Day Declared a Holiday," *Washington Post*, March 30, 2000, https://www.washingtonpost.com/archive/local/2000/03/30/dc-slave-emancipation-day-declared-a-holiday/1c0fa519-c076-4745-8f0e-683908b94b88.

[47] Imani Perry, *May We Forever Stand: A History of the Black National Anthem* (Chapel Hill: University of North Carolina Press, 2018).

not explicitly racialized, speak to a history of struggle and rising above that resonates with Black freedom struggles in the United States. Consider, for example, the end of the second verse:

> We have come over a way that with tears has been watered
> We have come, treading our path through the blood of the slaughtered
> Out from the gloomy past, till now we stand at last
> Where the white gleam of our star is cast

The lyrics speak to the unfathomable struggle and ultimate overcoming of a people, and the performance practice reflects this journey, as the final peak of the song is typically offered with a great fermata (pause) and collective breath. The song is emblematic of a specifically African American struggle against systemic racism and speaks to the rituals that Black people in the United States have engaged in to build their institutions and communities around a collective struggle and vision. Rather than singing "Lift Every Voice and Sing," though, Tillman sang the "Star-Spangled Banner," the more widely recognized national anthem of the United States, which was well performed and widely appreciated by the audience, through applause and encouraging shouts and verbal interaction.

Tillman sang the national anthem in the pop vocal style that has become common at many sporting events, especially the National Football League's annual Superbowl. Her singing featured a number of melismatic vocal runs and belting, both key features of the vocal performances popularized by Black pop balladeers such as Whitney Houston in the 1980s.[48] This style of singing has become ubiquitous in the pop music world, in Black and non-Black singers alike, especially in British pop-soul singers such as Adele and Sam Smith. Their manner of singing is descendant from gospel and soul traditions, which feature more melismatic passages, moans, slides, and emotive singing than the pop style, but have crossed over into pop. These melismatic runs that originated within the gospel music tradition but are a large part of the current pop music landscape are an example of musicologist Stephan Pennington's third phase of cultural appropriation, which he calls "obscured appropriation." Obscured appropriation occurs when a style or musical gesture is considered so universal that it has lost its roots.[49] Most white women pop singers,

---

[48] Mellonee V. Burnim and Portia K. Maultsby, *African American Music: An Introduction* (New York: Routledge, 2014).
[49] Jake Taber, "Q+A: Stephan Pennington Talks Music History, Cultural Appropriation," *The Tufts Daily* (blog), April 16, 2015, https://tuftsdaily.com/features/2015/04/16/qa-stephan-pennington-talks-music-history-cultural-appropriation.

from Ariana Grande to Christina Aguilera, have capitalized on gospelized pop singing, to the point where gospel's roots are largely unrecognized as the source. In global pop music, Black musical gestures are what make pop music popular, and therefore nonblack pop singers are obligated to draw upon these gestures, be it a vocal style or a trap beat, in order to be successful.

The scale that Tillman sang at the end of her Emancipation Day performance is indicative of this pop vocal style. Instead of ending on the tonic, or the home pitch, as the melody of the song dictates, she instead walks up a minor scale before landing on the dominant, which she then repeats with a lower passing tone, almost as if she's sliding into it. This scale is very similar to the one sung by Beyoncé at the 2004 NFL Superbowl, who, instead of ending with the word "brave" on the tonic, embellished her way up past the dominant to the superdominant, before ending, like Tillman, on the dominant. The similarity in these performances is not coincidental; it speaks to the style of singing that has become commonplace in the pop world, yet has its roots in the gospel music tradition, where the chest voice is taken as high as it can go, and melodies are frequently embellished. My point is this: although the "Star-Spangled Banner" is representative of a broader (whiter) conception of "America," common performance practices of this song, by Black and non-Black musicians alike, draw from, and even require, African American vocal traditions.

Beyond the musical aspects of Tillman's performance, there are also the cultural politics of the national anthem to consider. In 2016, football player Colin Kaepernick refused to stand for the performance of the national anthem at football games that he played in, citing the racial injustice that is experienced by Black people throughout the United States and around the world, specifically police brutality. After consultation with football player and military veteran Nate Boyer, he ultimately decided that kneeling rather than sitting for the anthem would be the best way to respectfully protest without disrespecting military service. His silent protest sparked a conversation around the anthem, patriotism, and the National Football League (NFL). The protests and backlash ultimately led to the NFL creating a policy that would fine players for protesting on the field, which many cite as a detriment to free speech.[50] These anthem protests became well known throughout the country, with many sports teams (professional and amateur) featuring players that are refusing to stand for the anthem. Fans, too, are refusing to stand for the anthem at

---

[50] Erik Ortiz, "New NFL Policy Will Fine Teams If Players Kneel during National Anthem," *NBC News*, May 24, 2018, https://www.nbcnews.com/news/us-news/nfl-announces-new-national-anthem-policy-fines-teams-if-players-n876816.

sports games, which causes tension, even physical violence, in the stands. I maintain here that the choice to perform the "Star-Spangled Banner" rather than "Lift Every Voice and Sing" in the midst of a global public conversation about anti-Blackness, first amendment rights, and what it means to be a patriot speaks to both the hegemony of the "Star-Spangled Banner" as well as DC Emancipation Day's unwillingness to commit to an emancipatory Black soundscape. The "Star-Spangled Banner," though it has specifically been tied to racism, slavery, and anti-Blackness, is so baked into what it means to be an American that it was still normal to perform it for an event specifically for Black emancipation. The national anthem is but one facet of a cultural hegemony that averts outright resistance by promising a freedom that is, at this point, blatantly false.[51] "Lift Every Voice and Sing," on the other hand, speaks specifically (although ambiguously) to the struggle of African Americans, and offers an unwillingness to compromise in a nation still trying to force itself into colorblindness. In the performance of the national anthem at the Emancipation Day concert, I heard a style of singing that originated within the African American community, yet also an absence of liberatory sonic practice simultaneously. How moving would that song have been if the gospel runs had been on the words "Have not our weary feet/Come to the place for which our fathers sighed?" Perhaps the crowd might even have sung alongside Tillman during her performance.

There were other moments within the Emancipation Day festivities that provide opportunity for intersectional listening. After Tillman's opening performance, Mayor Muriel Bowser offered a brief speech during the festivities, a portion of which is transcribed here:

> We celebrate Emancipation Day because we were the first jurisdiction in the United States where slaves were freed. But today, we know enslaved people then, and some, we know some enslaved people now. And that's because we have to continue to fight so that Washingtonians have every right of every American, and that's statehood for Washington, DC. So, when I count to three we're going to say, "Free DC!" One two three: Free DC! Free DC! Free DC! And so just like we're celebrating Regina [Hall], our homegrown success, we have to celebrate go-go music, and our own Rare Essence![52]

---

[51] Rinaldo Walcott argues that "postslavery and postcolony, Black people, globally, have yet to experience freedom," instead being caught within a long emancipation that confers freedom only through legislative and judicial means." See his *The Long Emancipation: Moving toward Black Freedom* (Durham, NC: Duke University Press, 2021), 1.

[52] Actress Regina Hall was present at the Emancipation Day ceremony, and is originally from Washington, DC.

Bowser's speech here immediately pivots from freedom from slavery to advocating for DC to be the 51st state in the United States, which is an ongoing fight in the life of the District.[53] She offered a chant of "Free DC!" that was meant to stir up the crowd and center the issue of statehood, which is perpetually on the minds of many District residents, who are unfairly taxed without representation in congress and the senate. However, in being unwilling to dwell on the fact of slavery, Bowser rendered herself unable to sincerely celebrate the occasion. At the beginning of the speech, when she arrived at the line about knowing people being enslaved now, I originally thought she was referencing mass incarceration, which has been called a modern-day Jim Crow.[54] The message about statehood, however, fits more centrally under mayor Bowser's political message, which is in tune with a wider group of people than just the Black residents celebrating Emancipation Day. In an effort to promote a unified, even colorblind city, Bowser shifted a conversation about Black freedom into a politicized moment of statehood advocacy.

In addition to the content of her speech, I also call attention here to Mayor Bowser's mechanics of delivery, specifically, the way she initiated the chant.[55] Bowser ended her speech with the "Free DC" chant, repeated three times after giving a one-two-three count-off. Considering not only presence but absence, there was a notable lack of antiphony in the mayor's delivery. Antiphony, or call and response, is a critical part of Black sonic experiences, and is an integral part of several African diasporic music genres, from gospel to go-go. This kind of antiphony is an Africanism, a cultural retention that endured the trans-Atlantic slave trade to become a part of Afro-diasporic cultural forms. Bowser's chant did not allow for the people to speak by themselves, a notable part of antiphony. She only called—and expected people to join her—rather than waiting for a complementary response. Afro-diasporic musical genres feature a large amount of repetition, which can be a method of heightening emotion, as well as a means of encouraging participation. If a phrase or lyric is being repeated, it is much easier to solicit participation from an audience, because they will be able to understand what is being said and repeat it. Bowser

---

[53] In 2019, the city got closer to statehood than it had in twenty-five years, with an official hearing in the House. There is not a great deal of hope that statehood will get past a Republican controlled Senate, but the hearing in the House was monumental nonetheless. Emily Cochrane, "For D.C. Statehood Advocates, a Hearing Marks Another Step Forward," *New York Times*, September 19, 2019, https://www.nytimes.com/2019/09/19/us/politics/dc-statehood-hearing.html.

[54] Michelle Alexander, *The New Jim Crow: Mass Incarceration in the Age of Colorblindness* (New York: The New Press, 2020).

[55] The mechanics of delivery, a framework constructed by ethnomusicologist Mellonee Burnim to analyze the performance of gospel music, allows us to consider the overlapping importance of time, text, and pitch. Mellonee Burnim, "The Black Gospel Music Tradition: A Complex of Ideology, Aesthetic, and Behavior," in *More Than Dancing: Essays on Afro-American Music and Musicians*, edited by Irene Jackson (Westport, CT: Greenwood Press): 147–67.

draws on this history with the repetition of a simple chant, but her unwillingness to invoke call and response evokes a larger history of Black voicelessness in DC. By only inviting them to participate with her own voice and not their own, Bowser's chant becomes almost disingenuous—she is asking for participation from a crowd to support an initiative that will benefit first the higher income white people that are flooding the city and making it their home. She is asking for a crowd to cheer in support of a statehood initiative that will serve as a test of trickle-down economics. Furthermore, as with Tillman's performance, this chant is not actually about emancipation or a legacy of slavery. While taxation without representation is indeed a violent enterprise, it is more comparable to colonialism than chattel slavery. Bowser's immediate pivot to statehood as freedom from a kind of slavery violently misremembers the horrors of chattel slavery and ultimately does a disservice to the occasion.

After Mayor Bowser's speech and a few other announcements, there was a brief DJ interlude from DJ Rico, a popular veteran DJ in the DMV who participates in go-go performances and local radio. The very first song he played for the crowd was Bruno Mars's hit "That's What I Like," which won three Grammy awards in 2018 for Song of the Year, Best R&B song, and Best R&B performance of the year. At the same Grammy awards in 2018, Bruno Mars won Album of the Year for 24K Magic, on which "That's What I Like" is featured. Musically, "That's What I Like" draws on multiple African American genres, from the new jack swing era of R&B that was popular in the 1980s and 1990s to the trap beats that have dominated hip-hop in the 2010s. Bruno Mars is an important figure in this conversation of emancipation, gentrification, and the racialization of sound because of his identity as a multiracial musician committed to cultivating a Black soundscape. Mars's Grammy wins placed him at the center of a conversation about cultural appropriation, and the tendency of awarding bodies such as the Grammys to award nonblack artists for making Black music. Unlike artists such as Miley Cyrus or Katy Perry, Mars is very thorough about acknowledging the genres, artists, and histories that he draws from in his acceptance speeches, which is appreciated by artists and scholars alike.[56] This is not to say that Black artists were not featured during the Emancipation Day festivities, as the audience was able to see live performances by Angie Stone, Brandy, Rare Essence, Classically Dope, the Allure Band, as well as a Luther Vandross impersonator. Leaning on listening as a speculative, intersectional method, Mars's prominence as the first artist

---

[56] Adelle Platon, "Bruno Mars 'Latina' Cover Story: Details from the Interview" *Billboard*, January 31, 2017.

featured in the DJ's set shows how difficult it is to foreground Black cultural production at an event that is supposed to be focused on Black emancipation.

The 2018 Emancipation Parade offered frictions that detailed how difficult it is for a gentrifying city to embrace the fullness of Black sonic freedom, instead leaning more toward a pro-development urban American sound. The goal of listening to gentrification via intersectional listening is to reach toward an emancipatory soundscape, which I understand as a process in which sonic space is created and maintained in the service of Black life. Emancipatory soundscapes oscillate in a queer space between the grounded "already otherwise" and the utopian "not yet."[57] The already otherwise reassures us that emancipatory soundscapes already exist, through practices of singing, worshiping, and noisemaking. These sonic worlds are already here. Emancipatory soundscapes also exist in the space of the "not yet," the ever moving toward, in a kind of aural consideration of what utopia might be. Emancipatory soundscapes, then, those spaces we need in which to imagine a liberatory Black life in a rapidly gentrifying Washington, DC, are both already here and yet always signaling to the possibility of what could be.

A Note on Methodology

On a cool day in the spring of 2018 I was descending the steps of Florida Avenue Baptist Church (FABC), having just spent about thirty minutes on the roof downloading data and changing the batteries of a sound recorder that was perched on the edge of the building facing the intersection of 7th Street and Florida Avenue Northwest. As I arrived at the bottom of the steps I saw Ms. Alease, one of the office workers in the church, waiting for me. From the moment I met her, Ms. Alease was like home to me, the quintessential Black church surrogate grandmother. When I came down from the roof she hugged me, asked how my mother was doing, asked how the work on the roof was going, and then began to playfully (but also seriously) admonish me for not wearing a coat. She quipped, "If you have the sense to have a dissertation you have the sense to put on a coat." I cherished this remark because it encapsulated the contours of navigating my ethnographic fieldwork, which was very much an academic endeavor but was made possible by navigating Black social relationships with vernacular training that I received at home, among family. This was my dynamic with Ms. Alease for the entire year, where she and Ms.

---

[57] See Crawley, *Blackpentecostal Breath* and José Esteban Muñoz, *Cruising Utopia: The Then and There of Queer Futurity* (New York: NYU Press, 2009).

Regina of the FABC supported my work and my well-being, offering heat in the cold weather, cold water in the heatwaves, and always a hug and a place to rest my feet. These encounters always stuck with me, because the "new" digital work I was doing was being facilitated by a very old culture of care in which I grew up. Ethnographic work is always a collection of different levels of knowing and practices, rather than a standard set of fieldwork activities.

Most of the fieldwork I conducted for this project in Washington, DC occurred between 2013 and 2019, employing three central methodologies: interviews, participant observation, and passive acoustic recording, which involves collecting a vast number of short recordings over a long period of time. I used this combination of methodologies in order to arrive at a kind of "thick data."[58] Thick data combines anthropologist Clifford Geertz's thick description with the big data that is often central to digital humanities inquiries, aiming for a generative kind of movement between the macro and the micro.[59] Generating thick data was essential for this project, as I was interested in telling the stories of individuals through interviews and participant observation but also through a sustained immersion into soundscape recordings. As ethnomusicologist W. F. Umi Hsu argues, "A deepened engagement with cultural content in multiple registers could enable us to identify patterns of social linkage and cultural meanings that are otherwise inaccessible in participant observation methods."[60] I engaged more meaningfully with the ethnographic work because of the soundscape recording aspects of the project.

I conducted dozens of interviews with a wide range of conversation partners: musicians, local neighborhood officials, church members, business owners, and more. These interviews were typically semistructured conversations, drawing on a mix of my own questions related to sonic impressions of the neighborhood as well as stories that people were willing to share.[61] Gaining access to interviews was often an exercise of positioning

---

[58] Tricia Wang, "Why Big Data Needs Thick Data," *Ethnography Matters* (blog), December 5, 2016, https://medium.com/ethnography-matters/why-big-data-needs-thick-data-b4b3e75e3d7.

[59] Although thick description is commonly engaged and remixed (thinking about Tricia Wang's "thick data" here), there have also been cases made for other methods of description. Namely, John Jackson's ethnography *Thin Description* challenges the possibility and necessity of thick description, instead offering an alternative mode of ethnography "where you slice into a world from different perspectives, scales, registers, and angles—all distinctively useful, valid, and worthy of consideration And the thinness of these slices is central." Thin description disputes that anthropologists or other researchers can know all there is to know about a particular topic or interaction, arguing rather that what folks have been considering "thick" is actually quite thin at times. See *Thin Description: Ethnography and the African Hebrew Israelites of Jerusalem* (Cambridge, MA: Harvard University Press, 2013), 16.

[60] W. F. Umi Hsu, "Digital Ethnography Toward Augmented Empiricism: A New Methodological Framework," *Journal of Digital Humanities* 3, no. 1 (2014): 43–61.

[61] My method of questioning is informed by a number of sources, including Barz and Cooley's *Shadows in the Field* and Headlee's *We Need To Talk*. More than anything, though, my interviewing practices are informed by my experience interviewing people. Since I began conducting fieldwork in 2013, I have conducted dozens of interviews, and each one teaches me something new about how to have conversations

myself in layers, typically beginning with my "official" classification as a PhD student or Smithsonian intern, working on a project focused on neighborhood change. Language was important here, as "gentrification" carries different connotations than "neighborhood change" in local discourses. Neighborhood change is a less racially charged term than gentrification, with the former indicating that the neighborhood has undergone some development and the latter insinuating that the development can be blamed on a particular group of (white) people. For example: at a neighborhood association meeting, I once described my project to a Black resident of Maryland as focusing on "gentrification and sound," and he remarked that it was very interesting, "because of that word that you just used," rather than repeating it himself. He distanced himself from the more charged term of gentrification while acknowledging his own interest in the project.

Two other facets of identification were key in gaining access to interviews: my Blackness as well as my being from Prince George's County, Maryland, located directly east of the city.[62] When soliciting interviews via email I realized early on that I was assumed to be white, given the name "Alison" and my status as a student at Indiana University.[63] During phone calls, I noticed that I was subconsciously code switching more than usual, drawing out my DC accent in order to be heard and coded as a Black woman from the area. In this way I was both insider and outsider for the duration of the project, at home in my proximity, racial identity, and family ties to the city yet distant in my academic credentials. Ethnomusicologist Deborah Wong reminds us that "the ethnographer is always an outsider."[64] Even as I did fieldwork in places familiar to me, I was always an outsider just by virtue of doing the fieldwork. I articulate

with people. For this project specifically, though, I approached nearly each interviewee with the same initial three questions: 1) Describe your history in DC (where you've lived, worked, etc.); 2) How did the city/your neighborhood sound in the past?; and 3) How does it sound now? Beyond these three questions, interviews were largely based on the experiences of the person with whom I was speaking. See Gregory F. Barz and Timothy J. Cooley, *Shadows in the Field: New Perspectives for Fieldwork in Ethnomusicology* (New York: Oxford University Press, 2008) and Celeste Headlee, *We Need to Talk: How to Have Conversations That Matter* (New York: HarperCollins, 2017).

[62] In conversation as well as popular media, Prince George's County has occasionally been called "Ward 9," as though it is an extension of DC's eight wards.

[63] To briefly compare demographics, Indiana's population is 83% white and 9% Black compared to DC's 40% white and 40% Black. Combined with a name like "Alison," which is coded as "white" along with names like Heather, Molly, or Emily, it seems reasonable to assume that I would be coded as white via email, especially within a research background. However, while many studies have shown that "white" names go further than "Black" names in the corporate world and in hiring processes, in this case I argue the opposite. Nilanjana Dasgupta et al., "Automatic Preference for White Americans: Eliminating the Familiarity Explanation," *Journal of Experimental Social Psychology* 36, no. 3 (2000): 316–28.

[64] Deborah Wong, "Moving: From Performance to Performative Ethnography and Back Again." in *Shadows in the Field: New Perspectives for Fieldwork in Ethnomusicology*, edited by Gregory Barz and Timothy Cooley (New York: Oxford University Press, 2008), 82.

these layers in order to complicate the notion of "fieldwork at home," which has been inconsistently theorized in ethnomusicology and is seemingly most often conducted by people of color.[65] As ethnomusicologist Melloneee Burnim argues, shared racial or ethnic identity with a group of people does not automatically create a culture-bearer. Regarding her fieldwork on gospel music, she emphasizes that racial/ethnic identity is not the only reason why she was trusted in her various research sites, but also because she was a culture bearer within the gospel music tradition and was able to offer these churches her services as a musician in return for conducting research.[66] My Blackness, then, did not always endear people to me. Fieldwork for me was at home but-not-home, where I was often familiar with the people and places around me but had arrived with a new set of expectations and questions that required me to become an outsider.

Participant observation for this project involved attending musical performances, neighborhood meetings, farmers markets, rallies, protests, and more. At these events, I was typically most interested in sound sources and tensions surrounding them. At an Advisory Neighborhood Commission (ANC) meeting one evening, half the attendees left the event halfway through because their hot-button agenda item had been completed. They then proceeded to be so loud in the hallway that one of the commissioners running the meeting had to step out to tell them to be quiet, that there were still more items on the agenda besides theirs. These tensions, stemming from who is able to be heard and whose sounds or voice are deemed important, were central for the project. More than any particular event, though, I spent a great deal of time in the intersection of 7th Street and Florida Avenue. Whether I was sitting at the bus stop on the corner, taking soundwalks around the neighborhood, eating in Halfsmoke, the restaurant on the corner, or just listening to the go-go music, I wanted to get to know the aural contours of that intersection as I was conducting passive acoustic recording. Also, many of my observations were digital rather than in person; that is, I listened to online radio, watched videos on social media apps such as Facebook and Twitter, and watched live streams of DC Council Hearings. In this way, my ethnography was necessarily digital because many of the city's conversations on gentrification are happening online, both privately and publicly. Throughout the book

---

[65] Jonathan Stock and Chou Chiener, "Fieldwork at Home: European and Asian Perspectives," in *Shadows in the Field: New Perspectives for Fieldwork in Ethnomusicology*, edited by Gregory Barz and Timothy Cooley (New York: Oxford University Press, 2008), 108–24.

[66] Mellonee Burnim, "Culture Bearer and Tradition Bearer: An Ethnomusicologist's Research on Gospel Music," *Ethnomusicology* 29, no. 3 (1985): 432–47.

I incorporate these materials where possible, including tweets, Facebook comments, and maps.

Passive acoustic recording was the most unconventional method for the project because the approach is most often used to listen to changes in more "natural" bioacoustic environments, such as forests, or to listen to whales underwater. However, this method of long-term passive acoustic recording has been established as an effective way of detecting patterns and changes in soundscapes.[67] As I began attempting to hear change in one intersection, I anticipated passive acoustic recording to be an innovative and dynamic way to hear change over time. From the beginning, this recording was carefully intertwined with ethnography, because in order to install the recorders, I first had to receive permission from the owners of those particular buildings, both of whom agreed after an interview with me. This agreement also came with the promise of letting me inside and on the rooves once a month to download data and change the batteries for the recorders, which allowed me to get to know various office staffs and grounded this project in people, rather than soundscape data. To explore the sonic changes and aural perceptions of the neighborhood, I installed two recorders on rooftops in the intersection that recorded one minute out of every five minutes, all day every day. The final tally of over 100,000 recordings is nearly impossible to listen or analyze manually, and yet the possibilities for the dataset are nearly endless.

Chapter Outlines

Ultimately, this book is about stories—of intersections, people, and sounds. Chapter 1, "I'm On My Way to Atlanta," starts our journey by examining how musicians in DC's larger music scene(s) interact with, challenge, and participate in narratives of gentrification within the city. I focus on the stories of three Black women musicians that I interviewed for the project: Be Steadwell, Carolyn Malachi, and Asha Santee. These musicians have distinct musical stories but have all collaborated together and are a part of DC's larger Black and queer music scene. Be Steadwell, born and raised in upper Northwest DC, released her album *Queer Love Songs* in 2018, which she considers to be a form of activism. Carolyn Malachi balances many roles as a musician, audio engineer, and educator. Asha Santee is a drummer and producer who was

---

[67] Bryan C. Pijanowski et al., "Soundscape Ecology: The Science of Sound in the Landscape," *BioScience* 61, no. 3 (2011): 203–16.

born outside of the city but has cultivated an intimate fanbase through her involvement with almost a dozen bands in the city.

Between Chapters 1 and 2, I offer a brief interlude that bridges the concerns of Black women raised in Chapter 1 and listening to the Shaw neighborhood in Chapter 2.[68] This interlude recounts soundwalks that I took during fieldwork and engages the complicated and subjugated nature of Black women's knowledge production. I explore a Black feminist practice here, utilizing soundwalks to humanize myself in a soundscape that would otherwise disregard my sonic perceptions in favor of white hearing as the default standard of sound.

Chapter 2, "Smooth Jazz and Static," explores how people in the Shaw neighborhood of DC understand change to be heard and enacted sonically. I argue that people in Shaw perceive gentrification through aural expectations, neighborhood legacies, and sonic tension. This chapter is framed and argued through the story of Breonna Taylor's murder in 2020, which has been linked to processes of gentrification by her family's attorney. I attempt to think through what deaths might be prevented if we listen critically and carefully to those that sound themselves as being marked for removal. This chapter is also grounded in the importance of the educational value of Black neighborhoods, where the stories people tell offer invaluable insight into the racialization of sound. I argue that gentrification is heard throughout Shaw, and that attention to these understandings demonstrates the importance of music and sound to this historically Black neighborhood.

Chapter 3, "7th and Florida," presents a soundscape analysis of 7th Street and Florida Avenue Northwest, the intersection in Shaw where I initially set out to conduct fieldwork. Here, I outline my methodology of passive acoustic recording and analysis. For nine months in 2018, I had two recorders installed on rooftops at the intersection that recorded one minute out of every five, all day every day, resulting in 288 recordings per recorder for each day. From this data, I track patterns among key instances of tension within the soundscape, such as sirens, go-go music, and traffic. This chapter also expands on my contribution to Black digital humanities, a mode of engaging the connections

---

[68] The two interludes in this book are inspired by a few different sources. In her book *Queer Times, Black Futures*, Kara Keeling offers a few different kinds of short writings between chapters: an interregnum, an interlude, and an intercession. These short pieces act as bridges between larger chapters, and introduce a briefly different genre of writing, a short story of some kind. In addition to Keeling's work, these interludes are also inspired by musical interludes. When I mentioned to my best friend that I was planning to include them, he told me, "You want to be a neo-soul singer so bad." And don't I? Neo-Soul and R&B interludes are unmatched. Frank Ocean, Sza, India Arie, they all have beautiful interludes that you wish were four minutes longer but also love because they're not. So yes, I do want to be an R&B singer, and still yet may reach that point in my life, but at the moment I am an ethnomusicologist writing about sound and drawing on musical form to get there. See Kara Keeling, *Queer Times, Black Futures* (New York: NYU Press, 2019).

and tensions between humanities tools in a way that foregrounds the intricacies and realities of Black life. My contribution to Black digital humanities is a toolset to question how the digital can help render the spatiality of Black sound, particularly within soundscapes that are vulnerable to silencing.

Chapter 4, "Life, Death, and Legacy in Go-Go Music," explores in depth the relationship between go-go music and gentrification in Washington, DC. Go-go music, DC's local subgenre of funk, has been the sound of working-class Black DC for over forty years. In this chapter, I set out to accomplish two goals within the larger context of listening to gentrification in DC. First, I listen to the ways in which gentrification has affected go-go music, from displacement, to increased police encounters, to go-go's intricate and complicated legacy in the city. Second, bearing my own use of "legacy" in mind, I utilize Christina Sharpe's theorization of "the wake" to argue against the notion that go-go is dead or dying, a violent yet familiar classification that ignores the hundreds of people on stage and in the audience every night at these shows. Along the way, I amplify lesser-known voices in the go-go community, people whose stories have not been told during the institutionalization of go-go. There is a common thread of conversation about go-go that refers to the genre as dead or dying. One of the core interventions of my work is to argue that this language is violent and does a disservice to those still performing go-go music.

After this trio of chapters, I offer another interlude on the work of musical artist Kokayi. In 2016, he was commissioned by the Funk Parade (an annual music festival on U Street to celebrate local funk artists and the vibrant history of the neighborhood) to create four songs based on crowdsourced sounds of DC, one for each quadrant of the city. This interlude briefly analyzes each song, as well as Kokayi's larger position as an internationally known artist that remains committed to the cultural life of his hometown. His commitment extended into organizing against the Amplified Noise Act, which is the subject of the next chapter.

Chapter 5, "Plainly Audible," tells the story of the Amplified Noise Act (ANA), a law introduced in the DC council in June of 2018 outlawing amplified music in the DC, punishable by fine, jail time, and/or the impounding of musicians' equipment. In this chapter, I recount the events of the ANA through council hearing transcripts, interviews, and my own observations. Residents and workers in Chinatown, tired of the noise levels of street musicians, petitioned the DC council to draft and pass legislation that would allow the police to enforce the noise standards, which they were seemingly unwilling or unable to do previously. These residents leaned on a combination of both legislative and criminal justice aspects of city policies in order to take care of what they considered a problem in their neighborhood. The danger of the ANA is that requesting permission for police to escalate encounters with street musicians is actively endangering the lives of the musicians, many of whom are Black. Whether considered too loud, stubbornly silent, dangerously aggressive, hypersexual, or resistant to categorization altogether, Black sonic production has been consistently stigmatized.

I conclude the book with notes on the sonic futurities of Black people in Washington, DC, and how sound can be used to enact an ephemeral kind of justice in the city through events like Moechella, which began in 2019 during the rise of the #DontMuteDC. While architecture and rent prices are not instantaneously shifted, Black sound can immediately, if temporarily, hold space for Black people, retransforming gentrified neighborhoods into temporary concert halls, protests, and gathering spaces. While this project is in no way a comprehensive study of gentrification in Washington, DC, my commitment to the particular offers an ethnographic and digital account of sonic, racialized change. My goal in this work is to contribute to the decriminalization of Black sound, amplify Black life, and support those who are trying to do the same.

Chapter 1
"I'm On My Way to Atlanta"

> There is not a single global, national, or local condition to which Black women's intellectual, spiritual, and emotional intelligences cannot be trusted to bring greater clarity.[1]
> —Tressie McMillam Cottom

> Above all else, our politics initially sprang from the shared belief that Black women are inherently valuable, that our liberation is a necessity not as an adjunct to somebody else's but because of our need as human persons for autonomy. This may seem so obvious as to sound simplistic, but it is apparent that no other ostensibly progressive movement has ever considered our specific oppression as a priority or worked seriously for the ending of that oppression.[2]
> —Combahee River Collective

Cities are often personified in popular and scholarly imaginations. From the common trope of New York as "the city that never sleeps" to Lewis Mumford's 1960s theorization of cities (Chicago in particular) as living organisms, cities are regularly prescribed limbs, organs, and personality traits. Science fiction author N. K. Jemisin took this personification even further with her 2020 novel *The City We Became*, offering a narrative of New York City embodied in five separate people, each embodying the traits of a specific borough. Manhattan, for example, is sleek and slightly cutthroat, while Staten Island is constantly feeling left out and increasingly wary of outsiders. Despite these consistent personifications, cities are very little without the people that live in them. As the Combahee Collective said about Black women's liberation, this is "so obvious as to sound simplistic," but cities are not people. People are what give cities their "personalities" and make them rich, vibrant places to be. However, many of these people are minoritized, segregated, disenfranchised, and displaced out of these spaces during processes of gentrification.

---

[1] Tressie McMillan Cottom, *Thick: And Other Essays* (New York: The New Press, 2018), 227.
[2] "The Combahee River Collective Statement," in *Home Girls: A Black Feminist Anthology*, edited by Barbara Smith (New York: Routledge, 2000), 73.

Intersectional Listening. Allie Martin, Oxford University Press. © Oxford University Press 2025.
DOI: 10.1093/9780197671603.003.0002

Musicians are key components of urban character development, shaping cities with their music and the communities they create. In this chapter I consider how musicians in Washington, DC shape the city as they themselves are influenced by processes of gentrification. For some, gentrification is an obstacle to their livelihoods; for others, an opportunity to grow their audiences. And others still consider gentrification to be another institutional crisis in a long line of institutional crises facilitated by anti-Blackness and disenfranchisement. The stories in this chapter are intentionally about Black women, many of them queer. I am thinking with Kemi Adeyemi's ethnographic work on queer Black women in nightlife spaces in Chicago, where she notes that the dance floor is where the right to the city is negotiated.[3] Black women, especially in nightlife spaces, are articulating the conditions of what it means to be a part of gentrifying city life. This decision to focus on Black women's stories is also in part pedagogical, as I ask, "what do the experiences of Black women musicians have to teach us about how gentrification operates in DC?" In her poetry collection *Dub*, Alexis Pauline Gumbs gracefully challenges her readers as the work begins: "When you think your heart will break, stay there, stay with it. But at the same time, when you think you gotta hold onto something (like who you think you are), let go."[4] Here, I am staying with the heartbreaking knowledge that Black women's experiences are so richly instructive for the study of gentrification and sound because of the ways that our oppressions are copious and compounded. And yet I am asking that we let go of the idea that a study of gentrification must begin with a certain Black person or event. We will not start with the riots of 1968, nor with the gatekeepers of music in DC, nor with the common position of Black queerness as aberration or afterthought.[5] We begin with musicians that are experiencing gentrification and being affected by the sonic, political, and cultural changes in the city. This is an unlearning, an unraveling of the stories that we tell ourselves about cities and the people that live in them.

---

[3] Kemi Adeyemi, *Feels Right: Black Queer Women and the Politics of Partying in Chicago* (Durham, NC: Duke University Press, 2022), 21.
[4] Alexis Pauline Gumbs, *Dub: Finding Ceremony* (Durham, NC: Duke University Press, 2020), xiii.
[5] After the assassination of Dr. Martin Luther King Jr. in April of 1968, Washington, DC was one of many cities across the United States to erupt in riots and rebellions of frustration against white supremacy. Many neighborhoods in DC experienced significant fire damage and property destruction, including the H St Corridor, Shaw, and the U Street Corridor, all of which are currently gentrifying. The riots have defined a generation of study about DC, and while important, they are not the only story there is to tell about DC in the 1960s and 1970s, which I explore further in Chapter 2 with the work of Shelleé Haynesworth.

"Gay Sex" and Affordability

During an interview, questions about what a person's neighborhood sounds like usually go in one of a few different directions. People talk often about music: the music they grew up with, the music they heard blasting in their neighborhoods, the music they hear in the city now. People often synonymize music with sound, explaining what their neighborhoods sound like with the music that they hear in that space. People also gift me with extraordinary metaphors to describe what they hear in their neighborhoods: electricity and energy, static, smooth jazz, silence, light. Rare, though, is the occasion when someone takes me on a soundwalk to experience the soundscape of their neighborhood with them.[6] Be Steadwell was born and raised in Upper Northwest DC, on the edge of the famous Rock Creek Park, immortalized in Donald Byrd and the Blackbyrds "Rock Creek Park" (1975).[7] During our interview she described the sounds of the park to me as she remembered them, fox cries and woodpeckers; but after recorders were tucked away and goodbyes were said, we ventured from her house into the park to hear the trees. On that day in May, Rock Creek Park sounded like a gentle sway of wind moving through the trees, like relative quiet on the edge of a busy city.[8] The presence of trees and green space is important to Steadwell, who told me that when she moved to Atlanta ("because I can afford to live there") she would want to be near a park.[9] On gentrification and affordability in DC, Steadwell expanded:

> I feel like I experienced it [gentrification] in every way. The most obvious way is that I can't afford to live here anymore. I do a lot of gigs where people want you to be background music for an event or people are having lunch or people are, you know.

---

[6] Soundwalks, as I discuss later in the text, are walks that are particularly attuned to sound. These walks can be recorded or not recorded, alone or with a group. The underlying factor of any soundwalk is that is intended to be a space of listening.

[7] "Rock Creek Park" is an ode to sex in the park, repeating an arrangement of the lyrics ""doing it in the park / doing it after dark / oh, yeah / Rock Creek Park" for over four minutes.

[8] Be Steadwell, interview with the author, 2018. It is also fair to say that Rock Creek Park sounds like segregation, as it has long served as the unofficial racial dividing between white and Black communities in DC. It has been said that there were no white people east of 16th Street, which borders the park. This unofficial line was reinforced by the racial covenants that were prevalent in DC housing practices in the early to mid-twentieth century. So as I hear Be Steadwell, a Black woman musician that grew up around the park, describe the sounds she hears there as home, I also hear the legacies of covenants and restrictive housing practices that were designed to keep her from doing just that.

[9] The irony of capitalism is that Atlanta is also steadily gentrifying. Housing prices are not as high in Atlanta as they are in DC, but they are steadily increasing and contributing to both sprawl and displacement. Elora Lee Raymond et al., "Gentrifying Atlanta: Investor Purchases of Rental Housing, Evictions, and the Displacement of Black Residents," *Housing Policy Debate* 31, no. 3–5 (2021): 818–34.

And it's such a clear apathy for the music that's happening, the musicians in the room.[10]

Herein lies one of the foremost cultural costs of gentrification: many musicians and cultural practitioners cannot afford to live in DC, which affects the many communities of artists that would make their homes there. Black music is a space of "perpetual creation," featuring embellishment, improvisation, and the interaction of audience members that participate in the creation of community.[11] Steadwell engages in this community-building through her musical performance, playwriting, and filmmaking. With minimalist production, a loop pedal, and an introverted neo-soul aesthetic, Steadwell creates new worlds wherever she performs that disrupt the unaffordability of life in DC.

The impossibility of an affordable life in DC immediately changes the musical makeup of the city, because who makes Black music in a city where Black people leave by the droves for more affordable lives? Who shapes, stewards, leads, and finances Black music in a city where the 2020 median income for white people was $149,000 but the median Black income is $49,000?[12] Legislative responses to these inequities often come in the form of promised "affordable" housing, which is in itself a fraught term because of the process of dictating what is affordable. The standards of affordability revolve around percentages of the Area Median Income (AMI), determined by the US Department of Housing and Urban Development. Housing programs are determined from household size and income percentage of the AMI, which was $152,100 for DC in 2023. Affordability is an issue for not only those who want to move into the city but for those who, like Steadwell, grew up in the city. Lawyer and community advocate Stanley Mayes outlined the problem with affordability and rising housing costs succinctly:

> The person who bought the million-dollar house said, by virtue of that act alone, that they could stand the carrying cost of a million-dollar house—because they

---

[10] Steadwell, interview with the author, 2018. As a former violinist in a string quartet, I have experienced this apathy for music and musicians. I once played a reception at the Newseum, a now closed private museum in DC that displayed a large collection of materials related to journalism. One of the draws of the Newseum was its floor to ceiling glass walls that looked out onto Independence Avenue, one of the city's most important thoroughfares downtown. During the event, when attendees saw that a motorcade was about to pass by, they nearly bowled over my quartet to get a good look at who it might be (length of motorcade corresponds to the importance of the person it's for).

[11] Samuel A. Floyd Jr, *The Power of Black Music: Interpreting Its History from Africa to the United States* (New York: Oxford University Press, 1996), 232.

[12] "DC Racial Equity Profile," Council Office of Racial Equity, January 2021, https://www.dcracialequity.org/dc-racial-equity-profile.

did it! Somebody who paid twenty-five thousand, thirty-five, forty, forty-five, fifty thousand dollars for a house never said they could afford an eight-hundred-thousand-dollar house. Never did they do anything to suggest that they could afford an eight-hundred-thousand-dollar house. So to tax them identically is to run the person away, in the fifty-five thousand dollar house. And it just makes it yet another opportunity for the person who can afford the million-dollar house. So—but that's politics. Those are political decisions.[13]

Mayes here considers the different financial situations of a person that moved into the city in the midst of gentrification, who is able to afford a million-dollar home and the associated taxes, as opposed to the person whose home has risen in value, who was never in a position to pay the taxes associated with a luxury priced home. The persistence of rising property taxes has compounded the difficulties of homeownership for Black people in Washington, DC. Local businesses also struggle with rising property taxes, which impacts artists. A prominent example is Sankofa, a Black-owned Pan-African bookstore in DC that hosts a number of different programs, events, and author talks for the community in their Georgia Avenue neighborhood, near Petworth and Howard University. In 2019, Sankofa faced closure because they were unable to afford their property taxes, and community members mounted campaigns to help save the store. As of 2022, Sankofa was approved for property tax relief. This is another example of Mayes's articulation of gentrification because related to what a person can afford: just as many residents in DC never gave any indication that they could afford a million-dollar home, many local business owners never intended to own and be required to pay taxes for multimillion dollar commercial or mixed-use property.

For many artists, their art is not a lucrative career. Streaming is not profitable, and live music performances have tanked during the COVID-19 pandemic. Artists like Steadwell are sometimes able to secure grant funding for their projects, as well as partnerships with various arts institutions in the city. Artists often apply for funding from organizations such as the DC Commission on the Arts and Humanities, the Humanities Council, the Wherewithal Foundation, the Anacostia Arts Center, and more. Grant funding alone is not enough to sustain artist communities, especially as the distribution of the city's arts funding has been critiqued as unevenly distributed.[14] While this

---

[13] Stanley Mayes, interview with the author, 2018.
[14] In 2021 the long-time chairman of the DC Council, Phil Mendelson, attempted to block the reappointments of Natalie Hopkinson and Cora Masters Barry on the Commission on the Arts and Humanities, because of their conduct on the council. They repeatedly attempted to draw attention to the uneven distribution of city arts funding, particularly in regard to race. Due to intervention by Mayor

funding supports artistic growth, it cannot solve the problems of property taxes or rising home prices. More than millennial aged artists like Steadwell, the inability for musicians to afford housing resonates with the aging Black musician community, many of them jazz musicians that made their careers in DC in the 1950s and 1960s. Rev. Dr. Sandra Butler-Truesdale, co-author of *Washington, DC Jazz* (2019), founded DC Legendary Musicians in 2002 to promote and protect the legacies of these musicians. In addition to fairly compensated performance opportunities, Butler-Truesdale is also focused on creating a "musician's village," a space in which these Black musicians can age in place, and be given guidance and advocacy regarding healthcare, and insurance.

In addition to concerns with displacement and affordability, Steadwell also describes an "apathy" for music amid what she describes as DC's culturally conservative soundscape. Music acts as window dressing for events, and musicians become props that are needed for vibrancy but not appreciated for what they bring to a space. This was echoed by emcee Dior Ashley Brown, a rapper and bandleader who spoke with me about the unfairness of asking musicians to liven up a space and subsequently vilifying them when they become "too loud." All over the city, the role of music has changed, and musicians oscillate between being wanted and unwanted depending on the sociopolitical context of the moment. Of gentrification in the late 2000s and early 2010s, Brown said:

> I will never forget. When we were going through that gentrified change . . . basically it got cold. I would be out and be like it is so dry out here. And it was in between this whole transition. Then once they started building all these businesses, they pushed out all the music. And then it was like "Oh, can we have you come perform here? Because we need people to come over here. We need people to see this." Yeah. Yeah I thought so.[15]

Both Steadwell and Brown describe the push and pull between artist's communities and the city, its developers, legislators, and their own patrons. People want music because it promotes the products they are attempting to sell, be it a home, a neighborhood, or a nightclub experience. Once the experience is sold, however, the musician becomes irrelevant, background music in a city that remains unaffordable. Despite the difficulties of living in the city,

Muriel Bowser, Mendelson's attempts to block the reappointments were ultimately unsuccessful, and they were reappointed to the commission.

[15] Dior Ashley Brown, interview with the author, 2018.

Steadwell has maintained an active presence in the city, including her active performance schedule, filmmaking and writing musicals. Her 2018 album *Queer Love Songs* offers an array of approaches to queer love, desire, and heartbreak. "Gay Sex," one of the most popular and frequently performed songs from the album, makes a mockery of both the patriarchy and patriotism, and is grounded in the argument of queer love as radical.

I offer an analysis of "Gay Sex" here that attends to the sonic activist positioning of the song and speaks to why the song's message is relevant to the soundscape of a gentrifying city. Pleasure is the connection here, where drawing from the work of adrienne marie brown I suggest that just as pleasure is essential to queer worldmaking, pleasure is also essential to living with and in opposition to gentrification in Washington, DC. brown, in conversation with Cara Page, looks toward "setting down suffering work, or awakening something that is more compelling than suffering."[16] I hear the song "Gay Sex" as an offering of a framework more compelling than suffering, as Steadwell approaches pleasure as both resistance and activism.

During live performances, Steadwell has called "Gay Sex" "a love song inspired by the Trump administration." The song begins with a drumroll reminiscent of a Civil War band, already making mockery of traditional American military songs and patriotism. After the drumroll, the production is minimalist and whimsical, consisting of percussion, bass, and Steadwell's own vocals. The first verse pulls no punches:

> Racist white dudes are not new
> Racist white presidents are old news too
> A burning cross in the night
> Is as American as apple pie

This opening immediately expresses a remembering of America that foregrounds its violent past, centering the oft-dismissed knowledge that the country was built on a foundation of white supremacy and genocide. Trump's administration, then, is a continuation of American values, rather than being shocking or aberrational in its racism. Steadwell's vocals here are light —airy, even, as she states matter of factly that none of this is new. Following this opening, she offers a musical aside before finishing the first verse, an adjustment of "America the Beautiful." Steadwell only sings the first line of the song, switching out the second half for her own lyrics: "Oh Beautiful, for spacious

---

[16] adrienne maree brown, *Pleasure Activism: The Politics of Feeling Good* (Stirling, UK: AK Press, 2019), 49.

skies/ and bleaching out bloodstains." This lyrical change continues to criticize the American project, contrasting a visual of beautiful blue skies with blood, presumably staining the American flag.[17] There's a harmonic shift in this critique as well, swapping out the upward walking melodic line that usually accompanies "And amber waves of grain," with a minor melodic gesture, which combined with Steadwell's looping pedal skills imitates blood staining (perhaps even dripping down) the flag. This brief gesture folds Steadwell's critique of America into the melodic and harmonic structure of the song. By switching out the upward melodic line for notes that are not in the original key, Steadwell furthermore sings herself into a queer kind of deviance by singing the "wrong" notes, bending the song from one of open, sonorous patriotism into a haunting glimpse into the underbelly of the United States.

The bridge between verse and chorus follows:

> But look at us, we're so strong
> We fall in love while the whole world tells us we're wrong
> Yeah, look at us and our hearts
> We fall in love while the world tears itself apart
> They will come to curse our names
> Try to make us feel ashamed (oh)
> Yeah, they will come to curse our names
> We'll just come and come again
> Again

Strength here is presented as the ability to fall in love when the world is telling you you're wrong specifically for doing so. In keeping up with the humorous tone of the song, she offers a double entendre for "come," where "they will come to curse our names" leads to "we'll just come (cum) and come again." The United States as an institution is so against queer life that to speak of queer pleasure and orgasm is to operate in dissonance with the place itself. Finally, we reach the chorus:

> Oh, let's go home and have gay sex
> We'll do it for the President
> The sons of the Confederates
> Oh, they wish they had love like this

---

[17] Civil rights activist Fannie Lou Hamer famously declared that "the flag is drenched with our blood. Because you see so many of our ancestors was killed because we never have accepted slavery." *Of Black America*, 5, "The Heritage of Slavery," directed by Vern Diamond, aired August 13, 1968, on CBS News.

40 Intersectional Listening

> Oh, let's go home and have gay sex (let's go home)
> We'll do it for the President (and have gay sex, we'll)
> The sons of the Confederates (do it for the)
> Oh, they wish they could fuck like us (President)

The chorus is the celebratory peak of the song, where gay sex operates as both pleasure and protest. The second verse offers a brief new story before returning to the bridge and chorus:

> This is my civil unrest
> There are so many ways one can protest
> Hold up your sign in the street
> And when you're done, bring your fine ass home to me

This short verse situates Steadwell as narrator within a larger culture of protest that has erupted since the 2016 elections, where she encourages her listener/lover to protest in the street and then return to her. This second verse expands the conditions of protest beyond gay sex, emphasizing that queer people not only protest through pleasure, but also through more traditional methods such as holding signs in the street and marching. The last bit of the song zeroes in even further to Steadwell's intended marks:

> These sad straight white boys crying into pillows
> "What we gonna do if we lose our privilege?"
> "Oh good Lord, whose country is this?"
> All these sad straight white boys crying into pillows
> "What we gonna do if we lose our privilege?"
> "Oh good Lord, whose country is this?"

Here, with one last parting shot before repeating the chorus three times, Steadwell takes on white male anxieties about becoming a minority population in the United States, which is set to happen in 2045.[18] While Steadwell makes it known that these "straight white boys" are exactly who she talks in the song, the song is indeed written for those who explore the potential of gay sex as a form of patriotism, understanding the potential for queer desire as civil unrest.

---

[18] William H. Frey, "The US Will Become 'Minority White' in 2045, Census Projects," *Brookings* (blog), March 14, 2018, https://www.brookings.edu/blog/the-avenue/2018/03/14/the-us-will-become-minority-white-in-2045-census-projects/.

"Gay Sex" is tongue-in-cheek when listened to alone, but it moves into giddy territory when experienced live, because people in the audience sing along and find joy in singing about their own pleasure in spaces not built for that kind of joy. The live performance of this song is perhaps its most intense and effective civil unrest, particularly at places like the Kennedy Center, where Steadwell performed the song on the Millennium Stage in 2018.[19] Opened in 1971 as the United States National Cultural Center, the John F. Kennedy Center is home to the city's premiere arts and cultural institutions, including the National Symphony Orchestra and the Washington National Opera. It is the arts and cultural hub of the city as well as of the federal government. Given the federal government's blatant homophobia within the Trump administration as well as many others, to perform "Gay Sex" at the Kennedy Center, the city's most premiere venue for "high" arts and culture, is indeed an act of civil resistance. Steadwell laughs, quite literally, in the face of the federal government's conservativism, flaunting her pleasure and understanding that queer desire is controversial enough to warrant an activist stance.

I want to make a connection here between the performance of "Gay Sex," and the experience of Washington, DC as an increasingly unaffordable city. Rising housing costs, rents, and property taxes in DC invite complaint, invite disbelief (especially regarding the wealth gap), and invite resistance and organizing against these increases. In 2023 apartment rents in Washington, DC are on average over $2,000 a month, and this varies widely depending on the neighborhood.[20] The performance of "Gay Sex" at institutions like the Kennedy Center recognizes the violence of the city as well as the country, and advances pleasure as a viable friction, a mode of being alongside resistance. Intersectional listening asks us to seek knowledge on the margins, and Black queer pleasure is a marginalized knowledge within gentrification discourses. Furthermore, studying gentrification and understanding the difficulties of making a home in an unaffordable city works best when we think outside of a framework of resistance only, and of musicians as merely of use to the city's cultural palate. Rather, thinking pedagogically, songs like "Gay Sex" show that Black women have been and continue to articulate their positionalities in the world, and yet knowing these things, continue to advance pleasure as a viable framework through which to move in the world. How then, does

---

[19] Millennium Stage is the Kennedy Center's free concert series, where every night there is a free show at 6 p.m. These shows feature local musicians, youth groups, and a variety of acts for an hour-long free performance meant to make the arts more accessible to DC. The Kennedy Center remains accessible by Metro, as they offer a free shuttle running from the Foggy Bottom Metro Station to the building.
[20] Jeff Clabaugh, "DC-Area Rents Still Rising despite National Trend Lower," *WTOP News*, April 19, 2023, https://wtop.com/business-finance/2023/04/dc-area-rents-still-rising-despite-national-trend-lower/.

pleasure address the problem of affordability? Pleasure, experienced in this case through gay sex, moves us out of a resistance only framework and into a mode of living alongside injustice. Throughout this text, I will refuse the sensationalizing that conversations on gentrification thrive on. There is no mention here of there being "no more Black people in DC," or genres being completely wiped out. Rather, understanding pleasure as key here shows us that while apartments are unaffordable, and while organizations are tirelessly acting to secure more affordable housing for folks, there will always be Black people loving on each other nonetheless.

Backbone of the City

While there are many musicians with plans to leave, there are also those who are determined to stay. The night I met Carolyn Malachi, she was hosting "AWE," or All Woman Everything, an open mic at Busboys and Poets, a restaurant and community event space with locations throughout the DMV. Founded in 2005 and named after Langston Hughes's time as a busboy (and poet), Busboys occupies a curious space in the DC imaginary, both connected to patterns of gentrification but also existing on a promise of community engagement and conversation. Throughout the restaurant, Busboys projects a vibe of trendiness, diversity, safety, and attracts a clientele that is ready for conversation and performances from a variety of local acts. They host regular open mics, community meetings, have artwork of Black luminaries on the walls, and feature clever cocktail names such as "DC Tap Water" and "The Color Purple."[21]

This particular event was intimate, held in the back room of the Brookland restaurant with low lighting and art of Black luminaries on the walls, with no more than twenty-five people in the audience at its peak.[22] Most of the audience were Black women of varying ages, who greeted each other and caught up as they settled in to order drinks and food. I was there at the invitation of Nicole Mosley, aka DJ Heat—Malachi's friend and popular local

---

[21] Tap water in Washington, DC was notoriously unsafe to drink in the early 2000s because of lead in various pipe systems. *The Color Purple* is a 1982 novel by luminary Alice Walker.

[22] Brookland is a neighborhood in Northeast Washington, DC, home to the Catholic University of America and many neighboring Catholic institutions. As of 2013, Brookland is also home to the "Arts Walk," a mixed used development space along Monroe Street that houses the Brookland Busboys and Poets location. The Arts walk was a contested plan because of the proposed height of the residential buildings, something that continues to be a sticking point between developers and various neighborhood advocates. Jonathan L. Fischer, "Need an Art Studio? New Spaces Are Coming to Brookland and the Former Warehouse Loft," *Washington City Paper*, November 16, 2012.

DJ, known for her status as the official DJ of the Washington Wizards and Washington Mystics, DC's professional men's and women's basketball teams, respectively. Heat was the featured artist at the open mic that night and had invited me to stop by during our interview earlier that afternoon. I was interested in learning more about Heat's performance style, as well as seeing Malachi, who I knew to be one of the most prolific artists in DC today. That night, dressed casually in a Hillman College sweatshirt, Malachi acted as both MC and performer, beginning the event with a piece of her own.[23] Her spoken word began with a disquieting opening line: "Does your wife know she married a rapist?" Those words sucked the air out of the room for a moment, but as we all began to breathe again, the women in the audience offered up verbal encouragement in moments that Malachi seemed to hesitate or had difficulty continuing, helping her get through. Through tears and affirmation, Malachi and the women in the audience demonstrated the kind of supportive environment that the AWE open mic sought to cultivate every month.

The AWE open mic generated what I imagine as a kind of "ephemeral justice" in a gentrifying city, a kind of encounter with Black life and death that is fleeting yet powerful in its impermanence. A justice moving toward permanence in a gentrifying city might involve more solid legislation on rents, developers and tenants' rights, soundproofing, policing, and other institutional forces that directly affect the lived experiences of Black people. Ephemeral justice, on the other hand, is something that sound and music can operationalize because they permeate property rights and property taxes. They enact a kind of accountability through sound that is temporary, because after the event is over, the space returns to whatever it was before. Denise Ferreira da Silva's framing of justice is instructive in this instance, because in refusing to resolve revolt and rebellion into objectivity, offers us guidance to think at the limits of justice. She asserts that we "require a plan of sorts, a certain procedure, but one not committed to resolving the conditions it exposes into a more effective measure, grid, account that can inform preemptive actions or preventive mechanisms. Knowing at the limits of justice ... unsettles what has become but offers no guidance for what has yet to become."[24] Much like sound itself, the limits of justice are speculative, unknowable through efficiency, effectiveness, or grid-like thinking.

---

[23] Hillman College is the fictional historically Black College featured in the television series *A Different World* (1987–1993). The show was groundbreaking in its portrayal of the Black university experience. Although originally a spin-off of *The Cosby Show* (1984–1992), a restructuring in the second season established *A Different World* as a cultural force in its own right. Hillman College remains, decades later, a recognizable place and (fictional) institution to those familiar with the show.

[24] Denise Ferreira da Silva, "To Be Announced: Radical Praxis or Knowing (at) the Limits of Justice," *Social Text* 31, no. 1 (2013): 44.

44 Intersectional Listening

Pursuing justice, listening to Black women, and holding on to gentrifying space require the speculative, require us to spend time at the limits of what we know, the limits of what we know to be possible. And in a city where there are no maternity wards east of the Anacostia River, which has effectively made Washington, DC the most dangerous place in the United States for Black women to give birth, the politics of AWE are at the limit of what we know.[25] At AWE, women were given first priority for performance, and everyone else was only allowed to perform after every woman on the sign-up sheet had performed. Even then, men and nonbinary people had to receive verbal consent from the women in the audience. This rule was enforced consistently, as I observed Malachi turn down a man that asked to be put on the sign on sheet at the beginning of the event. He eventually performed at the end, along with another man who was given permission by the audience. Black women are consistently silenced and overlooked, so to intentionally mark this space speaks volumes. By creating a space in which Black women are centered and listened to, Malachi is working toward another kind of world, where Black women's wants and needs are prioritized.

Malachi follows the tradition of many other Black women artists and community workers in DC's history who have used their resources and time to create space for each other, fellowship, vent, and hold space until they make their way back into a world that routinely refuses to acknowledge them. Throughout various iterations of urban renewal in Washington, DC, Black women have been on the forefront of protests and advocacy. From Etta Mae Horn's activism for welfare recipients in Barry Farm in the 1960s to Sabiyha Prince's work for Black residents amid gentrification, there is a long and storied history of Black women working for the working class in DC, most of whom are Black. This legacy was on full display at the AWE open mic, as Malachi, Heat, and the other performers made space for each other through an intentional acknowledgment and encouragement of Black womanhood. As gentrification progresses and communities work to live among drastic wealth and homeownership gaps while advocating against discriminatory economic practices, there is an incredible amount of work being done, especially

---

[25] To address this problem, the city has broken ground on a new hospital, Cedar Hill, that is scheduled to open in December 2024. Local community organizations such as Mamatoto Village have also stepped in to help families have positive birth experiences. Amanda Michelle Gomez, "Ward 7 Lacks Maternity Care Services. Mamatoto Village Wants to Change That," *DCist* (blog), June 7, 2022, https://dcist.com/story/22/06/07/dc-ward-7-mamatoto-village-new-location/; Samantha Kubota, Jesse Burkett-Hall, and Josh Bernstein. "DC 'Most Dangerous Place to Give Birth in the US' for Black Women," *WUSA 9*, October 17, 2018, https://www.wusa9.com/article/news/investigations/mothers-matter/dc-most-dangerous-place-to-give-birth-in-the-us-for-black-women/65-605243922

in musical and creative spaces, to create Black space whenever and wherever possible, generating a kind of ephemeral justice.

Malachi's commitment to making space for Black women is a part of her sense of responsibility for the cultural life of the city. She articulates an obligation to keep the local scenes alive, especially DC's go-go and jazz communities:

> We've always been the backbone of the city and our culture is vibrant. Our culture is what a lot of new folks come to this town for. It shifts and it moves but it's always us. It always looks back to the rest of the diaspora as well . . . I think in DC there is this sincere feeling, especially among we who are natives, this feeling that we have to keep our culture alive. So that beat comes at you, and us here and now, we gotta keep the past alive, we gotta keep the memory and the dreams of future us alive.[26]

Malachi demonstrates here that the personification of cities has always come from people, not simply an intangible "essence" of the cities themselves. "We've always been the backbone" speaks to the notion that DC's cultural reputation, as a chocolate city, a live band town and the home of go-go and jazz scenes (among others), is dependent on Black people remaining active in these spaces. Gentrification shifts the so-called personalities of cities because it makes it harder for communities to show up: by restricting access to space, limiting expression, and embracing the exploitative financial gains of rapid development. Malachi also expresses a sense of responsibility for the cultural health of the city, in that it is "always" Black people that come through to "keep the culture alive." Articulations of justice and responsibility are key in conversations on gentrification because they interrogate notions of accountability in the city. There is no one actor that is responsible for gentrification, as there is no "act" that encompasses this series of processes. Amid the questions of blame, though, Malachi and the community of musicians that she understands herself to be a part of, consider themselves responsible for stewarding DC's music and culture, for keeping it alive. What does it mean to keep a music alive, to have that responsibility on your shoulders?

One of the ways Malachi carries this responsibility is through collaboration with other local artists, especially within go-go music, which she endorses as the sound of the city. Go-go music, which I explore more in-depth in Chapters 3 and 4, is DC's indigenous genre of funk music that has been active since the late 1960s and 1970s. Many of the members of the go-go community are working-class Black people in Washington, DC who experience the effects of gentrification, making the genre a critical site of reflection for questions

---

[26] Carolyn Malachi, interview with the author, 2018.

on gentrification and DC's music scene. In 2017, Malachi collaborated with go-go artist Michelle Blackwell on "We Like Money," a song that celebrates the resilient spirit and hustle of DC natives. "We Like Money" combines Malachi's jazz influenced vocal style with go-go singer Michelle Blackwell's hard-hitting adlibs and an enduring pocket beat. Where go-go music typically features a heavy vocal, often in a woman's lower range, Malachi's voice floats higher above the beat, creating an interesting confluence of timbres. The song opens with a declaration of resilience:

> When the bill's long and the money is short
> When the bill's long and the money is short
> My people get creative
> We endure
> 'Cause we ain't tryna live like this no more

This opening, which bounces along within go-go music's signature pocket beat, would be appropriate at any stage of Black life in American history, as Black people's creativity amidst harsh living conditions is well documented, from culinary to musical innovation. Endurance is a useful metric regarding gentrification because over and over, discourses of gentrification seek a kind of sensationalism to support a certain narrative of loss and salvage. Endurance, though, recasts gentrification as the latest harsh condition in a centuries-long list of harsh conditions facilitated by anti-Blackness in the United States and around the world. In his essay "After Caravaggio," writer Teju Cole visits Italy to spend time in the same places that sixteenth-century Italian painter Caravaggio did during his controversial life, he says "I could no longer separate my exploration of Caravaggio's years in exile from what I was seeing around me in contemporary Italy: the sea was the same, the sense of endangerment *rhymed* [emphasis mine]."[27] How might senses and sentiments rhyme? Perhaps their endings rhyme, or maybe a more complicated internal rhyme in which the middle of a sentiment is the same as the middle of another sentiment in another time and place. The opening verse of "We Like Money" rhymes periods of Black financial stress with one another, because no matter what happens, Black people endure, creatively. This rhyming, an articulation of the predictable nature of racialized financial stress, facilitates Malachi's sense of responsibility for Black cultural life in DC. Gentrification may change the specifics, but the acts of financial violence and displacement are not new,

---

[27] Teju Cole, *Black Paper: Writing in a Dark Time* (Chicago: University of Chicago Press, 2023), 13.

especially not in DC, which experienced waves of urban renewal throughout the twentieth century.

Malachi's work presents gentrification as a multidimensional issue, one that is gendered, sexualized, classed, and racialized. At a show she headlined at City Winery, a multilevel venue in the gentrifying Ivy City neighborhood, she came out onto the stage at about 9 p.m. with her band playing her on. As she came on stage and saw just how many people were in the audience (at least 100), she startled briefly and began to fan away tears, taking a moment to gather herself before beginning the show. By way of explanation, she simply reminded us that it was a Tuesday night, conveying her sincere gratitude at being able to pack a venue in her hometown on a weeknight, which is not an easy feat for a musician. There were many instances of improvisation during the set, featuring similar methods of encouragement to the AWE open mic. Malachi improvised lyrics and affirmations throughout the show, reminding her audience to "spend time with someone who know how much your time costs," and that "ain't nobody badder than you at what you do." In addition to these kinds of affirmations, Malachi also offered commentary directly related to gentrification. She improvised a set of lyrics between songs, oscillating between the following two phrases: "Solid as a rock/____ can't stop me now." She filled the blank with the following: Gentrification, Kavanaugh, Trump, "fear of my vagina," and "fear of my complexion." This show was in October of 2018, and Brett Kavanaugh had just been confirmed to the Supreme Court despite credible allegations of sexual assault being brought forth to the Senate and his accuser, Dr. Christine Blasey Ford being questioned at his confirmation hearings. Women across DC, the United States, and the world watched in horror as President Trump, who himself has several credible allegations of assault, nominated Kavanaugh, who proceeded to engage in a stunning performance of white heterosexual male privilege during the hearings and was eventually sworn in. The Kavanaugh hearings became another in a long list of examples that prove that being a known perpetrator of sexual assault does not ruin a man's career. Her next improvised lyric, Trump, is a similar idea, as he even admitted to sexual assault on an Access Hollywood audio recording with Billy Bush. "Fear of my vagina" and "fear of my complexion" are a call for intersectional acknowledgment of the violence Black women face, especially in a country that rejects reproductive rights and continually fails Black women during maternity care, especially in DC. Including gentrification in this conversation is an acknowledgment that processes of development and neighborhood change enact a kind of violence onto Black women, be it through displacement, closing medical centers, or increased police brutality. Despite the pervasive messaging that Black men are the only people targeted by police brutality, Black women and nonbinary people are also regularly targeted, often experiencing sexual violence at the hands of the police, and the #sayhername movement began in 2015 to raise awareness for these offenses.[28] Gentrification creates a sense of suspicion around people in their own neighborhoods, and Black women are included in this suspicion. Gentrification, then, is very much a factor that increases violence against Black women, cis and trans. After these lyrics Malachi danced into the next musical transition, introducing a moment of levity into the show. Malachi's work is, in this way, multifaceted and nearly indescribable in its variation. One thing remains clear: she is committed to holding space for Black women and Black music even as the city around her continues to shift and morph, and not always for the better. Ephemeral as this justice may be, it is eternal, as the need for Black people to hold space for themselves amid ever changing urban conditions continues to rhyme.

Opportunity and Possibility

In addition to being an obstacle for artists to live and work in DC, gentrification also poses a series of ironic opportunities for musicians: artists grants (for those legible to granting institutions), new residents who want to explore the soundscapes of their new homes, businesses that want to draw in new clientele, and musicians themselves that come to live in the city. Artists like Asha Santee are doing their best to navigate these opportunities. A multi-instrumentalist, singer, and producer who has lived in DC since 2004, Santee expressed sadness at the displacement of Black people but an action-oriented mindset about what to do in response:

> It's like aight, this shit happened, so what are we gonna do? Are we gonna sit here and cry about it, or am I going to do my part and continue to build and grow so maybe one day I can start a home, and set up something for Black people, for underserved people? What am I gonna do besides sit here and blame and point the finger? Nah, we can't give them that much control and that much power over how we're going to react.[29]

---

[28] Kimberlé Crenshaw et al., "Say Her Name: Resisting Police Brutality Against Black Women," *African American Policy Forum*, January 1, 2015, https://scholarship.law.columbia.edu/faculty_scholarship/3226.
[29] Santee, interview with the author, 2018.

Santee refuses to give newcomers and those pulling the strings on processes of development power over how she reacts to gentrification. To this end, she is focused on growing her audiences in an effort to take the city back in a sense, looking to eventually sell out iconic venues such as the 9:30 Club, located in the U Street Corridor. This strategy of growing audiences leads to Santee approaching music and performance with a spirit of unbridled openness, where she emphasizes that we have to be open to various musical experiences for this to work, rather than staying only in our musical comfort zones. This manifests not only in the music that Santee listens to herself but in who she finds in her audiences: "I'm not going to side eye or question or exclamation point if there's a white person in my audience. I don't know what they going through, like if my song saves their life, or helps them be a better partner, or makes them fall in love with somebody, my job is done. Now we're together." While this togetherness is a significant goal for Santee within her artistry, there is also a compelling interplay between openness and specificity in Santee's work: she is vocal about wanting to bring people together but also offers an unapologetic, specific Black queer experience in her music.

Here I offer an impression into Santee's musical world in order to facilitate a larger discussion about how musicians in gentrifying cities approach the realities of cultural displacement. While some artists are repeatedly repelled by the apathy of their audiences, artists like Santee are intent on connecting with people that they would not necessarily connect with in daily life. Ethnomusicologists often struggle with how to break to our students that music is not quite the universal language we've been enculturated to believe it is, but Santee's style of music-making offers an intervention in this conversation. She complicates the dismissal of music as a universal language, building up her musical chops so she is able to perform with anyone, and yet offering musical performances that are specific to her experiences, pushing us to continually question what music gentrification makes possible. Openness and specificity exist simultaneously, and it is in part the specificity of her holding space as a Black queer woman supported by other Black queer folks that allows her to go in pursuit of various other musical opportunities and conversations. Depending on who and when you ask, she is a member of anywhere from five to a dozen bands of varying genres. And yet watching her perform her solo work, one is struck by the vulnerability of a woman talking to herself about love and heartbreak. Santee's musicality makes her able to collaborate across genres, in both her use of instruments and rhythms as well as her ability to command center stage or offer a supporting role.

When I interviewed Santee, she made my day when she asked if I wanted to hear songs from her new album and played them for me in her home studio.

Although a small space, her studio was dense, packed with speakers, a monitor, and several instruments, acoustic and electronic. The first song she played for me was "By Her Side," which is built around a keyboard motif and a repeated lyric: "She just wants to be/by her side/She just wants to be/right by her side." This lyrical meditation continues throughout the song, even as the beat drops about three quarters of the way through the song, taking the listener into another space with the same lyrics. As she explained to me, most of her upcoming album *The Process* is Santee talking to herself, leading to the kind of repetition she utilizes in "By Her Side." The repetition also serves another purpose, creating a Black queer soundscape; a sonic world where her loops, layers, and repetitions enmesh the listener in a sonic world that centers Black queer womanhood and relationships.

This intimate home studio experience is replicated whenever Santee performs live. At a queer open mic at Bloombars in 2018, Santee was the featured performer, offering a solo set of covers and original material. She opened with a cover of "Beauty" by Dru Hill, one of the most popular R&B slow jams of the 1990s. This cover had a similar soundscape to "By Her Side," including sparse production, and a beat built from scratch with a keyboard, loop pedal, drum machine, and her own voice. In addition to changing the soundscape of the song, Santee also made small lyrical changes. Artists often change the pronouns for a cover song to correlate their gender with that of the protagonist and adjust accordingly the rest to keep the song heteronormative. However, the shifts Santee made in "Beauty" were specifically made to change a song written about men loving women into a song about a woman loving a woman who *loves women*. She only changed one line in the chorus, from "I'm hoping I can make you mine/before another man steals your heart" to "I'm hoping I can make you mine/before another *girl* steals your heart." The change queers the object of her desire, pronouncing her a queer woman. This gesture creates a space for queer sonic intimacies, holding space for queer desire and relationships. Santee's own queerness is both announced and reinforced just from keeping the chorus the same:

> Walks by me every day
> Her and love are the same
> The woman that's stolen my heart
> And beauty is her name

During these performances, Santee occasionally explains to her audience what she's doing at any given point, especially regarding building beats. Depending on the audience, she also solicits support, asking them to please tell her to breathe, or to take her time. This request of audience participation is evocative of Black religious soundscapes, where people call out for the pastor to "preach!" or "take your time!" These sentiments also regularly occur during performances with her bandmate Patience Rowe when they perform as "Boomscat." Patience will ask the audience to say "Sing, Asha," creating space for breath and the release of any tension that is built up on stage. These expressions have seeped out of the church and into popular culture, where anyone who is about to give a word, preach, or perform, is subject to this kind of encouragement.

Santee's intimate performances strike a balance between openness and specificity, and the formation of intimacies during live performance as well as studio recordings works counter to the divergence of gentrifying neighborhoods. Gentrification erodes the intimacies of neighborhood life by removing the "local-ness" of various spaces and replacing them with chains, luxury apartments and condominiums, and in house amenities that take away the need to interact with one's neighbors and community. Santee's work poses the question of "what if everyone is my community in some way?" offering a path forward into the current state of DC. Santee presents the immediate generation of intimacy as a strategy against cultural displacement.

On a large scale, gentrification is about vision, and how people envision a city like DC. Rampant capitalism envisions DC as a city of sprawling condominiums and sleek neighborhoods, from the newly named "NoMa" to "AdMo."[30] Santee's vision is important because it imagines DC as a queer space, as a space where shows are diverse but in which she gets to make exactly the kind of music that she wants to make, even as different versions of the city shift around her, and some become more dominant and others recede into past.

Santee's openness is exhibited through a flexible and dexterous musicality in performance, on full display at a show she performed at in August of 2018 called "The 9." The premise of the show was to get nine acts onto the same bill at the Rock & Roll Hotel, with each act performing two or three songs each, and at the end nine brief encores. The result was a long show that gave a wide variety of artists a chance to shine on the same stage. I arrived on time even though she was billed toward the end of the show. I settled in preparing myself to wait hours to see her. To my surprise she played on over half of the sets on the bill, offering support on cajon, background vocals, or both simultaneously.

---

[30] NoMa refers to Northern Massachusetts Avenue, a moniker that has been critiqued as serving the purposes of gentrification because the area used to be referred to as New York Avenue, the same as the Metro Stop. AdMo refers to Adams Morgan.

I knew Santee as an R&B singer primarily, so it was enlightening to see her in various other capacities, collaborating with country singers, harpists, rappers, and everyone else on "The 9" set. This is Santee's openness in practice, where she creates connections between a variety of musical spaces in the hopes of making connections not only with other performers but with whoever happens to be in the audience. When it came to her own set, Santee offered a performance similar to the Bloombars set, with body mic, keyboard, drum machine, and loop pedal. Complementary to her openness as a performer and collaborator, Santee's music is intentional, intimate, and specific to her identity a Black queer woman. While stories of gentrification often paint a picture of Black people as victims to displacement, increased police harassment, and a wealth of other negative consequences, a deeper look (and listen) will reveal an intricate network of responses and strategies to engage with gentrification. These changes are continually affecting aspects of musicians' lives, from rent prices to securing gigs, but in a similar fashion, these musicians are shaping narratives of gentrification for themselves, and not necessarily suffering. Santee is an artist well aware of how gentrification is changing the city but is simultaneously exerting a refusal to be shaped solely by a narrative of displacement or loss. Instead, she intends to shape the narrative herself, through performance, collaboration, and flexibility.

Tarica June and Oh He Dead

While gentrification has negatively affected the livelihoods and musical practices of many musicians in Washington, DC, the economic and demographic shifts in the city have also created space for new artists altogether, like Oh He Dead. This band formed in 2015 because of a chance meeting between two musicians, one a Black native Washingtonian and the other a white transplant to the city. My meeting Oh He Dead was a chance encounter as well, an example of how even the best laid plans can go awry during fieldwork, spurred by a conversation, observation, or in this case, a band. After walking three blocks in a sideways downpour, I finally entered the Rock & Roll Hotel, a multilevel club and concert venue located in the H Street Corridor of Northeast DC. Like Shaw and the U Street Corridor, H Street has undergone rapid transformation since the late 2000s, moving quickly from a severely underserved neighborhood to one that is "up and coming."[31] I was there to see Tarica June,

---

[31] H Street, much like U Street and Shaw, has been defined by the 1968 riots that devastated the neighborhood. Many Black-owned businesses were burned out and left for years after the initial conflict.

a local rapper who was opening for Los Angeles based artist Sunny War. After unsuccessfully drying my shoes in the bathroom's air dryer, I squelched back to the main stage to see June. She's best known for her song "But Anyway," which went viral in 2016 because of its gentrification related themes and clever punchlines:

> The city's still filling up with those who dance off-beat
> more than a hundred forty characters and all of em weak
> they walk by, low eye, act like they can't speak
> they walk dogs—when I say that I don't mean their feet

"But Anyway" is full of moments like these, mocking white newcomers to the city for all manner of reasons—whiteness is uncool in the popular imagination. White people, broadly construed, are regularly mocked on social media for various degrees of blandness, from unseasoned food to dance moves. This mocking is occasionally subverted by an attachment to an ethnicity or nationality, such as Italian or Polish, which adds some "zest" to otherwise undifferentiated whiteness.[32] This popular conception of whiteness as bland and silly operates as a defense mechanism for how dangerous manifestations of whiteness as power actually are for people of color. June acknowledges the danger of the stereotypical white gentrifier later, with the more subversive lines about dog walking reference and lack of eye contact. Connections between animal cruelty and police brutality have become a popular trope, where white people are criticized for caring more about dogs than Black people, and not caring about police misconduct until the police hurt a dog. This is grounded in the dehumanization of Black people as well as the historical and contemporary use of dogs as weapons against protestors of color.[33] As for ignoring neighbors, this is yet another level of dehumanization, where white people refuse to even look at or acknowledge their Black neighbors, out of a combination of fear or general snobbery. This combination can quickly turn deadly, perhaps best outlined in Claudia Rankine's *Citizen* where she describes realistic scenarios in which white people call the police because they see an unfamiliar Black man in the neighborhood.[34] Police officers have acknowledged that they are called more frequently in gentrifying neighborhoods now because of this

---

[32] Emily Bazelon, "White People Are Noticing Something New: Their Own Whiteness," *New York Times*, June 13, 2018, https://www.nytimes.com/2018/06/13/magazine/white-people-are-noticing-something-new-their-own-whiteness.html.

[33] Sam Levin, "Guards for North Dakota Pipeline Could Be Charged for Using Dogs on Activists," *The Guardian*, October 26, 2016, https://www.theguardian.com/us-news/2016/oct/26/north-dakota-pipeline-protest-guard-dogs-charges.

[34] Claudia Rankine, *Citizen: An American Lyric* (Minneapolis: Graywolf Press, 2014).

fear.[35] Evoking these disharmonies, "But Anyway" captures the popular imagination of gentrification and displacement, making audible the combination of nostalgia and resentment that many people feel in gentrifying spaces.

I went to the Rock & Roll that night to see June perform "But Anyway" live in a gentrifying neighborhood, curious to see how the energy would transfer in a live setting. She didn't disappoint, entertaining the small crowd with a set that included "But Anyway" as well as a hilariously true song about the annoying persistence of DC parking and speeding tickets.[36] June's performance style embodies a kind of vigilant locality, where she positions herself as part of the old guard (despite her relatively young age) that needs to protect the city from the newcomers and maintain a particular way of life. She signals to this nostalgia through local, insider slang, references to place names, and well-trodden stereotypes of "the gentrifier." These kinds of performances are happening more frequently throughout the city, operating as spaces where artists can come and express their frustrations with how the city is changing around them.

Although I came specifically to see Tarica June, what I didn't know was that Sunny War had another opening act that night, a local band called Oh He Dead. There were five of them, a young Black woman with a striking head of gray hair and a raspy voice, with four men (two white, two Black) backing her on guitar, bass, drums, and vocals. They did a short set featuring covers and originals, with Amy Winehouse's "Valerie" getting the most attention from the audience. Their sound is perhaps best described as "indie soul," reminiscent of a less Southern Alabama Shakes.[37] I was struck by their sound and curious about their story, so I reached out after the show and eventually interviewed Andy Valenti, their lead guitarist and singer. He told me the story of how he and singer Cynthia Johnson (CJ) met and started the band in 2015. The meeting was serendipitous, spurred on by a mutual friend who asked if Valenti would help CJ with her songwriting:

She sent me a voice memo of CJ singing this song "Crying," that she had written. It was beautiful and completely done and didn't need anybody else's anything.

---

[35] Anne Branigin, "Exclusive: New Report Shows Gentrifiers Use Police to Terrorize Communities of Color—Without Even Calling 911," The Root, January 8, 2019, https://www.theroot.com/exclusive-new-report-shows-gentrifiers-use-police-to-t-1831576262.

[36] Luz Lazo, "Violating D.C. Traffic Laws Could Soon Cost You More," Washington Post, September 26, 2018, https://www.washingtonpost.com/transportation/2018/09/26/violating-dc-traffic-laws-could-soon-cost-you-more/.

[37] Rudi Greenberg, "Oh He Dead Was Once An Acoustic Folk Duo. Now It's An Indie Soul Band With A Bright Future," Washington Post, November 21, 2019. https://www.washingtonpost.com/goingoutguide/music/oh-he-dead-was-once-an-acoustic-folk-duo-now-its-an-indie-soul-band-with-a-bright-future/2019/11/19/cfb958d8-06f3-11ea-ac12-3325d49eacaa_story.html

Her voice is incredible, and the first time I heard it I was like holy shit. So, I texted her back as quickly as I could like yes, please, when can she meet. She had probably half a dozen songs that were in various stages of being written, and I just was helping her think through chord changes, typical song structures, where to put more syllables, and where to take syllables out. I think the second or third practice, we started harmonizing together on songs. It was an instant, kind of like [snaps fingers] connection with that. We both kind of smiled, like what was that? I think the fourth or fifth practice she finally got up the courage to ask if I wanted to be in a band, and it was so funny because in my mind I'm like "she's way better than me, she's just going to go off in the stratosphere and I'm gonna be here." She asked so sheepishly, she was really nervous that I would say no, and I was like oh my god, are you kidding me? Yeah. So that was in 2015.[38]

Valenti moved to the city in 2011 for work, and Johnson is from the area, making theirs a story of a newcomer and a native Washingtonian making music together. Oh He Dead has gained a lot of traction in the city's local music scenes and beyond, with one of their original songs, "Lonely Sometimes," going viral with a submission to NPR's Tiny Desk Concert and the band touring across the country. Hearing their story and following them at shows that summer, I continued to think about how gentrification has changed DC's music scenes, creating new groups, partnerships and opportunities. Here again, the realities of gentrification prove to be more complex than the displacement of Black people and musicians. What music does gentrification make possible, and how do we study this music without ignoring or trivializing the violence of displacement?

These strategies outlined here, from invitation to resilience to the creation of entirely new groups and styles of music, are all a part of DC's larger music scenes and the sonic history of the city. Unfortunately, the gentrification that began in the 1990s and continues into the 2020s is not the first wave of gentrification, and these musical responses are therefore not the first of their kind. For example, the Georgetown punks, a group of punk musicians from DC's legendary hardcore punk scene which developed in the 1980s, may not exist if the neighborhood of Georgetown had not been cleared of Black people in the 1940s and 1950s. The music created in cities is inextricably tied to the history of those places, and the strategies of those who have faced waves of slum clearance, eminent domain, and urban renewal throughout the twentieth century and into the twenty-first.

---

[38] Andy Valenti, interview with the author, 2018.

This complexity, as explored through intersectional listening, is imperative to a discussion about gentrification and sound. For while I presented the musicians featured in this chapter separately, they exist together within a web of artistry and collaboration in the city. I met Be Steadwell first, and she encouraged me to reach out to Asha Santee, having collaborated with her on a number of projects, including *Queer Love Songs*. And although it was DJ Heat that initially introduced me to Carolyn Malachi that night at the open mic, Asha Santee's group Boomscat opened for her show at the City Winery in October. DJ Heat and Santee are both part of the touring musicians group for R&B musician Mýa (who went to the same high school as me). These connections only scratch the surface of how Black women artists are working together and supporting each other in DC. These women, although continually struck by the intensity of gentrification, are fighting back and shaping narratives for themselves, sounding a futurity of the chocolate city into existence as they work and build together.

Interlude: Notes on Soundwalking as Black Feminist Method

In July 2018 I visited Oxford, Mississippi for the first time, to attend a workshop at the Southern Foodways Alliance on conducting oral histories.[1] Upon walking with a friend back to our accommodations on the University of Mississippi campus, we heard a voice calling to us from far away, up a hill somewhere. It was a catcalling voice—that much I definitely recognized—but I also felt sure that I heard the word "nigger." My friend, who is also a Black woman, heard the taunting sounds of the voice but not that word specifically. At the time, I considered this to be one of the difficulties of Black womanhood: I was unable to distinguish which of my two most prominent identity markers (Blackness and womanhood) the speaker was using to harm me in that moment. I found it ironic that I came to Mississippi to learn best practices for listening to other people's stories, but could not hear my own story, could not say for sure what had happened to me. As I think about it now, I know that these two identity markers were never able to be separated. I was always being catcalled as a Black woman because that is what I am, my uncertainty was simply being unable to tell for sure if they used a racial slur or not. The lack of slur would not have removed my Blackness from the equation, would not mean that I was being catcalled as a "woman." There is no such thing as an unracialized woman, and the production of the category of woman is equally as caught up in the production of Blackness. Hortense Spillers taught us this: that Black women "describe a locus of confounding identities."[2] In the same breath, Spillers also gave us the grammar to pierce the violent imposed inventions of Black womanhood, where "in order for me to speak a truer word

---

[1] Oral histories are interviews that typically take into account a person's life story. The interviewer is often largely absent from these recordings, as oral histories are typically about preserving the account of the person being interviewed. Given the value placed on written transmission over oral transmission in the Western world, oral histories are key methods to gather information about a person, people, or event that may not be written down. Similar but not altogether the same as ethnographic interviews, I attended this workshop to learn more about how I might engage the people I was interviewing in Washington, DC and beyond to listen to gentrification.

[2] Hortense J. Spillers, "Mama's Baby, Papa's Maybe: An American Grammar Book," *Diacritics* 17, no. 2 (1987): 65–81.

concerning myself, I must strip down through layers of attenuated meanings, made an excess in time, over time, assigned by a particular historical order, and there await whatever marvels of my own inventiveness."[3] In the time since that visit I have used the ambiguity and distance of that catcall to both listen to and speak a truer word about myself, namely that being sonically uncertain of the violence being directed toward me at any given moment is not a failure on my part, nor a reflection of how well I know myself. Rather, the uncertainty of sonic violence directed toward Black women is an opportunity to listen more closely to how that violence made me feel, and how it affected the way I move around the world.

Since that time, I have become less interested in hearing more clearly and sharply the violences aimed at Black women and instead I have spent more time coming to embrace the speculative sonic ephemerality of Black womanhood, and utilizing this uncertainty on soundwalks. Soundwalks are any walk that is particularly attuned to sound and are a popular method for understanding the everyday sonic life of a place. Reminiscent of Michel de Certeau's "Walking in the City," soundwalks offer the kind of embodied experience missing from other more static soundscape recordings.[4] They can be recorded or unrecorded, guided or unguided, as long as participants are encouraged to listen deeply to their surroundings, which often involves listening closely to oneself and engaging deeply with one's inner thoughts. Soundwalks were popularized with a group of scholars in Canada that included R. Murray Schafer and Hildegard Westerkamp, who, in developing the tradition of sound studies and soundscape ecology, devised soundwalks for people to take to study the sounds around them. Visual culture has decreased the importance of sound in everyday life, and soundwalks recenter sound, sonic health, and soundscapes as important facets of the places that we make our lives in.

As a part of listening to gentrification, I have reimagined soundwalks as Black feminist method, as a procedure for centering and amplifying the knowledge, contributions, and logics of Black women and Black womanhood. Soundwalks allow me to center the complex, incomplete sonorities of Black womanhood, and they are enough in their incompleteness. Patricia Hill Collins has explained that Black women's knowledge is subjugated.[5] From

---

[3] Spillers, "Mama's Baby, Papa's Maybe," 65.

[4] In Walking in the City, de Certeau takes to task geographers and urban planners that are only considering the city from a bird's eye view. He insists that looking at New York from the top of the Empire State Building does not actually reveal to a person how the city is made. Rather, the city is made and remade from those that walk the city every day. Michel de Certeau, "Walking in the City (1980)," in *Cultural Theory: An Anthology*, edited by Imre Szeman and Timothy Kaposy (New York: Wiley, 2010).

[5] Patricia Hill Collins, *Black Feminist Thought: Knowledge, Consciousness, and the Politics of Empowerment* (Routledge, [1990] 2002).

the mismanaging of pain management to the terrifying statistics about Black maternal health (particularly in Washington, DC) to the #sayhername campaign that was specifically created to lift up the names of Black women and girls harmed by police brutality, Black women are often not trusted to articulate the conditions of our existence. Since I first read *Black Feminist Thought*, I have understood this to mean that my knowledge is tainted somehow, too specialized or not specialized enough, and not considered fit for application by a broader audience. Soundwalks as method, though, rely on my own subjugated knowledge. What did *I* hear? As Black feminism centers and humanizes Black women, I utilize soundwalks to humanize myself in a soundscape that would otherwise disregard my sonic perceptions in favor of white hearing as the default standard of sound.

Soundwalks, rather than stationary recording, speak to the possibilities of Black feminist methodologies because they privilege the motion of my body. I walk along the sidewalks, I cross the streets, I press the crosswalk button and wait in the intersection (or don't). The entire method is predicated on my movement, it cannot exist without me placing my body and my "locus of confounding identities" in direct conversation with various spaces, and the people and objects in them. Soundwalks immediately force and require a consideration of my perspective when in so many other modes of research and knowledge production, I do not exist as a fully formed subject. In recording my movements and documenting how gentrifying space reacts to my movements, I am able to better understand what gentrification sounds like, because gentrification does not exist as a process without imposing onto and being imposed onto by various subjects. By placing myself into gentrifying space and recording the ensuing engagement, I am better able to hear some of the many ways in which gentrifying space presses onto Black women.

Casting soundwalks as Black feminist method puts my work in conversation with other such methods, which is important because I am exploring the potential of Black feminist method not to create a proprietary theoretical stream but rather to be in conversation with scholars writing before, alongside, and after me. For example, Savannah Shange has written extensively on abolition as Black feminist method, where abolitionist anthropology "is an ethic and a scholarly mode that attends to the interface between the multisited anti-Black state and those who seek to survive it."[6] Black feminist methods are procedures, tools, modes of being that insist on the survival of Black women and queer people, because we cannot be free if Black women are not free.

---

[6] Savannah Shange, "Black Girl Ordinary: Flesh, Carcerality, and the Refusal of Ethnography," *Transforming Anthropology* 27, no. 1 (2019): 10.

Tamura Lomax calls for us to dwell in "the gray" as a Black feminist method in Black religious studies.[7] Across disciplines, geographies, and histories, and time, Black feminist scholars are puzzling through what it means to do this work and be safe, what it means to fashion a better world for Black women. A reimagining of soundwalks is one of my contributions to this effort.

Soundwalks lend themselves well for this kind of work because as a Black woman walking in a variety of urban and suburban environments, there is a particular kind of sonic awareness already because of the reality that I am consistently unsafe. If I am outside, if I am walking past a group of people, particularly a group of men, I walk with the vigilance that I could be harmed at any moment, listening intently for anyone behind me. This awareness is heightened if I am walking outside at night, and it is heightened even still if I am alone. In 2018 Danielle Muscato asked a question on Twitter: "What would you do if all men had a 9pm curfew?"[8] The answers were heartbreaking and simple, many of them saying that they would take a walk at night, run at night, run with both headphones in, etc. A recorded soundwalk, operating as Black feminist method, draws attention to this already heightened aspect of my surroundings.

I began soundwalking in DC to further my exploration of gentrification and sound. These walks could be anywhere between five minutes and an hour depending on where I was going, the pace of my walking, weather, and any other combination of factors. I walked a few different neighborhoods in the city, mostly keeping to the H Street Corridor, LeDroit Park, the U Street Corridor, and Shaw, as I tried to think about what a neighborhood's character sounded like and how I fit into that. During the day, these neighborhoods oscillate between a quiet residential neighborhood and a busy city space. Traffic, horns, and sirens are frequent, yet so are the sounds of children at recess and old men chatting outside on their stoops or outside of corner stores. Conducting soundwalks as a Black woman in gentrifying neighborhoods was a curious space to tarry in. I was in some ways an outsider as a nonresident, mindful of who and what I recorded at any given moment because part of what makes gentrification such a tense and terrifying process is the lack of control that residents (particularly renters) have regarding their own surveillance. I was also an insider, a Black woman in this space where being a Black woman is not (yet) anything out of the ordinary. In fact, as the months went

---

[7] Tamura Lomax, *Jezebel Unhinged: Loosing the Black Female Body in Religion and Culture* (Durham, NC: Duke University Press, 2018).

[8] Danielle Muscato [@DanielleMuscato], "Ladies, a Question for You: 'What Would You Do If All Men Had a 9pm Curfew?' Dudes: Read the Replies and Pay Attention. #metoo #Kavanaugh #Cosby #feminism #maleprivilege #privilege," Twitter, September 25, 2018.

on, more of my recordings featured me speaking to people on the street, some I had come to know and some still strangers to me.

One of my favorite interactions on a soundwalk came early on in my research, in late February of 2018. I was walking quickly, running late for an interview, listening intently to what was going around me, when I walked past a Black man, seemingly in his thirties, on a narrow sidewalk. The exchange went something like this:

Man: Whoa, whoa, why you running up on people?
Me: My bad, my bad!
Man: It's okay. Hey sis, you know how to make grits?
Me: [laughing], Nah, I don't know how to make grits.
Man: What about pancakes?
Me: Yeah, I can make some pancakes.
Man: Ayyyee, I'm tryna get some breakfast!!
Me: I don't know about all that!

The exchange, not quite a catcall but not quite comfortable either, consistently faded in volume, because during the entire time we spoke, I continued to walk away from him. I was in a position of wanting to speak, because I know the politics of being an outsider in a gentrifying neighborhood and not greeting folks as you walk by. However, I also know the dangers of being a Black woman walking alone, and so I negotiated a lighthearted exchange while making my way to my destination. My soundwalks, then, act as a sonic record of gentrifying space as well as my attempts to keep myself safe (gentrification sounds like Black women trying to keep themselves safe). This duality is a key part of considering soundwalks as Black feminist method, because they allow for the consideration of multiple sonic perspectives of the neighborhood, rather than one seemingly authoritative record.

Soundwalks are rhythmic, and the most noticeable thing on the recordings is the pace of my walking, the swish of a coat. Depending on how I'm holding my phone, my breath is audible in some parts of the recording. As I move, you can hear the city move with me, with cars, buses, and people. The juxtapositions in the city are decidedly audible as sounds float against and pass each other. In a recording from November of 2018, as music being played is fading out, I hear two men talking about a postnasal drip treatment that they do twice a month. Swirling around that conversation is the sound of construction, a loud jackhammer, and beams of metal and steel being struck together. And then comes the sound of children at a playground, screaming and laughing. As the city makes and remakes itself through concrete and glass, Black people are standing on the corner sharing advice about health and wellness, and children, the city's future, are testing their lungs on a cold day. Listening to gentrification allows us to hear the city's friction, where if looking at these things from a bird's eye view, there would only be new construction on the map, only stores and traffic patterns and other things that can be flattened into two-dimensional space. There is something both poignant and incisive about hearing, in the midst of change, Black people sharing suggestions to keep themselves well.

Just as Black feminist thought amplifies my "tainted" knowledge, it also mutes the authoritative "objective" knowledge of the stationary recorders I employed for other aspects of listening to gentrification. When once describing the stationary recording process to a colleague at a digital humanities workshop, they celebrated the idea that I would be able to "objectively" hear what was occurring in the neighborhood, instead of relying only on pieced together accounts from community members. The colonizing impulse of definitive knowledge production is seemingly inescapable, but intentionally positioning soundwalks in the lineage of scholars like Collins and Spillers gives me access to generations of refusal and articulations of refusal. I refuse the false familiarity of objectivity, instead casting the sounds of the stationary recorder placed on a rooftop to be as partial and positioned as the recordings of my footsteps as I move around the neighborhood.[9] I have never wanted the recorders or recordings to hold a kind of power of truth over the words and impressions of my interlocuters. All of these accounts—my soundwalks, the soundscape recordings, the interviews—are different accounts of what the neighborhood sounds like on any given day, and of what gentrification sounds like at any given time. These accounts are not to be discarded in favor of a more truthful one, but rather to be listened to in concert with one another, taking special care to hear and spend time with harmonies and dissonances in accounts. I am consistently more interested in counterpoint and relationality between sounds than in a one-to-one understanding of what a sound means or what gentrification sounds like. Soundwalks are a moment in time, and their interpretation changes over time. For example, listening to myself cough on a recording in 2018, I cannot help but think about COVID-19 and how the pandemic has changed perceptions and stigmas about public illness.

Although I have been asked so that students can listen, observe, and better understand how the city sounds at one of its most vibrant points, I refuse to lead classes on soundwalks through my fieldwork sites in the Shaw

---

[9] Abu-Lughod, Lila. "Writing Against Culture," in *The Cultural Geography Reader*, edited by Timothy Oakes and Patricia L. Price (New York: Routledge, 2008).

neighborhood.[10] I am unwilling to lead a class of majority white students through that space, because the line between observation and gawking feels unrecognizable in this context. How could we come and observe without disturbing the space? There are people there living their lives, folks that oscillate between listening to go-go music and hanging out in front of the corner store for several hours in the day, folks that are houseless making space for themselves in the intersection, as well as those just waiting for bus, going from one job or location to another. I would not invite a group of people, particularly white people, into that space or any similar space to observe those rhythms first-hand. Once while giving a virtual talk to a group of students in Finland, one of them asked me about my training, and specifically about how I had been trained in data ethics. I told them that I had not been trained in data ethics, but rather that Black Studies was my data ethics training. Scholars such as Simone Browne and Rashad Shabazz make clear the stakes of surveillance and carceral space for Black people, and studying with scholars like Valerie Grim taught me that if I am going to study and engage with Black people I have a duty to be as ethical as I know how to be. If I know better, I should do better. In Chapter 2, as I listen to the gentrification of Shaw from various vantage points, soundwalks were very present in my understanding of what it meant to move through gentrifying space, and what it meant to feel unwelcome in more ways than one.

---

[10] Although I have steadily refused to lead them in DC, I have used soundwalks in the classroom to help my students think about their various positions in the world. In *Teaching to Transgress*, bell hooks explains that "we must intervene to alter the existing pedagogical structure and to teach students how to listen, how to hear one another." In a course called "Hearing Race and Place in the US," I assigned students a soundwalk halfway through the semester, and wanted my students to think about how their various intersecting identities, how they operated in the world, influenced what they heard and how they were heard. bell hooks, *Teaching to Transgress* (New York: Routledge, 1994), 150.

Chapter 2
Smooth Jazz and Static

On March 13, 2020, twenty-six-year-old Breonna Taylor was murdered by police officers in her home in Louisville, Kentucky. The fatality was linked to a "no-knock" search warrant issued by the Louisville Police Department, which allowed for the unannounced entry of armed plainclothes officers into the home, where they eventually shot and killed her. Taylor's death sparked protest and outrage across the world, especially because none of the officers were indicted or charged for her murder.[1] The global call to #sayhername that began with Sandra Bland in 2015 has re-erupted, as Black women ask how justice may be enacted in their names.[2] One important—if underreported—aspect of the case has been the family attorneys' claim that Taylor was murdered as a part of Louisville's gentrification process. The attorneys argue that the Place Based Investigations Squad that killed her was focused on properties on Elliott Avenue, where she lived, because they stood in the way of a multimillion-dollar reinvestment project slated for the neighborhood. These claims have been vehemently refuted by the mayor's office, which claims that no such connection exists. Despite the city's claim that the allegation is false, both the family's lawsuit and Louisville's *Courier Journal* attest that "in a three week span earlier this year [2020], eight homes on Elliott Avenue were demolished by the city's contractor . . . Only nine homes had been demolished on Elliott Avenue in the past 16 years combined."[3] Furthermore, the city of Louisville has also purchased homes for $1 after making arrests at various properties.[4] The increased demolitions on Elliott Avenue combined with the

---

[1] One of the officers involved was indicted for "wanton endangerment" because of the shots he fired into neighboring apartments, but none were charged directly for her murder.

[2] #Sayhername began as a call to center and lift up the names and stories of Black women that have been harmed and killed by police violence, because too often these conversations are solely about Black men, ignoring injustice again Black women and nonbinary people. The calls for justice in the form of arrest in Breonna Taylor's case have been fraught, because they come during a time when the United States has entered an unprecedented conversation about the abolishment of policing and prisons. The Black feminist politics that calls for justice and the Black feminist politics that advocate for an end to carceral punishment require a careful consideration of what we understand justice to mean.

[3] Phillip M. Bailey and Tessa Duvall, "Breonna Taylor Warrant Connected to Louisville Gentrification Plan, Lawyers Say," *The Courier-Journal*, July 5, 2020.

[4] Natalia Martinez, "City Buys Home Rented by Breonna Taylor's Ex-Boyfriend for $1 as New Allegations Arise," *WAVE*, July 6, 2020.

city's purchase of homes after arrests raised suspicion that the city might be using the police to remove people that stand in the way of various development projects.

The United States has a long, violent history of clearing out communities of color to advance development projects, from highway construction to university expansions.[5] Taking Breonna Taylor's death and the Place Based Investigations squad as a starting point, Brent Cebul reminds us that when we talk about the ways in which the police have destroyed Black communities and entire "lifeworlds," we must remember that "policing is but one branch of the state."[6] The violence of policing is allowed and encouraged by the fiscal and political agendas of the state, in this case potentially to facilitate gentrification. The connections between policing and the fiscal aims of the state (including gentrification) are not isolated to Louisville. In Ferguson, Missouri, investigations in the wake of Mike Brown's murder uncovered that Black residents were charged more for parking tickets and traffic violations than any other demographic in the state. In Los Angeles, researchers at UCLA reported that billions of dollars of cash bail is levied by the Los Angeles Police Department every year, disproportionately against Black and Latinx residents.[7] The list goes on, as cities around the United States use the penal system to further financially destabilize the poor and working class.

Keeping these violent relationships between development, municipal finances, and police violence in mind, the provocation is this: If we situate Breonna Taylor's tragic murder within a framework of gentrification, of places and people being marked for removal, what then might we hear? What should we listen for? The immediate sonorities of Breonna Taylor's death likely involved chaos: screams, over a dozen gunshots, yelling, the last breaths of a dying woman. What of listening before the chaos of death? What did it sound like when the judge signed the warrant? Pen moving against paper authorizing the use of a battering ram in the middle of the night. What did it sound like when the police officers surrounded her door, readying themselves to execute the plan that would end her life? Did they talk to each other? Were they trying to be quiet, muffle their feet? If we mark these things that precede the murder as violent, can we prevent the murder altogether? Can we prevent, for

---

[5] Fernando Orejuela, *Rap and Hip Hop Culture* (New York: Oxford University Press, 2014); Davarian Baldwin, *In the Shadow of the Ivory Tower: How Universities Are Plundering Our Cities* (New York: Bold Type Books, 2021).
[6] Brent Cebul, "Tearing Down Black America," *Boston Review*, July 22, 2020.
[7] P. R. Lockhart, "'A Multibillion-Dollar Toll': How Cash Bail Hits Poor People of Color the Hardest," *Vox*, December 6, 2017.

example, the signing of the warrant in a gentrifying neighborhood if we mark even the discussion of rapid redevelopment as potentially murderous?

In this chapter, I offer not an argument but rather an attempt to demonstrate that listening to aural experiences of gentrification in a neighborhood makes audible the ways in which Black people and Black neighborhoods are marked for removal, be it through state-sanctioned murder, displacement, or otherwise. Drawing on interviews, historical accounts of Black neighborhoods, and my own participant observation, I listen to and parse out the civic and legislative procedures that lead to and anticipate the eventual—seemingly inevitable—screams and last breaths. If we listen to the pen moving across the paper that authorizes the police to murder someone without so much as announcing themselves, if we mark that action as violent, then perhaps we might be able to prevent the scream and the last breaths. I situate this as an attempt rather than an argument because the history of the United States and whiteness in and as the United States tells me that this may not be possible. And yet Darrais Carter writes that we who work to develop a Black Studies mind are writing against our own demise, practicing experimentation that lends itself to unlimited possibility.[8] So here I experiment with the im/possibility of an attempt rather than the surety of an argument in order to listen against the demise that gentrification promises to Black neighborhood life.

The work of this attempt is to listen critically to the processes of gentrification that punctuate everyday life in the Shaw neighborhood of Washington, DC, and to take seriously how people understand the shifts in their own neighborhoods. I connect these experiences to the audibility of Black neighborhoods as constructed sonically, and further insist that affording attention to these constructions make audible the often violent sonorities of gentrification. These changes are heard throughout the Shaw, and attention to these auralities offers insight into the racialization of sound, further demonstrating the importance of music and sound to this historically Black neighborhood. This work continues to operate within a framework of intersectional listening, as I listen to the constellation of identities and matrices of marginalization present in processes of and conversations surrounding gentrification. Furthermore, drawing on sociologist Mary Pattillo's insight that "the neighborhood is not an island," I contextualize experiences of Shaw with

---

[8] In her "Black Studies Manifesto," Darlene Clark Hine outlines what she calls the "Black studies mind," namely the mindset of those that seek to carry out Black Studies. She identifies five important characteristics of a Black Studies mind: intersectionality, nonlinear thinking, diasporic perspectives and comparative perspectives, oppression and resistance, and solidarity. Darlene Clark Hine, "A Black Studies Manifesto," *The Black Scholar* 44, no. 2 (2014): 11–15. See also Darrais Carter, "Black Study," in *The Fire Now: Anti-Racist Scholarship in Times of Explicit Racial Violence*, edited by Azeezat Johnson, Remi Joseph-Salisbury, and Beth Kamunge, 38–43 (London: Bloomsbury Publishing, 2018).

sonic experiences within DC and from other cities around the country.[9] Part of this contextualization is historical, and I begin with attention to the importance of the Black neighborhood as an idea, followed by an examination of how the sonic components of prominent Black neighborhoods have been treated across the literature.

Black Neighborhoods

Every neighborhood is different, held together by various spatial, social, and financial relationships. Even amidst this diversity, as units of analysis, the value of Black neighborhoods cannot be overstated. These spaces hold the majority of Black people in the United States and carry historical and cultural legacies of Black life. Most of the historically and contemporary Black neighborhoods in the United States were created and maintained by institutional racism and segregation, and have in turn informed Afro-diasporic cultural practices on a global scale. Black neighborhoods are sites of innovation, as communities invent cultural landscapes in the midst of intense oppression time and time again. This process of making a way out of no way has been known by many names, theorized and analyzed and examined in a number of neighborhoods across the centuries. In her analysis of sonic Black and brown coalition building in Los Angeles, Gaye Theresa Johnson calls this practice "spatial entitlement," which refers specifically to ways in which "marginalized communities have created new collectivities based not just upon eviction and exclusion from physical places, but also on new and imaginative uses of technology, creativity, and spaces."[10] Johnson details that even amidst urban renewal and the demolition of minoritized neighborhoods, Black people were making sonic claims on space, deploying fashion and the radio to work against the spatial oppressions being imposed onto them. Spatial entitlement, then, describes the strategic use of resources to imagine and materialize remedies to class, race, and gender-based oppressions. In the Midwest, Marcus Anthony Hunter et al. outline a similar process of "placemaking" in Chicago, which they describe as "the ability of residents to shift otherwise oppressive geographies of a city to provide sites of play, pleasure, celebration, and politics."[11] In

---

[9] Mary Pattillo, *Black Picket Fences: Privilege and Peril Among the Black Middle Class* (Chicago: University of Chicago Press, 2013), 5.
[10] Gaye Theresa Johnson, *Spaces of Conflict, Sounds of Solidarity: Music, Race, and Spatial Entitlement in Los Angeles* (Berkeley: University of California Press, 2013), x.
[11] Marcus Anthony Hunter, Mary Pattillo, Zandria F. Robinson, and Keeanga-Yamahtta Taylor, "Black Placemaking: Celebration, Play, and Poetry," *Theory, Culture & Society* 33, no. 7–8 (2016): 4.

a different context, Kemi Adeyemi takes up this exploration of placemaking in Chicago as she describes queer partying aesthetics in rapidly gentrifying neighborhoods. She details queer dance parties in joyful detail, noting her own participation in these parties. There are moments, in bars taken over by white newcomers, where folks are still yelling "the kids don't even know! the kids don't even know!" as they jump up to dance to Luther Vandross in the club.[12]

Both spatial entitlement and Black placemaking detail the fraught dialectic between marginalization and innovation, where people of color have created cultural forms because of and in spite of oppressive conditions. The creation of these forms is deeply connected to the aurality of Black neighborhoods, which has not been sufficiently amplified in ethnographies about Black life in the United States. In an effort to read and hear the archive against the grain, I explore the sonic facets of several key ethnographic texts on Black neighborhoods, engaging the importance of the sonic in the pasts and presents of Black neighborhoods.

Neighborhood ethnographies have revealed the ways in which Black people are recognized to be musically talented but not "formally" educated and, therefore, unable to engage in suitable pedagogical practices. These sentiments are couched in an inability to consider Black music as rigorous or requiring instruction, and leads to the dismissal of Black musicians as music teachers. W. E. B. DuBois reports his findings on this phenomenon in *The Philadelphia Negro* (1899), which remains one of the earliest and most influential studies of a Black urban neighborhood. Adamant that discrimination against Black people in the North was as prevalent as it was in the South (if not as gruesome), he set out to explore the spatial organization of Philadelphia's Black 7th Ward, studying residents' daily lives, occupations, and recreation. Of sonic practices in Philadelphia, DuBois speaks specifically to how segregation affected musical training and education for Black residents.

Acknowledging that most music schools would not admit Black students, DuBois recounts the level of surprise aimed at Black music teachers, who were often not patronized because this was not an occupation considered to be fit for Black people.[13] The discrimination against Black music teachers makes clear that formal musicianship and teaching were considered to be high arts, and outside of the realm of Black expertise. Specifically, this discrimination is in reference to the teaching of Western art music. Black music genres, from

---

[12] Kemi Adeyemi, *Feels Right: Black Queer Women and the Politics of Partying in Chicago* (Durham, NC: Duke University Press, 2022), 39.
[13] William Edward Burghardt Du Bois and Isabel Eaton, *The Philadelphia Negro: A Social Study* (Philadelphia: University of Pennsylvania Press, 1996), 347.

spirituals to gospel music, have historically been considered as lacking formal training requirements, rather than the acknowledgment that formal Black music training often takes place in churches and juke joints rather than in music schools or through private lessons.

Ethnographies have also revealed Black practices of hybridity through music, especially in the case of gospel music, which remains one of the most stunning innovations of Black people in the United States. Drake and Cayton's *Black Metropolis* offers insight into the intracultural tensions that facilitated the creation of the genre.[14] Although they conducted ethnographic fieldwork on all aspects of Black life in Chicago, from education to employment, the details provided about Black Chicago worship practices are of particular importance to the sonic dimensions of Black life. Drake and Cayton detail how Southern charismatic worship practices had to be reconciled with Northern ideas about religion and "proper" worship. Charismatic worship was considered excessive and unseemly by many northerners, but it was this combination of migration and new, hybrid worship practices that led to the creation of gospel music by musicians like Thomas A. Dorsey, who migrated to Chicago from Georgia in 1916.[15]

In addition to sociology, ethnographic works within folklore and anthropology have also been key to understandings of Black neighborhood aurality. In *Mules and Men* (1935), Zora Neale Hurston offers sound and silence as modes of resistance, engaging both the trickster and the griot characters of Black folklore. Hurston's take on storytelling is unmatched, and she shrewdly recognizes herself as both insider and outsider, given her role as a Black folklorist doing fieldwork "at home" in Florida. Of Black storytelling, she offers an insider's account of Black evasive measures: "The white man is always trying to know into somebody else's business. All right, I'll set something outside the door of my mind for him to play with and handle. He can read my writing but he sho' can't read my mind. I'll put this play toy in his hand, and he will seize it and go away. Then I'll say my say and sing my song."[16] Particular sounds and stories are given to folklorists and other white outsiders as a means of distraction while personal songs are kept within the interior of the Black mind. Here, too, we are offered a difference between writing and singing, or sounding. In many cases writings are given to outsiders, whereas inside is where the Black storyteller will say their say and sing their song. Sonic expressions of language

---

[14] St. Clair Drake and Horace R. Cayton. 2015. *Black Metropolis: A Study of Negro Life in a Northern City.* University of Chicago Press, 2015 [1945].
[15] Mellonee V. Burnim and Portia K. Maultsby, *African American Music: An Introduction* (New York: Routledge, 2014).
[16] Zora Neale Hurston, *Mules and Men*, reprint edition (New York: Amistad, [1935] 2008), 3.

are maintained in secret, in interiority, where written expressions are given away as distraction. Sonic expressions of language are also often coded, hearkening back to spirituals with hidden messages, stories with double meanings, and toasts and signifying that are witnessed by outsiders but not fully understood.

Shaw

It has taken a fair amount of time in this chapter for me to arrive to Shaw, the Black neighborhood that is the focus of this chapter. This journey is intentional, and moving through the stories that places like Los Angeles, Chicago, Philadelphia, and Eatonville have to tell is intended to recognize the labor of ethnography, of the (Black) ethnographers that have been tasked with collecting and amplifying these stories. Ethnography is often a troubling charge, mutually extractive at best and singularly violent at worst. In these works, though, through Hurston's folktales and DuBois's social science, Drake and Cayton's interviewing, and Adeyemi's work on the dance floor, we see the amplification work that Black ethnography is capable of. These ethnographies, few among many, each offer something in the way of illuminating the importance of sonic practice in Black neighborhoods.[17] It is through listening to the archive in this way that we can get a better understanding of what role sound has had historically, and what roles sound plays currently, in places like Washington, DC. This exploration is also meant to engage the connections between Black neighborhoods across the diaspora, where although neighborhoods have their own particular histories and stories to tell, there are a number of connections to be made, whether in joy or in grief. Ethnographies are connected, and so are ethnographers. These connections are drawn across families, geographies, and migrations. My uncle in Oakland talked to me about gentrification before he sold his house there; my cousins in Atlanta still live in the house that their grandparents bought; and I was too young to have a say in my great-grandfather's house being sold in DC. There are intersections between gentrification, property, violence, joy, and music being drawn across the United States and the diaspora at any given time, and

---

[17] Many essential ethnographies of Black life exist. See John Langston Gwaltney, *Drylongso: A Self-Portrait of Black America* (New York: The New Press, 1993); Elijah Anderson, *Streetwise: Race, Class, and Change in an Urban Community* (Chicago: University of Chicago Press, 2013); Pattillo, *Black Picket Fences*; and Sabiyha Prince, *African Americans and Gentrification in Washington, D.C.: Race, Class and Social Justice in the Nation's Capital* (Farnham, UK: Ashgate Publishing, 2014).

the plethora of work on Black neighborhoods allows us a glimpse into these neighborhoods and their soundscapes.

But now, to Shaw. Located in the Northwest quadrant close to downtown DC, Shaw is a large, beautiful neighborhood, over 400 acres in total. There's a little bit of everything in Shaw: shops, hotels, historic rowhomes, music venues, clubs, churches, restaurants, and cafes. There are wide avenues featuring fast-moving heavy traffic and narrow, tree-lined streets with historic homes, many of which are currently being rented out through various means, including Airbnb. The neighborhood is home to a number of diverse populations, including a large West Indian population and Ethiopian community. Washington, DC has the most Ethiopian people outside of Ethiopia, and they are concentrated in Shaw and the U Street Corridor. Google describes the neighborhood as "hip":

> Shaw is one of the city's hippest enclaves, with craft cocktail bars, beer gardens, indie clothing boutiques and trendy global restaurants. This historically African-American neighborhood is home to the 1910 Howard Theatre, where jazz greats like Ella Fitzgerald and D.C. local Duke Ellington once performed. Today the venue hosts all sorts of music concerts and other events.[18]

In these kinds of descriptions, which are abundant among apartment building and Airbnb listings, Shaw's Blackness is past, while its present and future rely on language of trendiness. This trendiness and hipness are further complicated by the fact that Blackness is, in and of itself, trendy.[19] Despite descriptions on Google or Airbnb, Shaw is indeed a Black neighborhood, past, present, and future.

Like Philadelphia, Chicago, and Eatonville, Washington DC has been the subject of study by anthropologists, sociologists, and geographers alike, with the Shaw neighborhood being particularly popular. Historically populated by formerly enslaved African Americans, Shaw was a part of the rich cultural and intellectual fabric of the nineteenth and twentieth centuries, an extension of DC's famous "Black Broadway." The neighborhood is named after Shaw Junior High School, which bears the name of Robert Gould Shaw, a Union Civil War colonel. Shaw was an epicenter of African American cultural and economic success in the mid-twentieth century, serving as a hub for Black performers that were not able to stay in hotels and perform in venues elsewhere in the city

---

[18] "Shaw Washington DC," Google (accessed January 11, 2024).
[19] Brandi Thompson Summers, *Black in Place: The Spatial Aesthetics of Race in a Post-Chocolate City* (Chapel Hill: University of North Carolina Press, 2019); Derek S. Hyra, *Race, Class, and Politics in the Cappuccino City* (Chicago: University of Chicago Press, 2017).

because of segregation. Stanley Mayes, a long-time African American resident of the neighborhood and key player in its renovation, reminisced about the performers he used to see:

> When Black entertainers were in town, they couldn't stay at the white hotels. So, they all stayed along the U Street Corridor. At any given time, you could just look up and you might see Pearl Bailey walking down the street, whoever it may be . . . it was nothing exceptional to see all of these various sundry entertainers all the time. James Brown, you name it. They were appearing at the Howard Theatre . . . if they didn't have other housing, I guess, the only place they stayed was at the Dunbar hotel. So, the Dunbar Hotel being at 15th Street and the Howard being between 6th and 7th Street they would be back and forth up and down that corridor. And then all of the clubs all along the way. Ramsey Lewis, he appeared and Miles Davis used to appear with some degree of regularity at the Bohemian Caverns, and then the Benghazi Club, Club Benghazi, they, different people, from time to time, you got to see everybody. Roland Kirk, you just name it, they were all just regular people up and down the street.[20]

The U Street Corridor that Mayes mentioned is located northwest of the Shaw neighborhood, and remains a vibrant cultural hub. The neighborhood has featured many a demonstration on its northern end, including the Caribbean carnival that used to take place in the city every year but has since ended. In addition to the carnival, residents used to participate in Georgia Avenue Day, which featured vendors, music, and other festivities. Now, rather than the carnival of old, the neighborhood is a participant in Open Streets DC on Georgia Avenue, which is a new, pandemic-era initiative that closes down major arteries of the city to cars so that residents can walk along the streets and do activities such as yoga. These initiatives are celebrated by many that want the city to be safer and more accessible to pedestrians and bikes but are criticized by residents with cars that feel as though they get "stuck" on one side of the city or another, or have to sit through large amounts of traffic because major roads are closed for long periods of time.

Between the area's early twentieth-century popularity and its current status as a gentrified neighborhood, both the Shaw neighborhood and U Street Corridor were badly damaged after the 1968 riots following the assassination of Martin Luther King Jr.[21] The riots are often cited as the reason for the demise of these neighborhoods, which remained blighted until the 1980s and

---

[20] Stanley Mayes, interview with the author, 2018.
[21] Blair A. Ruble, *Washington's U Street: A Biography* (Baltimore: Johns Hopkins University Press, 2012).

1990s, when they began to be rebuilt and eventually gentrified. The riots occupy a dominant position within public memory of these neighborhoods (and the city as a whole), but others have recognized a demise not centered around them. Shelleé Haynesworth, filmmaker and native of the city, offered this counterhistory:

> I'm not on board with that narrative, that the riots were the reason why we lost our economic footprint on U St, that's not true. It was before that. What's never told is that... once the external community discovered that we were creating this vibrant, culturally and economically vibrant community, they came in, as they always do. They don't want us to succeed. And that's the accountability that has to happen in this country, for us to move forward. It's not that we don't want to, it's that every time we try to do that they undermined it.[22]

Haynesworth disrupts the commonly accepted narrative that the 1968 riots were what destroyed culturally and economically successful neighborhoods in DC, including the U Street Corridor. In particular, she identifies "external" forces as the reason for the demise of the neighborhoods, which I interpreted as white residents and financial institutions during our interview.[23] Haynesworth refuses the pathologizing that surrounds memory and legacy in Black neighborhoods. Black people and institutions are often understood as inherently dysfunctional, and Haynesworth refutes this dysfunctionality, instead clearly identifying the layers of cultural and economic jealousy that undermined the solidarity of the neighborhood.

Music and sound have historically played important roles in Shaw's Black solidarity. In addition to the entertainers featured on Black Broadway, music was also used as an important activist tool. In the 1960s, Shaw was slated for urban renewal by the DC government, the same process inflicted onto neighborhoods in Southwest DC in the 1950s, in which the city government utilized a deadly combination of eminent domain and language of slum clearing to raze entire neighborhoods. Recognizing a similar process beginning in Shaw, Walter Fauntroy, community activist and pastor of New Bethel Baptist Church in Shaw, organized the Model Inner City Community Organization (MICCO), "a coalition of about 150 churches, civic groups, and businesses that aimed to give Shaw residents 'a voice and a hand in the

---

[22] Shelleé Haynesworth, interview with the author, 2018.
[23] DC's Black Broadway is not the only neighborhood to have been disrupted by outside agitators. In 1921 white residents of Tulsa, Oklahoma destroyed what was known as "Black Wall Street" in a devastating display of racial violence.

rebuilding of their community."[24] MICCO employed a multipronged strategy of aural resistances in order to save Shaw from urban renewal. For example, in attempting to incorporate community input for their urban renewal plans, organizers used a sound truck equipped with the voice of Martin Luther King Jr. and other local leaders in order to convince people that a survey would be worth taking, while they were trying to involve Black people in the neighborhood revitalization process. They thought that drawing on the voices of these leaders would convey the message to people that these surveys were legitimate and to be taken seriously by the community. In addition to the sound truck, member Mary Morton composed the "MICCO Theme Song," set to the melody of spiritual "Michael Row Your Boat Ashore."[25] The use of gospel music here is both notable and ordinary, because MICCO is but one of the many organizations during the civil rights movement to utilize gospel as a grounding force. MICCO's work was centered in the organizing power of the Black church, with a charismatic pastor at its helm.

Shaw's rich histories of activism, entertainment, and racial turmoil have led to a wealth of attention from anthropologists and sociologists. Three ethnographies in particular have utilized Shaw as a site of analysis and fieldwork, all offering rich descriptions of sonic life in Shaw from the 1960s to the present day. The first, *Tally's Corner* by Elliot Liebow, follows the lives of "streetcorner men" in Shaw as Liebow examines their lives, employment, and relationships with family, friends, and partners. Through his thick descriptions, Liebow paints a depressively gripping portrait of working-class Black life in the 1960s.[26] Following shortly after, anthropologist Ulf Hannerz published *Soulside* (1969), a study of streetcorner men, families, and various other groups of people in Shaw in order to understand "soul," or the essence of Black people.[27] Though essentialist in its premise, Hannerz's work was critical for the 1960s because of the way he argued against the culture of poverty thesis. Hannerz considered systemic factors that influenced "ghetto culture," rather than resorting (only) to a pathologizing of Blackness. The most recent ethnography on Shaw is Derek Hyra's *Race, Class, and Politics in the Cappuccino City* (2017). In this work, Hyra uses ethnography to tease out the racial, gendered, and classed intersections that come to light within processes of gentrification. Hyra's argument is that processes of gentrification mirror the composition of a

---

[24] Chris Myers Asch and George Derek Musgrove, *Chocolate City: A History of Race and Democracy in the Nation's Capital* (Chapel Hill: University of North Carolina Press, 2017), 349.
[25] Walter E. Fauntroy Papers, George Washington University Special Collections, Washington, DC.
[26] Elliot Liebow, *Tally's Corner; A Study of Negro Streetcorner Men* (Boston: Little, Brown, 1967).
[27] Ulf Hannerz, *Soulside: Inquiries Into Ghetto Culture and Community* (New York: Columbia University Press, 1969).

cappuccino, where a less expensive Black coffee gives way to a more expensive coffee and milk drink, white on the inside and brown on the outer edges.[28] The cappuccino metaphor has its limits, because it seemingly codifies the violence of removal by characterizing displacement as a transition to a more expensive coffee drink. I recognize the displacement of people in Shaw, but am more interested in listening to and amplifying those still in the neighborhood, and those fighting for their right to sound in these spaces.[29] Rich as these ethnographies are, they do not center or theorize from the perspectives of Black women. My ethnographic process is one that, through intersectional listening, understands women (specifically Black women) to exist outside of the orbits of men. So much of Liebow and Hannerz's interest in the streetcorner and "ghetto culture" was centered on Black men alone, with women being considered only through kinship and relationships with men. Instead, I draw on the work of Patricia Hill Collins, recognizing that Black women create entire galaxies for and among themselves, away from the gazes of those who would objectify them.[30]

Stories of Loud and Soft

At a spring brunch for women writers of color, I was asked to give a brief introduction of myself and my research project to the thirty or so women in attendance. The brunch was held in Petworth, a DC neighborhood located only a couple of miles north of Shaw. I stated briefly that I was interested in exploring the connections between gentrification, race, and sound, and a Black woman immediately responded, "Are you going to talk about how loud these white people are?" After the laughter subsided, she and others went on to offer their sonic experiences of gentrification, from loud people going to bars at night to Black people having the police called on them for walking in their own neighborhoods. These kinds of informal interactions are commonplace, as people hear their neighborhoods and the city around them quite viscerally. While not the only element of sound to consider in a gentrifying neighborhood, the language of louder and softer is a good place to start, and opens the door for a conversation about perceived changes in dynamic levels. However, the meanings of louder and softer are never simply constructed and

---

[28] Hyra, *Race, Class, and Politics in the Cappuccino City*, 77.
[29] Hyra's work makes a number of fruitful interventions beyond that of the "cappuccino city," such as the ways in which neighborhoods capitalize on the legacies of Black Broadway through "Black branding."
[30] Patricia Hill Collins, *Black Feminist Thought: Knowledge, Consciousness, and the Politics of Empowerment* (New York: Routledge, 2002).

are instead made and remade within the context in which they are evoked. Loudness can carry pride, joy, and abundance, but can also be assigned to groups of people to mark them as wrong or needing removal.[31] Softness, on the other hand, can signal peacefulness, high socioeconomic status, or can lead to accusations of misplaced femininity. These are infinitely complex descriptors, and yet they remain useful within conversations about gentrification and sound. What follows is an analysis of a few key impressions of community members, who described to me how Shaw's dynamic levels have changed over the course of their time there.

While not a resident of Shaw, James Stokes attended Gospel Spreading Church in the neighborhood from 1958 until his passing in 2021. His relationship with the church goes beyond Sunday worship; in 1995 he became the church's accountant and has also served as their summer camp director. Originally from Sanford, Florida, Stokes settled in the DC area after leaving the military, and part of his reason for staying in the city was feeling drawn to Gospel Spreading Church.[32] Founded in 1945 by Elder Solomon Lightfoot Michaux in Hampton, Virginia, Gospel Spreading has many branches, including the DC branch on Georgia Avenue, at the northern edge of Shaw.[33] The church plays an important role in the neighborhood not only because of its longstanding history with the community, but also because the church owns its own building as well as two more on Georgia Avenue. Owning these buildings gives the church a significant amount of power in this gentrifying neighborhood, as several churches in the area have sold or lost their buildings before moving their congregations to Maryland.[34]

During my conversation with Stokes, he made note of the following changes:

> It's definitely gotten louder. And see, we didn't have all these high-rise buildings back here behind the church, and so you got a lot of walking traffic coming through,

---

[31] Fredara Mareva Hadley, "In Defense of Loud, Black Summers," *REVOLT*, July 30, 2016, https://www.revolt.tv/article/2016-07-30/18627/in-defense-of-loud-black-summers.

[32] During our interview, I asked Mr. Stokes where in Florida he was from and he responded "Sanford, Florida. The Trayvon Martin situation down there. So I'm from that area." That brief admission from a man who left Sanford in 1958 reminded me that so many of us have had our histories and homes changed by the violences inflicted onto Black people.

[33] Elder Lightfoot Michaux was one of the most popular radio evangelists of the twentieth century. He was known for his holiness revivals and active congregations within the Gospel Spreading community. Suzanne E. Smith, "Tuning Into the 'Happy Am I' Preacher," *Sounding Out*, March 5, 2015.

[34] One of the most significant churches to make the move to Maryland was Metropolitan Baptist, established in 1864 by formerly enslaved Black people in DC. As Hyra outlines in *Cappuccino City*, the church's move to Prince George's County, MD, was facilitated in large part by a battle over where church members would park. As I learned in my own ethnographic work, parking is a pivotal issue in the livelihoods of Black churches, music venues, and other spaces that cater to people that do not reside in DC.

and a lot of people are not interested in the church, and they can do all the talking loud in front of the church, they pay that no attention. It's definitely a difference.[35]

He went on to express frustration that new buildings obstruct the skyline, which prevent the city's annual 4th of July fireworks from being visible from the church balcony. Stokes here connects sonic and visual changes within the neighborhood, where new high-rises feature rooftop bars and lounges that lead to an increase in noise. The high-rise buildings he referenced are a part of the city's attempt to accommodate its rapidly growing population. To the delight of both developers and government officials, DC is on track to reach a population of one million by 2045, a metric that has worried many advocates for the poor and working class in the District. To make room for this demand, the city is increasing density parameters for both residence and commercially zoned areas around the city, including Shaw, which in some blocks has increased from approximately 2,000 to 10,000 residential units in the span of a few years. Advocacy organizations such as Organizing Neighborhood Equity and Empower DC are pushing back against this increase in population and density in zoning, in part because more housing at market rates will do nothing to alleviate the District's homelessness and affordable housing crises. Furthermore, these advocacy organizations allege that the housing demand is inauthentic, because many of the apartment buildings and condominiums being constructed in the city are not full. Rather, they argue that the supposed demand serves to give developers carte blanche to build all over the city.

I had the opportunity to visit one of these new rooftop lofts as an audience member of a Sofar Sounds show in June of 2018. Sofar (Songs from a Room), is an organization operating across multiple cities worldwide, including London and New York, that puts on intimate shows featuring up and coming musicians from a variety of genres. Potential audience members for Sofar sign up online for a particular date and time and receive an invitation to the show if they are chosen from the lottery, at which point tickets can be purchased. Sofar shows are "secret," with locations not being revealed until 24 hours before the show. The show I attended was in a high-rise apartment building only a few minutes from Gospel Spreading Church, and the audience was primarily white millennials. Two acts from across the country performed for an audience seated on the floor in front of them, with an option to head outside and see a beautiful view of the city.[36]

---

[35] James Stokes, interview with the author, 2018.
[36] Three acts performed at the show that night (the third was an Americana band named Wildeyes), but I only stayed for the first two acts. The very limited seating at Sofar shows is usually staked out by audience members over an hour before the show, and the majority of people sit on the floor. My ethnography in this

King Willow, a two-sister pop duo from San Francisco, opened the show. Both sisters played acoustic guitars, occupying a kind of indie-folk-pop space. Next up was Jake Wesley Rogers, an artist from Nashville, Tennessee who played his set seated at a keyboard. Rogers embodied a pop-soul genre space, similar to the music of Sam Smith or Adele. Between those two performances, the two acts received different reactions from the audience based on their performance styles. King Willow, for example, stood during their performance and played acoustic guitars during both songs, and received applause after each song. Rogers, on the other hand, sat at the keyboard and played his set, and received a small amount of vocal interaction from audience members during his performance as well as standard applause afterward. The genres and performance practices each artist evoked during their performance seemed connected to the amount of interaction they received. I'll suggest here that Rogers received more interaction during his set because he created a more soulful soundscape within the context of the Sofar performance. By soulful soundscape, I am referring to his emphasis on ballads, melismas, and the vocal passion that soul and R&B artists have transformed into a global commodity.[37] Rogers created a moment within Sofar in which vocal performance was crucially important and vocally encouraged by others.

For comparison, consider the performance space at singer and vocal coach Stevie Mackey's "Taco Tuesday," a gathering in which young, mostly Black, singers perform covers of popular songs in Los Angeles, California. At Taco Tuesday, virtuosic vocals are regularly on display, from singers like Amber Riley and Avery Wilson, and people regularly whoop and yell when they hear something they like. This kind of soundscape is descended from the charismatic worship practices and blues sensibilities that created gospel music, and Rogers brought a slice of that kind of a soundscape with him to his Sofar performance. I make note of the difference in audience interaction in order to ruminate on how Black sonic practices travel in and out of gentrifying spaces. While that Sofar show was an overwhelmingly white experience, the reactions during Rogers's performance shifted something in the air—even if only for a moment—and gestured to the Black aesthetic practices that serve as the foundational architecture of pop music today.

My Sofar Sounds experience was intimate, much more so than more notable Shaw venues like the Howard Theatre or 9:30 Club, and this level of intimacy

---

case was limited by my body's inability to sit for hours on a hardwood floor. For more on bodies, ability, and fieldwork, see Johanna Carolina Jokinen and Martina Angela Caretta, "When Bodies Do Not Fit: An Analysis of Postgraduate Fieldwork," *Gender, Place & Culture* 23, no. 12 (2016): 1665–76.

[37] Burnim and Maultsby, *African American Music*.

created a notable quietude. The show was more presentational than participatory, with the audience clapping and showing their appreciation between songs rather than during songs, even though pop music is typically known to have the opposite dynamic, where audience members are encouraged to show their appreciation throughout performances.[38] Shaw has a long history of more bombastic entertainment options, from the Little Harlem nightclub that Duke Ellington frequented to the Broadway Theater, a popular African American entertainment venue in the 1920s.[39] Rather than the large spectacle of a theater, though, Sofar offers a particular, intimate experience that seems to rest more on exclusivity and intimacy than audience participation. I offer this reflection on the Sofar experience and its quietude to expand the discussion of dynamic levels in gentrifying space, and also to blur the lines of what "counts" as gentrifying space. For even as gentrification changes the soundscape of the streets themselves, it also changes the types of music venues that the neighborhood welcomes as well.

Where an increase in population and density have made the environment louder to some, others consider newcomers to have dictated a new level of acceptable noise, making the space quieter. During an interview with journalist Sam Collins, he described how his neighborhood has changed sonically:

> I live on a pretty tight knit block. Dogs barking, people jogging. It sounds a bit quieter though, a lot of the young boys ain't really out there no more, other than like, when the sun's out. But it's like, not a lot of activity among young people, to be honest with you. The young people, I don't know where they got to go, where they can go . . . because they don't like stuff too loud. They think that you're being abrasive if you're loud. People just laughing, or even just like squabbles. Say if people are arguing or in the midst of a very spirited debate about something, they might confuse it as a conflict, about to explode and they might not want to walk over there and see and inquire but they'll call the police quick. I think stuff's gotten quieter. Stuff's definitely gotten quieter.[40]

---

[38] Ethnomusicologist Thomas Turino defines differences between participatory and presentational performance. Participatory performance blurs the lines between audience and performer, encouraging participation and verbal response. Presentational performance, though, holds the line between stage and audience, expecting participation only at designated times, such as applause at the ends of songs or pieces. Thomas Turino, *Music as Social Life: The Politics of Participation* (Chicago: University of Chicago Press, 2008).

[39] Shellée Haynesworth, "Explore the Community," *Black Broadway on U*, https://blackbroadwayonu.com/explore/ (accessed September 14, 2024).

[40] Sam Collins, interview with the author, 2018.

Collins describes typical sounds of the neighborhood, from joggers to the grass being cut, but also suggests that Black sounds are often considered by non-Black residents to be violent or abrasive, and results in a level of policing that forces the neighborhood community to lower the volume. Herein lies the crux of a conversation about gentrification, race, and sound: white people regularly enlist the police to force Black people to be quieter. Collins maintains that white residents are uninterested and unwilling to parse aggressive from nonaggressive sound, instead deciding that any Black sound above a certain dynamic level is dangerous and therefore requires police intervention. Feelings of forced quiet are common in gentrifying cities, from New Orleans to New York.[41] People become unable to play music at night or even let their children outside to play at various hours, because the sonorities of these activities carry deadly consequences.

Black sounds that are indeed "loud" are not automatically aggressive, and this dangerous correlation leads to Black death at the hands of the state. Gentrification creates opportunities for those in power to utilize the police as a weapon against Black people, and these opportunities are often sonically motivated. To call the police on people having a "spirited debate," as Sam intones, can lead to the death of the people in the debate. Time and time again, the police prove themselves to be agents of escalation first, de-escalation later/never. Just as with the murder of Breonna Taylor, though, there are decisions and consequences before the explosion of death. Violences before death. Gentrification facilitates these anticipatory violences, when people move in and demand that a new standard of sound be adopted. This is a kind of cultural displacement, where those that can still afford to live in the city choose not to because they want to be in a place where they will be accepted. Displacement is not only eviction, but rather the slow erasure of knowing that you no longer belong in the place that made you and that you made.

In addition to its insistence on Black death and displacement, the correlation between Blackness and loudness is dangerous because it evokes a two-dimensional understanding of Black sounding. Kevin Quashie has argued against the common narrative that all of Black life is about loud resistances, instead asking us to consider the possibilities of quiet, which "is not incompatible with black culture, but to notice and understand it requires a shift in how we read, what we look for, and what we expect, even what we remain open to."[42] Quashie is writing against traditions that consider Blackness and Black

---

[41] Lance Freeman, *There Goes the Hood: Views of Gentrification from the Ground Up* (Philadelphia: Temple University Press, 2011); Nathan Tempey, "New Harlem Resident Declares War On Jingle-Happy Mister Softee Man," *Gothamist*, July 21, 2017.

[42] Kevin Quashie, *The Sovereignty of Quiet: Beyond Resistance in Black Culture* (Rutgers University Press, 2012), 6.

artists to be only public, only existing to make comment on race and racism. The possibilities and importance of a Black quiet interior complicate the notion that the sonic dimensions of gentrification are only about the silencing of Black life. In addition to silencing Black public life, gentrification also forces Black people to speak up about their position and status in a neighborhood, announce themselves as nonthreatening, and intrudes upon their quiet in order to appease newer residents. Claudia Rankine excavates this phenomenon in *Citizen: An American Lyric*, detailing how white residents cannot fathom the presence of Black people (often those assumed to be Black men) in their neighborhoods without assuming criminality and involving the police:

> You and your partner go to see the film *The House We Live in*. You ask a friend to pick up your child from school. On your way home your phone rings. Your neighbor tells you he is standing at his window watching a menacing Black guy casing both your homes. The guy is walking back and forth talking to himself and seems disturbed.
>
> You tell your neighbor that your friend, whom he has met, is babysitting. He says, no, it's not him. He's met your friend and this isn't that nice young man. Anyway, he wants you to know, he's called the police.
>
> Your partner calls your friend and asks him if there's a guy walking back and forth in front of your home. Your friend says that if anyone were outside he would see him because he is standing outside. You hear the sirens through the speakerphone.
>
> Your friend is speaking to your neighbor when you arrive home. The four police cars are gone. Your neighbor has apologized to your friend and is now apologizing to you. Feeling somewhat responsible for the actions of your neighbor, you clumsily tell your friend that the next time he wants to talk on the phone he should just go in the backyard. He looks at you a long minute before saying he can speak on the phone wherever he wants. Yes, of course, you say. Yes, of course.[43]

This is the interruption of Black life via forced amplification, where the quotidian acts of babysitting, childcare, and pacing during phone calls are all (mis)read as a task for the police to handle. It forces people to speak and announce their legality in their own homes and neighborhoods. This forced amplification is as much of a problem as silencing, because it intrudes on the inner lives, dreams, and imaginations of Black people. Quiet is needed, and yet it is not allowed if a neighbor feels threatened. The needs of those protected and served by law enforcement trump the needs of those that they need protection from, in this case the Black friend in the front yard.

---

[43] Claudia Rankine, *Citizen: An American Lyric* (Minneapolis: Graywolf Press, 2014), 15.

The perceived sonic change of a neighborhood is not always simply louder or softer; sometimes, it can be neither, or both. Long-time resident Stanley Mayes observed the following changes:

> In some ways the neighborhood is quieter, in some ways it's more raucous. It's more raucous because people are less attendant to or pay less attention to the community because they don't take ownership in the community. They don't care in a matter of speaking that it's somebody else's neighborhood. It's quieter because when those things are not happening the people who are in don't tend to associate with the other people in the community as much and so whereas before kids would be out on the street playing ball in the middle of the street or people would be sitting on each other's stoops laughing and joking or somebody else would be having their own individual little dance party out on the street and all, playing their music a little bit louder and everything, because they're sitting on the stoop, so they got a speaker in the window and you two doors down and you got to hear it too. Those sorts of things are kind of gone, but you got a different sort of beat going on.[44]

Mayes outlines an intricate process in which Shaw is changing because of the presence of new residents as well as what seems to be generational differences. The neighborhood is quieter because it lacks the community sounds he was accustomed to, with the common practice of sitting on a stoop, spending time with neighbors and passing the time. The newer residents, as described earlier by Sam, do not necessarily engage in this kind of community based aurality, where people have agreed to collectively experience the full sounds of their neighborhood.[45] The nightlife and amenities that have accompanied their arrival, however, have led to an increase in "raucous" noise, where clubgoers spill out into neighborhoods and disturb residents. Combined, these residents seem to be describing at least two different groups of gentrifiers: newcomers that come to settle and live in the neighborhood, forcing a new acceptable level of noise, and newcomers that do not necessarily live in the neighborhood but arrive simply to visit the new amenities in neighborhoods like Shaw, which was one of the fastest growing nightlife hubs in the country in the 2010s.

---

[44] Stanley Mayes, interview with the author, 2018.
[45] This process is similar to the blurry distinction between the public and private sonic worlds of Buenaventura, Colombia, outlined by Michael Birenbaum Quintero. In Buenaventura, the line between public and private cannot be assumed, and "subjects are expected not only to deliberately immerse themselves in the shared sound environments, but also to actively project their own sonority out into it." Furthermore, the limits of neighborhoods are constantly being reshuffled. Michael Birenbaum Quintero, "Loudness, Excess, Power: A Political Liminology of a Global City of the South," in *Remapping Sound Studies*, edited by Jim Sykes and Gavin Steingo, 135–55 (Durham, NC: Duke University Press, 2019), 145.

Smooth Jazz and Static

In addition to descriptors of loudness and dynamics, some of my interlocutors considered gentrification through the filter of particular genres of music, and these conversations relied on a complex set of meanings that disclosed racialized elements of sound and music. One such discussion was with Rev. Dr. Earl Trent Jr. of Florida Avenue Baptist Church (FABC), which has been a cornerstone of the Shaw and LeDroit neighborhoods for over a hundred years. The church was established in 1912 by twenty-three former members of Vermont Avenue Baptist Church, another historically African American church in DC's Logan Circle neighborhood. Regarding the sonic practices of Shaw outside of the church, Rev. Trent expressed his understanding of the sonic changes in the neighborhood through an extended jazz metaphor:

> Before gentrification really took hold there was this sound. We had kind of a gritty sound with lots of sirens, lots of sirens, and lots of yelling... if you wanted to put it in a beat, I think that syncopated, that odd syncopation, that would have been the driving rhythm of the city. How has it changed? It's like smooth jazz [laughs]. The edge is not there. There's definitely less sirens, the noise that exists in the city has been muted, during the day. At night this place changes, I'm not down here at night that often... but at night there's a buzz but there's not a swing to it... there's no lilt to it, it's just buzz. It can be loud, it's drunken loud but it's more like hockey game loud. You know Black folks get loud and they... we still lyrical about it. This is just [claps off-rhythm]. That kind of... you don't hear that staccato, "you talking about my mama, I'm going to talk about you." That kind of rhythmic lyrical kind of thing. Don't even hear the sirens like we used to.[46]

Blurring the boundaries between music and sound, Rev. Trent's comments convey an understanding of what Blackness and non-Blackness sound like. The sounds of Black Shaw before gentrification are associated with grit, edge, sirens, yelling, syncopation, lyricism, and rhythmic complexity. Non-Blackness (and I allow myself to make the assumption of whiteness here), on the other hand, is linked to lack, smoothness, smooth jazz, muting, hockey, and a loud buzz. The sonic excess through which Trent understands Blackness is evocative of Olly Wilson's foundational "heterogeneous sound ideal," which includes five principal characteristics found across Afro-diasporic music:

---

[46] Earl Trent Jr., interview with the author, 2018.

1. Rhythmic complexity: approaching music making via rhythmic and metrical contrast.
2. Approaching singing or playing instruments in a percussive manner
3. Emphasizing antiphony, or call and response
4. Creating a high density of musical events within a given time frame; filling up musical space
5. Incorporating physical motion as a part of music making.[47]

Trent's description (and in person performance) of the intersection before gentrification embodies the heterogeneous sound ideal. He performs the staccato conversation, using a percussive timbre in speech. He also bemoans the lack of rhythmic and musical complexity in white soundscapes. Overall, he describes a rich sonic density, in which Black people fill up all of the sonic space available to them, and then some. This density is consistent with larger cultural understandings of minoritized people as compared to white communities. Communities of color are perceived to have "flavor" and "rhythm" in ways that white communities are not. In this case, the perceived cultural density of Black Shaw comes through sonically.

Within this dense musical space, however, how do we account for the connections between Black sound and a perceived edge or grit? I locate these descriptors within DC's 1990s drug crisis, during which the Shaw neighborhood experienced high crime rates and rampant disinvestment. Trent describes this grit through sirens, which mark emergency, crisis, and crime, and are seemingly a good fit for a neighborhood that has been plagued by its destruction in the riots of 1968 for decades afterward. By presenting edge and grit as something to be missed, Rev. Trent reproduces the connections between crisis and Black people, but he also soundly rejects the idea that whiteness, sonically linked to aspirational "peace and quiet," is somehow better than Blackness. Furthermore, he exposes the loudness of whiteness through commentary on hockey games and the drunken loud buzz that now permeates the neighborhood at night. In addition to its sonification of "edge," the dig at smooth jazz in these remarks is compelling because of the fraught racial politics of jazz music. Smooth jazz in particular is not always respected as "real" or "authentic" jazz, whether played by Black or non-Black musicians. For example, when describing how radio stations in New York describe the jazz that they play, Travis Jackson notes that "real jazz" was used to describe styles such

---

[47] Olly Wilson, "The Heterogeneous Sound Ideal in African-American Music," in *New Perspectives on Music: Essays in Honor of Eileen Southern*, edited by Josephine Wright and Samuel Floyd, Jr., 327–38 (Warren, MI: Harmonie Park Press, 1992).

as traditional, straight-ahead, and bop.[48] Other stations that claimed the label of "smooth jazz" leans more toward contemporary, R&B influenced styles of jazz. Following this pattern, Rev. Trent uses "smooth jazz" to address a watering down of the neighborhood, in which its "edge" and "grit" have been lost. Edge and grit are utilized to link Black neighborhood sounds to both crime and pure ideologies of jazz, and in doing so strengthen the notion that to move closer to an authentic Black sound is to move closer to "criminal" activity.[49]

Within his use of genre, Rev. Trent also offers descriptors of loudness and rhythm. The neighborhood has gotten quieter since gentrifying, with the noise having been "muted." In his rhythmic descriptors, he assigns Black people a level of rhythmic complexity not afforded to white people. Black sound is expected to have a beat, to be syncopated, and to have a defined staccato rhythm, even when couched within a drunken argument. White sound, however, is described as one of absence: just a buzz; no swing, no lilt, no rhythm. In addition to absence Rev. Trent also describes excess, using the hockey game metaphor to get to whiteness as raucous. The metaphor succeeds because within the constellation of racialized sports in the United States, hockey is coded very strongly as white, in addition to institutions like golf and NASCAR.

In addition to comparisons of the neighborhood soundscape to the buzz of a hockey game, Shaw's buzz was articulated by another of my conversation partners, Shelleé Haynesworth, albeit in a different context:

> Well from my era and if you want to go back further, in the Black Broadway era, it was jazz. It was bebop, it was big band, it was blues. It was R&B, rhythm and blues, back then. And funk at some point. And now I would say static, that's the sound for me. It's very noisy, because in addition to the land grabbing, I feel that what's happening in this gentrification space is it's also grabbing for culture. And that's part of this cultural appropriation, it's like who's going to define it [the sound of the neighborhood/city]? And that's why I said it's static. There's so many different agendas happening. So many people coming in but ultimately I don't see us benefitting as a community.[50]

---

[48] Travis A. Jackson, *Blowin' the Blues Away: Performance and Meaning on the New York Jazz Scene* (Berkeley: University of California Press, 2012).

[49] I want to trouble the idea of crime here, noting that just because something has been deemed a crime or someone a criminal does not mean that they have done anything "wrong." The United States has made criminals of Black people from its inception, regardless of their actions, in part because a criminalized class of people is easier to control. Michelle Alexander, *The New Jim Crow: Mass Incarceration in the Age of Colorblindness* (New York: The New Press, 2020).

[50] Shelleé Haynesworth, interview with the author, 2018.

Haynesworth, too, begins with describing the music as clearly defined African American musical genres, and yet the incoming sounds sound noisy to her, like static. The noise here, rather than a lack of rhythmic complexity described by Rev. Trent, is related to excess: too many agendas on the musical and cultural landscape in DC, particularly in Shaw. She describes a kind of white noise with no clear frequency or benefit to Black residents, citing cultural appropriation as an important facet of gentrification, speaking to the ways in which several aspects of cultural life (including music) have been appropriated from African Americans into something more palatable for a whiter audience. Issues of ownership and appropriation are common in Shaw, from the chronic mismanagement of the historic Howard Theatre to the annual Funk Parade, which began in 2013 and features funk musicians from around the region. Both of these institutions have been criticized for their attempts to appeal to incoming (white) residents rather than African Americans. The Howard Theatre was reopened in 2012 after being redeveloped by Black real estate developer Chip Ellis and was the site of the city's first Community Benefits Agreement, struck to keep some of the local Black-owned businesses in place, who could not afford to do so under market rate.

Regarding their difficulty staying in the neighborhood, locally owned businesses and Black churches are in a similar predicament. Churches have experienced difficulties with lower congregation numbers, maintaining parking lots, as well as the music played in the church itself. These difficulties, which result in social and financial strain on churches, speak to the notion that incoming residents, because of both racial identities and class status are able to dictate acceptable levels of engagement in any given neighborhood. In the case of Florida Avenue Baptist Church, while their congregation has decreased, their parking is taken care of by Howard University Hospital. According to Pastor Trent:

> Like most of the churches around here, the challenge is always parking. We're fortunate, because of our longstanding relationship with the hospital, so we use their visitor's lot on Sundays, so that gives us access to parking. During the week it's a little different, we have a small parking lot. That's a bigger issue for the churches in the city. If you don't have parking, it's hard to draw folks.[51]

The music ministry inside the church has changed as well, with the neighborhood changing outside of it.

---

[51] Trent, interview with the author, 2018.

We had a "more than jazz" on 4th Sundays where at 5 in the afternoon we would have, we would invite different musicians in and have a jazz set. That was before the Howard Theatre was renovated. Bohemian Caverns was just starting to be renovated, Twins did not exist. So, there was nothing here to really preserve our music, and that's what we say: we are preserving. This is our tradition.[52]

Here Rev. Trent locates the church as a jazz venue, tasked with preserving "our" music, in this case African American jazz. Before the renaissance of renovations that accompanied gentrification, the church occupied a central part of jazz in the neighborhood, having their monthly jazz set. In addition to their quest to preserve jazz, Florida Avenue Baptist also preserves its own tradition through the gospel music played during services. Just as with MICCO's uses of gospel in the 1960s and 1970s, gospel music practices inside the church are connected to sonic practices outside of the church, in part because gentrification threatens sound both inside and outside, whether considered private or public. Both Rev. Trent and Haynesworth here are offering localized, sonic theorizations of gentrification. Both consider not only the sounds of pregentrification Shaw, in Haynesworth's case going back to the era of Black Broadway, but also offer sonic metaphors to make aural sense of the changes happening in the community, be it through language of smooth jazz or static.

The Sounds of Local Government

Beyond individual interactions and venue operations, processes related to gentrification are often battled out in local politics, which is a crucial arena in DC because of the city's status as a federal city rather than a state. In addition to the thirteen-member council and mayor's office, there are neighborhood, citizens, and civic associations, as well as Advisory Neighborhood Commissions (ANCs) that serve as key political bodies. Many of these groups have particular racialized histories in the city, as citizens associations were historically white, and civic associations were Black. Advisory Neighborhood Commissions are larger bodies that attend to districts within DC's eight wards, where each ward has between three and seven ANCs, each with an individual elected commissioner. ANCs were enacted via referendum in 1974, as a part of the Home Rule Act that gave the District the right to self-governance. ANCs are a powerful force in the city, voting on matters from transportation to nightlife, and especially liquor licenses. In an interview with the late local civil rights leader

---
[52] Trent, interview with the author, 2018.

Sterling Tucker, he remarked the following about the relationships between the various structures in DC politics:

> Those strong-in the Black community they were civic associations, in the white community they were called citizens associations . . . It was a strong collection of organizations. The annual meeting of the civic associations was one of the big events in Washington every year. Now you don't even hear about them. I was concerned when we got the elected Advisory Neighborhood Commissions, I was hoping that that would not replace the civic associations. ANC is a political structure. Civic associations are a private structure. I was hoping they would work hand in hand so the private structure would have a political structure to help carry the message.[53]

As neighborhoods in the city continue to shift, ANC demographics have begun to include more white commissioners, as newcomers jump into local politics. However, there are still a large number of Black commissioners, many of whom are involved in local activism and organizing. In my interview with Anthony Brown, a Black commissioner in Shaw, he described his reasons for getting involved in local politics: "My experience with the ANC basically just coincided with my being here in Shaw because of my interest in what was going on in the area, things were happening and changing so fast, so I wanted to be on the inside of that figuring out what's going on. Nosy. [laughs]." For Anthony, being the ANC commissioner of a gentrifying neighborhood, having lived in the city all his life, served as a way of not preventing change but being a part of and shaping these changes. This speaks to a key facet of neighborhood change in places like Shaw: because of the disinvestment in these communities, many residents, Black and otherwise, do want change. These residents want more city services, they want grocery stores, amenities, and more. Speaking to the balance between improvements and accessibility, Anthony spoke to the push for increased affordable housing among new developments in Shaw:

> If you walked into a market-rate, you see all this stainless steel, granite countertops, and wood floors and all that. If you're walking into . . . that same development, an affordable unit, you should not be able to tell the difference. We make sure that . . . if they're going to give it to market, they're going to give it to the affordable. So that everybody has the same standard of living, you know?[54]

---

[53] Sterling Tucker, interview with the author, 2016.
[54] Anthony Brown, interview with the author, 2018.

Brown insists that the developments that are being brought into the community must serve the entire community, not just the people that are able to pay market price to live there. This insistence, through conversation and through voting on projects in his capacity as ANC commissioner, is an important component to amplify in the conversation on race and gentrification. I was at an event once where someone said that "Black people were asleep at the wheel" and essentially allowed gentrification to happen. Voices like Brown's prove that to be untrue. As with everything regarding gentrification, the stories are much more complicated than they might appear. Many Black residents have done everything in their power to prevent the city from becoming more exclusive than it already is, from voting to petitioning to serving on local committees. Despite their best efforts, though, development in the city has run rampant and ignored the appeals of the residential stakeholders. Much of this negotiation, successful or not, happens first in local meetings.

Meetings of local groups like ANCs are rich placemaking sites, where people create the communities best for themselves and their families based on what they understand a good neighborhood to be. In her study of DC's Mount Pleasant neighborhood, linguistic scholar Gabriella Modan cites these neighborhood meetings as sites of positioning in which people construct various stances for themselves and others, often within a moral framework.[55] In the case of the meetings I attended, people often positioned themselves using the number of years they had lived in the neighborhood or positioned another person doing the same. The number of years a person has lived in the neighborhood operates as a means of currency, where residents with more years have more institutional memory and can speak over "newcomers" or "gentrifiers." Neighborhood meetings, then, operate as spaces where residents construct their neighborhoods, both with themselves and with those around them.

The soundscape at any given community meeting depends on several factors: the agenda, the group hosting the meeting, the time of day, outside political climates, and above all, who attends the meeting. What became clear to me early on is that the people attending these meetings do so in order to have their voices heard and their interests represented, which can manifest in a variety of ways. In some cases, meetings involve heated exchanges between community members, who speak at and over each other to get their points across. One such discussion involved the installation of bike lanes in LeDroit Park, a small historic neighborhood located just north of Shaw. A District

---

[55] Gabriella Gahlia Modan, *Turf Wars: Discourse, Diversity, and the Politics of Place* (New York: Wiley, 2008), 297.

Department of Transportation (DDOT) representative had just given a presentation at the meeting about traffic studies and was taking community questions, many of which were about the recently installed bike lanes in the neighborhood. Bike lanes are a contested topic in the city, often considered an amenity for white newcomers, installed en masse, where long-term residents ask for amenities that are not received.[56]

During this discussion residents were clearly speaking to each other, sometimes over each other, questioning the need for bike lanes and the speed of their installation. At one point, a white woman began to speak to an older Black man about the utility of bike lanes. She positioned herself as a mother who appreciated the increase in bike lanes for safety purposes.[57] As she spoke, one of the meeting leaders invoked a rule reminding her that residents could only speak directly to the chair of the meeting or the visitor on the agenda, but not directly to other residents. The white woman was disappointed by the invoking of the rule and pointed out that the older Black man was allowed to speak directly to her just moments before. This type of exchange is not uncommon, and highlights the need for intersectional listening: being a long-term resident afforded the older Black resident a type of social capital that the white woman, considered a "newcomer," did not have. When speaking at any local meeting, people almost always positioned themselves by how long they have lived in the neighborhood. Second, his identity as an elder allowed him the authority to speak directly to her. How then might we consider white women, positioned as mothers, to be silenced in these community meetings? White women occupy an interesting assortment of roles in gentrifying spaces. In some instances they can be antagonistic, as evidenced by the common stereotype of the "Karen" often attached to videos of white women behaving aggressively in public places. In other cases, their presence is interpreted are read as signs that a neighborhood has fully gentrified. More than once, men during interviews or conversation have shared their surprise at white woman walking alone (or with a child) in a particular neighborhood that was once deemed "unsafe." The general sentiment seemed to be that if white women feel comfortable in a place (in turn, if white men are comfortable with their women relatives in a place), then the place is well and truly gentrified.

---

[56] On the relationship between protected bike lanes and gentrification, see Perry Stein, "Why Are Bike Lanes Such Heated Symbols Of Gentrification?" *Washington Post*, November 12, 2015. Derek Hyra also notes in *Cappuccino City* that bike lanes and bike infrastructure in Shaw have increased dramatically between 2005 and 2015.

[57] Parenthood can also operate as a form of currency in these discussions, much like race or the number of years lived in a neighborhood.

In addition to these heated exchanges at meetings (of which there were many), there was also the correlation of noise level to interest level at community meetings, which hearkens back to earlier discussion of dynamic levels in gentrifying spaces. For example, at a Shaw ANC meeting in March of 2018, the most sonically striking portion of the meeting was the mass exodus of people after a particular zoning issue was completed. The meeting had begun standing room only, with every chair full and about twenty people standing in the back of the room. After the ANC voted in favor of a development company that was asking for a building exception for a condo project, almost everyone that had been standing in the back and half the people seated abruptly left the meeting. When they left, though, they didn't leave the building, instead lingering in the lobby and conversing with one another. Their talking was so loud that one of the Advisory Neighborhood Commissioners went into the lobby to tell them to be quiet because they were disrupting the meeting. They quieted down but still were not silent, and the meeting continued on with the sounds of their conversations in the background. People typically show up and speak about issues that pertain to them specifically, and few people are committed to these meetings as a whole, if they are not advocating for a particular issue. Also, the noise of the developers was not an isolated incident. Representatives from developers and business interests all over the city came to these community meetings, stacking the room to support their cause. While they did not typically speak over residents in individual exchanges, their sheer numbers spoke volumes. Developers and their supporters can be intimidating, visually and sonically. They can steamroll issues through written and spoken testimony, making things happen that those unable or unwilling to attend neighborhood meetings cannot.

Beyond the Shaw neighborhood, DC Council hearings also have notable soundscapes, especially those that feature large numbers of developers and real estate professionals. At one such hearing in which the city's comprehensive plan was discussed, more than two hundred people signed up to be on the witness list, and the hearing lasted for almost thirteen hours. For many activists this hearing was a key battle in the fight against gentrification in DC, because the Comprehensive Plan is a key document that lays out the city's zoning plans and language to uphold these regulations. Led by the DC Grassroots Planning Coalition, activists with "Stop the Comprehensive Scam" stickers offered testimony opposing the proposed changes to the comprehensive plan, which they argued made the language in the plan too flimsy, allowing developers too much interpretive freedom and residents not enough support to fight zoning decisions in court. One of the primary complaints about the proposed changes to the comprehensive was about the sizes for low-, medium-, and high-density properties. In the new plan, each of those categories was being inflated to include more stories or levels than its previous iteration. This was a tactic that would severely change neighborhoods, allowing for ten-story buildings where there were once only five-story buildings allowed. Developers of course claimed that they needed this extra space to account for all of the new people coming into the city, but opposing advocacy groups like Empower DC maintained that the expansions were for financial gain rather than actual housing because many of the recently built apartment and condo buildings are actually partially empty.

After a severe testimony by activist and lawyer Guy Durant, who opposed the proposed changes to the comprehensive plan by referring to developers as "Devil-Lovers," he played a quick, not even two-second clip of Joni Mitchell's 1970 song "Big Yellow Taxi." This moment was over before it even began because his microphone was quickly cut off by the officials running the meeting, but it spoke volumes nonetheless, and the song and its utility were recognizable (to me, at least) even without the lyrics. "Big Yellow Taxi," written by Mitchell after a trip to Hawaii, is well-known for its environmentally concerned lyrics and arguments against development and construction.[58] The chorus is the most well-known portion of the song:

> Don't it always seem to go
> That you don't know what you've got 'til it's gone?
> They paved paradise
> Put up a parking lot

The connection to DC's development heavy comprehensive plan is clear, as condominiums and construction projects pepper the city skyline. Durant used music here as a direct form of resisting the strict decorum of the council hearing, where applause and outbursts are specifically discouraged (although they happen frequently anyway), and also aligned himself with larger environmental and climate change struggles by utilizing that particular song. "Big Yellow Taxi" framed his fight as one against developers paving the city's green space to build condos and parking lots.

---

[58] There are a number of interesting layers to peel back within Durant's use of this song to protest developers, primarily regarding Mitchell's relationship to race. Mitchell appeared in Blackface on the cover of her 1977 album *Don Juan's Reckless Daughter*. She was playing a character called "Art Nouveau," who she conceived of after watching a Black man walk down the street. She appeared as this character a number of times in the late 1970s, with the final appearance in a film in 1982. There is a notable irony in her song being used to defend land and, in turn, Black life. Even within this irony, there is an immediately recognizability to the song that cements its purpose in this instance. Joni Mitchell, "Big Yellow Taxi" (Reprise: *Ladies of the Canyon*, 1970).

The sounds of local government described here, from small neighborhood meetings to marathon council hearings, mark the sonorities of the gentrification in the neighborhood. Time and time again, people sound their ambitions and frustrations with the neighborhood and are in turn silenced, amplified, and sometimes altogether sounded over in the name of expansion and development. These are a complex set of relationships and ideas about the directions of a neighborhood, and about who should decide what occupies what spaces, and what sounds should be accepted or rejected.

Conclusion

Breonna Taylor's death sparked protests around the world as well as an unprecedented response from media outlets. During these protests against police brutality and anti-Black racism in cities across the United States in the summer of 2020, protestors marched past new buildings chanting things like "Black people used to live here!" and "fire, fire, gentrifier!" These chants call for us to make the same connections that the Taylor family attorneys have attempted to make: gentrification and the state-sanctioned killings of Black people are inextricably linked. The stories I have shared from Shaw tease out these connections as people understand themselves within complex histories of race, sound, and neighborhood life. Be it through resisting development or attempting to shape it themselves, Black people in these neighborhoods are fighting for their right to be there, and for the amenities and sounds that they deem essential.

The sounds of gentrification in Shaw are similar to the sounds of gentrification across the United States: things get louder, quieter, the wants and needs of folks with capital are amplified, deals are facilitated, people are displaced. The intervention in gathering and unpacking these stories is to expand our language about gentrifying sound. Softness can be a violent imposition, and loudness a welcome sign of freedom. The stories discussed here are meant in no way to be exhaustive, but instead to offer a small glimpse into how people hear change in their neighborhoods. Returning again to the concept of placemaking outlined by Hunter et al., placemaking involves a shifting of oppressive geographies to create sites of affirmation and life. The geographies espoused by gentrification, those that silence and dictate white sonic expectation as law, are being shifted daily by Black residents that continue to sound out their place in the neighborhood. For example, while confronting the silencing occurring in his neighborhood, Sam Collins hosts *All Eyes on DC*, a monthly talk show that he started in 2012. The show, which focuses on building solidarities around Black nationalist concerns throughout the diaspora, features a different panel of Black experts every month that dialogue around a particular theme, such as music, cryptocurrency, or gentrification. Working against the static that she hears, Shelleé Haynesworth created "Black Broadway on U," a brilliant multimedia project which details untold stories from the Black Broadway era in Shaw and the U Street Corridor. For this project, Haynesworth has interviewed a number of Black elders in the area, documenting and mapping their stories in an interactive digital environment. Stanley Mayes runs his shoeshine shop in the heart of Shaw, the existence of which furnishes rich conversations, much like a barbershop or a stoop. I offer these examples to resist the bait of salvage ethnography, the practice of documenting a community after or in anticipation of its death. While I do catalogue the strategies and techniques used to silence Black people in this gentrifying neighborhood, I do not present this as the end of Black sound in these spaces. I instead catalogue the shifting of oppressive geographies and do what I can to amplify this work. In the next chapter, I narrow my focus to a particular intersection in Shaw: 7th Street and Florida Avenue Northwest, the site of DC's 2019 #DontMuteDC movement, which fundamentally changed the city's conversation about gentrification and Black cultural displacement.

Chapter 3
7th and Florida

June: 11:20 a.m. Go-go music is playing in the intersection, a woman's voice is singing and riffing off of Keri Hilson's 2010 song "Pretty Girl Rock." Although the music is prominently featured in the intersection on this particular morning there are a lot of traffic sounds. The woman is riffing on the chorus of "pretty girl rock, rock." She gives affirming statements before each refrain, such as "all my ladies do the pretty girl rock," "let it go with your pretty girl rock." As she is vamping on this chorus, a car blows its horn loudly. The song is in the key of B minor, the car's horn is a B. The car is in harmony with the song and comes in at a rhythmically appropriate time to do so, augmenting the song being played out of the speakers.

Since 1995, "Central Communications" MetroPCS cellphone store owner Don Campbell has engaged in a simple, yet subversive ritual almost every morning: when he opens the store, he sets speakers outside of the front door and plays go-go music, DC's local subgenre of funk.[1] The music continues for the duration of the workday, from about 10 a.m. to 8 p.m., and is the source of many a spontaneous dance party. Howard University students, harried office workers taking a lunch break, and the folks that hang out in

---

[1] Although named Central Communications, the store is a MetroPCS affiliate and commonly referred to as "The MetroPCS Store." This chapter asks for you to direct your attention toward your attention; that is, to consider how this text feels possible (or impossible) to read. I am thinking here with many: Nick Seaver's work on attention, Marisa Parham's brilliant essay break.dance, the notion of sound writing as a palimpsest-like endeavor, socratic poets, Katherine McKittrick's rich footnotes. Mostly, though, I am thinking with the music of St. Lenox and with the intersection itself. In St. Lenox's song "Thurgood Marshall," the music video features several narratives operating at once. The words being flashed across the screen, one line at a time, are not the same lyrics being sung in the song itself. There are also musical elements to attend to, as well as the visuals in the music video. The intersection of 7th and Florida is similar to the "Thurgood Marshall" video, namely that there are always a number of narratives passing through at once, and it can be difficult to focus on just one, or to choose to flit from one to the next. In this chapter, I emulate the intersection by offering multiple narratives in the same space. The top of the page features descriptions of recordings from the intersection, presented without explicit argumentation. The bottom of the page is reserved, as is custom, for footnotes that explicate, offer further thoughts, and generally expand on the thoughts in the body. The body of the text is, as promised, a soundscape analysis of 7th Street and Florida Avenue. This can be read in any way that feels best, or not at all. See Morten Axel Pedersen, Kristoffer Albris, and Nick Seaver, "The Political Economy of Attention," *Annual Review of Anthropology* 50, no. 1 (2021): 309–25; Marisa Parham, "break.dance," *Sx Archipelagos*, no. 3 (2019). https://archipelagosjournal.org/issue03/parham/parham.html; Katherine McKittrick, *Dear Science and Other Stories* (Durham, NC: Duke University Press, 2021); St. Lenox, "Thurgood Marshall," *Ten Hymns from My American Gothic* (Anyway Records), 2016.

Intersectional Listening. Allie Martin, Oxford University Press. © Oxford University Press 2025.
DOI: 10.1093/9780197671603.003.0005

September: 5:55 a.m. This is the intersection at its foundation: Crosswalk beating every second or so, a light breeze, bird calls, traffic from beyond the intersection. On this particular morning grasshoppers and bug sounds are faintly audible. It could be the countryside, if not for the crosswalk. An engine begins to rev through the intersection, drowning out the bugs. It revs and revs until it moves away from the intersection, and it can only be heard in the distance.

front of the convenience store next door all dance to the music throughout the day. Over the years, products and personnel in the store have changed, as has the music itself, but the intersection of 7th Street and Florida Avenue Northwest where Central Communications is located remains famous for that go-go music.[2] Throughout the years Campbell has received complaints about the volume of the music, and even been asked to turn it off altogether. He always refused, confident in his compliance with DC noise regulations, and knowing well enough to turn down the volume temporarily if the city sent a representative with a decibel meter. In April of 2019, things changed, though, when a complaint was sent directly to T-Mobile's corporate office, which owns Campbell's MetroPCS store. The complaining parties threatened to sue T-Mobile directly if the music was not turned off, and it was rumored that residents of the apartment building across the street, the Shay, were the complaining parties.[3] Opened in 2015, the Shay is a luxury apartment complex that bills itself as a centerpiece of the best amenities DC has to offer:

> Welcome to The Shay, an apartment community designed for modern, vibrant living in Shaw—Washington, D.C.'s most exciting neighborhood. Just a few blocks from legendary venues like 9:30 Club and Howard Theatre, The Shay is surrounded

---

[2] As the store started in 1995 before cell phones became widespread, it was originally a pager store. Furthermore, they used to play R&B and hip-hop in addition to go-go music, for a time. Now, though, the store is exclusively go-go music. Gregory McNeil, interview with the author, July 2016. Also note that while I refer to the intersection as 7th and Florida, some also refer to it as Florida and Georgia, 7th and Georgia, or another combination. The intersection marks the place where 7th Street turns into Georgia Avenue. South of the intersection is 7th Street, north is Georgia Avenue. Florida Avenue runs east to west through the intersection before it turns into U Street after 9th Street.

[3] Marissa J. Lang, "'A Different Kind of Cellphone Store': Business Was a D.C. Staple Long before Go-Go's Brief Silence," *Washington Post*, April 12, 2019, https://www.washingtonpost.com/local/a-different-kind-of-cellphone-store-business-was-a-dc-staple-long-before-go-gos-brief-silence/2019/04/12/735a7498-5d23-11e9-a00e-050dc7b82693_story.html.

August: 11:15 p.m. The sounds of nightlife are audible in the intersection. There is fast dance music coming out of a club. Chatter and laughter from people in the space. The scene shifts when emergency vehicles attempt to get through the space. Rather than putting on their full sirens, they send "whoops" out into the air intermittently. The starts out with a few quick "whoops" before they end, but intensifies to a fever pitch, where the whoops from at least two vehicles are rising in pitch and frequency. Emergency vehicles were trying to get through, and they could not, and so they beeped incessantly until it was over, they were through, and the club's music could be heard again. There were no people audible on the recording after that.

> by a neighborhood imbued with music, culture, and art. From inspired shopping and bustling nightlife to top-notch restaurants and live music, these sleek and stylish apartment residences are surrounded by DC's best boutique bodegas, coffee shops, brewpubs, bars, and more. With the excitement of 9th Street and U Street just a short walk away, life at The Shay is truly where culture meets cool. Lease now and live in the best new apartments in Shaw DC.[4]

The Shay came under fire early in its existence because of how it seemed to flaunt gentrification in the face of the neighborhood. There was once a poster on the side of the building with a white woman in Victorian or Edwardian costume that said simply "She Has Arrived." The poster, and the building it was attached to, announced themselves proudly with little thought to how that kind of statement could be read by their new neighbors. In part because of this poster, which has since been removed, residents of the Shay were rumored to be the complaining parties and ultimately the catalyst for the forthcoming Don't Mute DC movement. The Shay did nothing to refute the claims that gentrification is a modern-day form of colonialism, and instead seemed eager to lean into the accusation of newcomer, outsider, wealth, and whiteness. As the complaint was relayed to Campbell, he finally acquiesced and turned the music off, unwilling to lose his livelihood. It didn't take long for the neighborhood to notice that the music was off, and less than two weeks later Howard University student Julien Broomfield under the Twitter handle @heroinej_ tweeted in support of Central Communications and started the hashtag #DontMuteDC. Her sequence of tweets directly blamed gentrification:

---

[4] "The Shay | Luxury Apartments in Shaw DC," accessed May 25, 2023, https://www.theshay.com/.

June: 12:00 a.m. Nighttime in the intersection, and a voice, presumably of a Black person, playfully sing-songs "nooo no no no no," almost a perfect arpeggio. Afterward, a seemingly unrelated group of people come by, and you can hear one voice call someone: "Sharon! Sharon! Walking! You're seriously going to get run over by a car." [A common theme in listening back to nightlife conversations is being unsure if someone is talking to a person or a dog.]

> I'm not a fan of gogo but the dudes down at MetroPCS on Georgia have stopped playing their music. Apparently, the new yt [white] neighbors were complaining about the "noise." Simply saying gentrification is sickening is an understatement.
>
> Use the hashtag #DontMuteDC when you tweet about this! We have to start somewhere![5]

These tweets started an overwhelming avalanche of support for Central Communications. The same day that Broomfield tweeted, activist Ron Moten and scholar Natalie Hopkinson started a petition titled "Don't Mute DC's Go-Go Music and Culture." Thousands of tweets and over 80,000 signatures later, the music was turned back on. #DontMuteDC morphed from hashtag to movement seemingly overnight as activists, artists, politicians, and countless others focused on 7th and Florida and the Shaw and U Street Corridors as a battleground against gentrification and cultural erasure. In this chapter I offer a soundscape analysis of 7th and Florida, the place where I initially set out to do dissertation fieldwork in 2018. This intersection, more than any other part of the city, was where I contemplated the question over and over, "what does gentrification sound like?" and was given more answers than I could have fathomed.

While the music at Central Communications is certainly the defining element of 7th and Florida, there are several other features that provide a rich space for a cultural soundscape study. Given its proximity to Howard University and Howard University Hospital, the intersection is heavily trafficked by students, residents, and people who work in the area. The northern half of the intersection is home to a florist, beauty supply store, restaurant, and church offices. At the southwest corner of the intersection was a CVS pharmacy (now closed), complete with a small parking lot that was always at least half full of cars. There are Metro Bus stops at the southwest

---

[5] @heroinej_, Twitter, April 6, 2019.

June: 12:35 a.m. Car breaks and engines fight for dominance in the soundscape as a lone siren wails in the distance, probably at least two blocks away. Is it moving closer to the intersection or further away? Music plays faintly in the background, its source unclear. It sounds like a children's lullaby being played on a xylophone or marimba-like instrument.

and northeast corners of the intersection, where people mill about and wait for the bus. In addition to foot traffic, 7th and Florida is one of the busiest intersections in the city for vehicular traffic, also ranked in the top ten for traffic accidents between 2015 and 2018.[6] Where Florida Avenue leads directly to U Street and further into the heart of the city, moving south on 7th Street leads into Chinatown and moving north leads into Howard's campus and later Petworth, all prominent neighborhoods in the city, complete with residences, businesses, and tourist attractions alike. The result is a bustling intersection that is never silent, if only for the crosswalk signal that beeps 24 hours a day.

My approach to the relatively small size of the intersection as a unit of analysis is informed by Lila Abu-Lughod's "ethnography of the particular," which she offers as a strategy of ethnographic writing that focuses on an intentional specificity rather than falling into the dangerous trap of generalizing culture.[7] She argues that "the effects of extralocal and long-term processes are only manifested locally and specifically, produced in the actions of individuals living their particular lives, inscribed in their bodies and their words."[8] Focusing on one intersection allows for a more specific level of locality and highlighting the sonic shifts in this intersection makes audible the changes that reverberate through the neighborhood and throughout the city during processes of gentrification. The intersection, thus, manifests as an example of not only gentrification, but of the urban renewal, rebellion, disinvestment, and growth that preceded it. Although Abu-Lughod originally suggested ethnography of the particular as a writing strategy, I found it particularly apt

---

[6] Max Smith, "DC Dangerous Intersections 2018," WTOP, February 27, 2019, https://wtop.com/dc/2019/02/the-most-dangerous-d-c-intersections-of-2018/.

[7] Ethnography of the particular is but one strategy that Lila Abu-Lughod offers in "Writing Against Culture," in *The Cultural Geography Reader*, edited by Timothy Oakes and Patricia L. Price (New York: Routledge, 2008 [1991]), a piece that critiques Clifford and Marcus's 1986 volume *Writing Culture*. One of the other strategies is to emphasize terms such as "practice" and "discourse" as a shift away from the finality of culture. The final strategy is shift the work of anthropologists to include connections, specifically between the anthropologist and the place in which they study.

[8] Abu-Lughod, "Writing against Culture," 150.

Immediately as the recording begins, a driver is honking intensely as they go through the intersection, practically laying on their horn. There is also a Black woman's voice rapping N.E.R.D.'s "Lemon" from the speaker in front of Central Communications. A Black man, who is actually in the intersection, is rapping along, but with different words. They're rapping over a go-go pocket beat, and cars are driving by. A heavy engine idles at the intersection, then accelerates after the light turns green. As vehicles drive past, the pocket beat remains. In the distance, there is a siren blaring for a few moments, though it never passes directly through the intersection. The man that was rapping along with the woman on the speaker has begun to rap on his own, because the speakers are currently on the breakdown, and there are no voices on the pocket now. He raps "Lock It, Lock it in the Pocket," on repeat. His voice is momentarily drowned out by another heavy engine, but upon it leaving the intersection he seems to have moved on to rapping, "get money, get money." More engines, more brakes, more horns. The song changes, seemingly beginning a new set altogether. Now the song is a go-go cover of Frankie Beverly and Maze's "Before I Let Go." The man that was rapping is now saying "Hey baby, hey baby," but it's unclear who he's addressing. A metrobus stops, with its customary hiss-and-beep combination. A woman's disembodied voice comes from the bus, announcing that "the base fare is two dollars." She sounds like Siri. While trucks idle at the traffic light, the music is muffled.

for a research site, as a way to recognize early urban anthropology ethnographies such as *Tally's Corner* (1967) and *Soulside* (1969), but to steer clear of the generalizing and pathologizing impulses that so framed that early work. I was also drawn to the intersection because of my previous experiences in that space, especially as an intern at the Smithsonian Anacostia Community Museum in 2016. That summer, I spent afternoons in the back room of Central Communications with sound engineer Gregory McNeil, asking about the intersection, the neighborhood, and the recordings he played for passersby. Although McNeil no longer works at the store, it was interviews with him as well as the suggestion of Natalie Hopkinson that assured me that 7th and Florida was the best place in DC to hear gentrification. The intersection is an immeasurably rich space, full of people, stories, and histories. And yet because of the #DontMuteDC movement, the primary story of the intersection has become that of Central Communications and the silencing of go-go music and culture, which is well documented in the work of writers such as Hopkinson, Brandi Thompson Summers, and Alona Wartofsky. Beyond #DontMuteDC, though, there have been other less publicized conversations being had in the space about sound, race, and gentrification. These threads of conversation are where I begin this soundscape analysis, as I treat the intersection as a kind of

August: 3:25 p.m. The band Be'la Dona is playing at Central Communications, vamping on a chorus over a pocket beat. You can hear a singer and the lead talker Karis. Brakes squeak on top of the music, arriving in harmony for a second before moving back into dissonance. A strong wind makes the recording clip. The drummer stutters for a moment but it's unclear whether it's the drummer on the recording or the wind making a disruption in the recording of the intersection. The chorus isn't easily made out, could be some variation of "on time" or "all night."

sonic palimpsest, where the most current, central stories overshadow earlier traces that remain.

Palimpsestic Listening

A palimpsest is typically understood as a page of a book or manuscript in which old writing has been removed to make room for new, but vestiges of that old writing remain. Thinking beyond the written page, many objects and spaces can be cast as palimpsests, particularly cities, which are constantly influenced by the previous traces of themselves. How, then, can we hear cities as palimpsests? In outlining a guide to palimpsestic listening, sound studies scholar Richard Cross notes that "a sonic palimpsest connotes a complex of auditory experiences in which both foregrounded and effaced sounds vie to be heard."[9] Cross goes on to think through how cities can be heard via palimpsestic listening and how digital traces might speak to analog histories of places. Palimpsestic listening and intersectional listening are connected, wherein both practices seek to listen beyond the first layer, past what is immediately visual or audible. As the go-go music being played at Central Communications is presented as the focal point of the intersection, what other sounds are vying to be heard? What sounds and sonic experiences linger at 7th and Florida and its surrounding blocks?

Institutional Traces

One such trace in the intersection's sonic palimpsest is go-go music's often tense relationship with the rest of the city and its various institutions. Julien

---

[9] Richard Cross, "Towards a Practice of Palimpsestic Listening," *Organised Sound* 26, no. 1 (2021): 145.

February. Vybe band is singing a cover of "Prototype" into the intersection. It gives the song more groove but keeps its laid-back introspective air. Melisma and traffic swirl into the intersection together. On the line "you are the prototype," the lead mic of Vybe, Derrick, does a five-note run that floats into the sky like a kid letting go of a helium balloon. Traffic swirls around the music, car engines and larger vehicle engines as well, maybe a bus or a truck.

Broomfield's tweets alluded to this relationship, because although she did indeed launch the #DontMuteDC movement in 2019, she first distanced herself from go-go music with the clearly stated "I'm not a fan of go-go" in the beginning of the tweet. As fierce an advocate as she was in that moment and has become in subsequent years, she made the rhetorical choice to begin with distance. As part of the Howard University community, Broomfield was a part of the complicated, occasionally fraught, relationship with both Black popular music and Black residents of DC. These complications stem largely from the pronounced socioeconomic differences among Black residents of the city, as DC has long been home to a Black elite, with the intellectuals and doctors at Howard University being a key focal point. Poet Langston Hughes complained about this elite class of the city in the 1920s, writing of his time with relatives who introduced him to prominent members of Black city society: "All my shirts were ragged and my trousers frayed. I am sure I did not look like a distinguished poet, when I walked up my cousin's porch in Washington's Negro society section, LeDroit Park . . . Listen, everybody! Never go to live with relatives if you're broke! That is an error."[10] Hughes instead aligned himself with the poor and working class of the city instead, frequenting 7th Street in Northwest.

As Hughes's grievance attests, DC has long faced a significant wealth gap not only among different racialized groups but also within Black communities as well. As the largest and perhaps most prestigious HBCU in the United States, Howard University is a key focal point of this social stratification in DC, as it continues to shape not only Black intellectual life in DC but also in the United States. Founded in 1867 and named after (white) general Oliver O. Howard, the university was part of a reconstruction effort to educate the newly emancipated Black population of the United States. In the process, Howard University became home to a prominent group of Black intellectuals that included Alain Locke, E. Franklin Frazier, and Mary

---

[10] Langston Hughes, *The Big Sea: An Autobiography* (New York: Knopf, 1945), 163.

August: 1:30 a.m. The intersection is relatively quiet, just traffic and the ever present sound of the crosswalk beep. But then there is a deep pitched voice saying "awwwww" with a rising pitch, building anticipation for the beat drop. The beat does drop, and an afro-beat song plays faintly into the intersection. It's most notable feature is the beat, featuring heavy maracas instrumentation.

Church Terrell. In addition to influencing Black intellectual and cultural life, Howard owns a great deal of property in the city, from its own 256-acre campus to commercial lots to several residences in various neighborhoods. Working with a number of development partners, the university owns and manages these properties all around the city, including at the intersection at 7th and Florida.

Across the street from Central Communications stood a CVS Pharmacy which has, as of 2022, been closed. Howard owns that building, so they will be instrumental in charting a path forward for the intersection depending on how they decide to lease the space. As of January 2023, the space is listed on their "Current and Future Projects" website as partnering with Quadrangle, a large private real estate and development firm in Washington, DC that owns upward of eighty properties in the city. On another corner of the intersection is a beauty supply store that sells everything from braiding hair to makeup. The store was formerly installed at Georgia Avenue at another property that Howard owns, but in 2014 the university declined to renew their lease. The owner of the store was then forced to look for new space and eventually settled on the second floor of what used to be a Popeyes restaurant. She recalled their 2014 move:

> [We were] On Georgia [Ave.] . . . for maybe like 8 or 10 years. And then, that was owned by Howard University, so then they didn't want any stores, like beauty supply stores, because they wanted to upgrade, to a higher market I guess. They didn't want something messy, I guess. I don't know. So, they kicked us out of there, and we couldn't stay there, so we were looking for somewhere close by, and this location was empty, so we got the upstairs. But it took us a couple years to open it, because we had to do construction, and there were problems with the permits and stuff. So that's how we opened this one and it's been about four and a half years now since we opened this one.[11]

---

[11] Anonymous, interview with the author, 2018.

May: 12:55 a.m. A siren wails during the entire recording, moving closer and closer to the intersection until it finally starts to move through. When it moves through it becomes exceedingly loud, drowning out everything in its path until it makes it through. After it leaves, everything else returns: the people hyping each other up down the block: "aye, aye, aye, eowww eowwww," the crosswalk, the metrobus. All of those are on hold until the siren can make its way through. The emergency emerges.

The owner's recollection of the move is similar to many other stories of local business owners and renting residents as well in gentrifying neighborhoods. When landlords and building owners decide that they have a different vision for the space, the existing tenants have to go. In this case, fortunately, she was able to find another location nearby, but the disruption was still palpable. The store may be further interrupted still, because in late 2021 Howard purchased the building that currently holds both the beauty supply store and the restaurant Halfsmoke. Howard's complicated, occasionally disruptive relationship with business owners in the city extends to their relationship with go-go music and go-go bands. Go-go has long been understood to be the music of the Black working class in DC, a working class that Howard has not always supported. Go-go bands often come from humble beginnings, such as Junkyard Band's early days playing on actual junk, or Backyard Band's emulation of Junkyard by playing on trashcans. The relationship between Howard and go-go music is complex, and these intricacies are made audible through the memories of those who moved through the institution. For example, in conversation with Natalie Hopkinson, a Howard alumna and former professor at the institution, she talked to me about those who are ashamed of go-go music both at Howard and in the city more broadly:

> I do think that there's something wrong with the idea that you think that it's something to be embarrassed of or that where you go outta your way to distance yourself from it. Or to put it down or to say, "Oh, that's something that those people do." You know, because there it's like, you're not just putting it down. You're putting down the whole history and the whole set of traditions that are associated with it. I mean, you're—you're distancing yourself from yourself. From your own identity. I mean, and for me part of it was like, "This is an identity that all people of Africans descent share." You know, in some way we are all connected to it in some way.[12]

---

[12] Natalie Hopkinson, interview with the author, 2013.

June: 11:25 p.m. A quiet night in the intersection, with the crosswalk keeping times. There are sounds intermittently: traffic passing by, muffled low pitched voices, what sounds like the bounce of a basketball, a shoe scuffing or brake squealing. At some point there is another high-pitched whine in the background, almost like a squeaky grocery cart.

As an ethnographer studying go-go music, I have seen this embarrassment firsthand, with countless questions over the years about why I study "that trashcan music." Howard, as a bastion of the Black middle and upper classes in DC, has actively participated in this shame around go-go music.[13] In an Atlantic article in 2012, journalist Abdul Ali wrote, "When I attended Howard University in the mid-2000s, the very sound that is native to the area was held at arm's length. One would have to leave campus to hear go-go."[14] Others have better memories, though. In a conversation with Hopkinson, author Ta-Nehisi Coates reminisced about being entranced by go-go music on Howard's campus. Aside from early exposure from his mother, who worked at a DC high school, he experienced Junkyard Band playing at a Kwanzaa show on campus his freshman year. He noted that some folks at Howard were often "skeptical" of go-go, but that "you would have to be some kind of asshole to not move [to go-go]."[15] This nostalgic push and pull with Howard sometimes coming out supportive of go-go but at other times dubious, is reminiscent of the rest of the city's Black establishment's approach to go-go. Councilmembers and mayoral candidates regularly employ go-go bands at campaign rallies, trying to garner support from neighborhoods in Wards 7 and 8 for their electoral goals. They are then often accused of ignoring go-go musicians after they are elected and turning away from legislative pressures on liquor license difficulties and high insurance costs that make go-go bands unable to play at venues. These complexities make it challenging to paint a clear picture of how

---

[13] Howard has also participated in shame around other Black music genres, particularly gospel music. Gospel artist Richard Smallwood, as a student at Howard, had to compose and rehearse in secret because his gospel passions were not supported within the music curriculum. For this reason, many of his gospel songs feature embellishments, ornamentation, and entire passages inspired by Western Classical music. He would switch into western music at the drop of a hat, so as to not be discovered. Alisha Lola Jones, "Honoring the Legacy of Richard Smallwood." (Lecture, Union Temple Baptist Church, June 11, 2016).
[14] Abdul Ali, "How Washington, D.C., Turned Its Back on Go-Go, the Music It Invented," *The Atlantic*, July 2, 2012, https://www.theatlantic.com/entertainment/archive/2012/07/how-washington-dc-turned-its-back-on-go-go-the-music-it-invented/259147/.
[15] Ta-Nehisi Coates and Natalie Hopkinson, "Launch Go-Go Museum and Café," Facebook, June 3, 2020, https://www.facebook.com/watch/live/?ref = external&v = 255939005653474.

November: 12:55 a.m. The crosswalk has a partner here, an audible partner. Perhaps it is that someone pressed the actual crosswalk button to prompt it? There is a steel plate in the intersection; it thunks every time a car drives over it. A car horn blows in the distance, maybe a block or two away. People yell, complain at each other. Sounds like nighttime. An engine revs. The wind starts to clip the recording. Someone wails on their horn right at the very end.

Howard University and other institutions have interacted with go-go music over the years, but clarity is not the goal. Rather, the goal is to imagine the depth of relationships between this music and the institutions with that have interacted with its community, and to show how sound becomes as classed as it is racialized. Be it through accent, percussive timbre, or dialect, sounds speak to classed understandings of Blackness in DC.

Public Opinions

More than institutional histories and relationships, public opinions of the music being played at 7th and Florida also linger in the space, vying for attention. These opinions are important because the everyday public display of go-go music at Central Communications is representative of that which is being marked for removal from the city. This is not a music or a musical community that fits into an easily commercialized package, and cannot be captured in a mural or only put on display at an annual music festival. The go-go at 7th and Florida is not easy to ignore, which means it tests the patience of those who have a particular aversion to cultural practices that are "loud" or "in-your-face." To get a sense of how the music was being received by key members of the community at 7th and Florida, I asked many of my conversation partners directly about their thoughts on the music at Central Communications and got a range of responses, paraphrased below:

- The music is a public safety issue, because the volume may prevent people from being able to hear sirens or the beeping at the crosswalk.
- The music is just a part of the culture in Shaw, and it's not going anywhere.
- The music is too loud to be played outside and playing music outside is unusual to begin with.
- The lyrics of go-go music are vulgar, and folks would rather not hear such language.

November: 12:15 a.m. There is a squeaking noise in the opening of the recording, like a car door working too hard or some other piece of machinery. It squeaks two or three times, and then there is conversation from at least three people, probably more, which grows louder and then softer again. Snippets: "First of all!" "Alright!" A car sounds its horn, more traffic goes by, another squeaking noise, but in motion this time. It is a windy day, cutting across the recording.

- The music is some people's favorite part of the neighborhood, and people enjoy listening to it as they pass.
- The music is "too damn loud!"

This sample of opinions on the music being played at 7th and Florida speak to several lingering sonic histories in the city. For example, the notion that go-go music is a public safety issue has been put forth for decades in Washington, DC, and has led to the banning of go-go music at many clubs altogether. While the aforementioned comment about being able to hear sirens and the supposed violence that go-go brings within live venues are on different sides of the spectrum, both are still under the umbrella of a public safety issue, because they insinuate that the presence of go-go music makes people less safe. The alleged vulgarity of the go-go music being played at 7th and Florida is also reminiscent of sounds and constructions of Blackness that have been effaced by time. In an interview with sound engineer Gregory McNeill, who played the music in the intersection from around 2007 to 2017, he mentioned that he took great care to play music that was suitable for the public, offering the following commentary:

> I'm thinking about the kids walking by, and women, everyone that's walking by, that doesn't know about go-go. So, you can't play the hardcore go-go and somebody's walking by going "what in the world?" . . . I can definitely play EU, because Sugar Bear never cusses. Never, he never cusses . . . a lot of the grown and sexy bands, I can automatically play them, because there's no cussing.[16]

Sugar Bear has been the lead talker (bandleader) of EU for over thirty years. Originally, he was just the bassist in the band, until his charisma and charm

---

[16] Gregory McNeill, interview with the author, 2016.

October: 1:00 p.m. The traffic is almost deafening on the recording. Trucks and wind and engines are the only thing audible on first listen. After a second listen, a voice starts to float through, seemingly a man's voice, singing long, legato notes. October 3 was a Wednesday so it's reasonable to assume that go-go music is being played at Central Communications. There are a number of reasons why the volume could have been low: complaints, weather, the number of trucks moving through at any given time.

got him moved to the frontline of the band to act as lead talker. Since then, Sugar Bear has been the face of EU, going so far as to be billed as "EU featuring Sugar Bear" for almost a decade.[17] As the band's sound engineer, McNeil knows that Sugar Bear never curses, hence marking the band as a safe choice for the public.

In my own observations of the intersection, I have heard many bands that are classified as "Grown and Sexy," a subgenre of go-go named not for adult content but for its smooth R&B sound and an aversion to young go-go fans. Grown and Sexy bands brand themselves as mature to keep themselves in business at clubs and venues that are hesitant to support younger generations of go-go musicians and fans, who are known to be more energetic, loud, and at times, rowdy. How can we reconcile a Black business owner's accusation of vulgarity with Central Communication's supposed commitment a sound suitable for the general public? Listening intersectionally requires listening on the margins, listening to the opaque, and I suggest that Black voices, presented at a certain frequency within a certain rhythmic pattern, and at a certain volume, are perceived as vulgar regardless of whether or not they are actually using profanity. The same observation goes for perceptions of loudness. Voices that are interpreted as Black are often simultaneously interpreted as loud because this is how we understand Blackness to sound. The impetus to label Black music and sound as vulgar, both intra and interracially, is one of the stabilizing forces of Blackness as a racial category.

---

[17] EU, like a few other bands in their generation, made it big before eventually returning home for a prolific career in the DC area. They are still nationally famous, though, being featured as hometown talent for Regina Hall and Taraji P. Henson's opening performance for the 2019 BET Awards. Hall and Henson combined the message of the #DontMuteDC movement with the HBCU aesthetic of Beyoncé's storied Coachella performance, inviting EU along to perform their hits like "Da Butt." Although some disagreed with the performance and EU as the choice representative, the greater DC area was bursting with pride for at least a week, both on and offline.

November: 1:35 p.m. A truck idling at the intersection provides some texture and percussion to the go-go cover of "Don't Mind" by Kent Jones. The song features lyrics about women speaking different languages and the singer saying that they don't mind any of the languages, and that they love all women from around the world. The truck engine gives the song more movement, more bass, more bounce. The truck eventually drives away, bouncing over bumps in the street and almost drowning out the song entirely before it's gone.

The historical and current opinions and reactions to go-go music show that despite the popular support it received and continues to receive as a result of the #DontMuteDC movement, this is not a universally loved music genre. Part of the flattening of the gentrification conversation comes from presenting homegrown cultural forms as universally loved and supported, and this is detrimental to a richer, fuller conversation about what gentrification sounds like. These opinions are, however, an insightful glimpse into how the continued public display of Black sound has emboldened some and disturbed others, and how the intersection sits at the nexus of a conversation about Black sound and city space. As I move through the space at 7th and Florida, now forever marked as the home of the Don't Mute DC movement, I am struck by these traces: of Howard University's presence in the area, of how many people who have supported the intersection in public would rather have the music turned off for peace and quiet. The supposed vulgarity, the classed aspects of go-go music, float across the intersection with every pocket beat. One of the key parts of 7th and Florida as sonic palimpsest is hearing these traces of class tension throughout the space.

Traces of Black Refusal

Refusal is another one of the sounds vying to be heard at 7th and Florida, both in the protests of the #DontMuteDC movement and in less obvious places. I engage Tina Campt's definition here as she articulates refusal in the context of Black visuality:

> refusal: a rejection of the status quo as livable and the creation of possibility in the face of negation i.e. a refusal to recognize a system that renders you fundamentally illegible and unintelligible; the decision to reject the terms of diminished subjecthood with which one is presented, using negation as a generative

May: 1:35 p.m. The traffic that sounds at the beginning of the recording sounds almost like a drum roll, like an introduction for the crisp, solid pocket that comes in afterward. There are seemingly two voices rapping on the pocket, one with lyrics that are mostly unintelligible, and the other coming in with adlibs: "Hah!" and "Yeah!" The wind clips the recording, women chat in the intersection, the pocket goes on and on. The drum set and congas are the focal point of this moment, and everything dances around them.

and creative source of disorderly power to embrace the possibility of living otherwise.[18]

As I discussed in Chapter 2 in the stories about the Shaw neighborhood, one of the responsibilities of listening to gentrification is to listen to the ways in which Black people have been marked for removal, and even more so, how Black people explain and articulate how they have been marked for removal. Refusal, as Campt shares, is a response to, and a rejection of, negation and forced intelligibility. People in the intersection at 7th Street and Florida Avenue are in many ways rejecting the status quo, rejecting gentrification, and rejecting having been marked for removal. This was evident during the height of the #DontMuteDC protests, where rallies, performances, fashion, and music videos demanded that residents be heard and not silenced. Activist Ron Moten was often seen in the space wearing t-shirts with slogans like "I'm not a gentrifier. I've been here" or images of DC license plate reading "Go-Go: DC's Official Music." One of the songs that was produced in conjunction with the movement was "Don't Mute DC," which featured lyrics like "Can't divide us/We gon' keep on fighting/we want freedom in the streets. Won't gentrify us/we gon keep on thriving/and we want some equity." All of these gestures, from the songs to the continued call for hundreds of people in the street to gather to the fashion choices speak to Black refusal, a very specific refusal in this case to be removed from the intersection or removed from the city's soundscape more broadly. More than just maintaining the music at Central Communications, the intersection became louder, more Black, and more boisterous. The complaining parties got much more than they bargained for, because the sound from the intersection swelled. More than the immediate increase in volume, there was also a refusal to be forgotten

---

[18] Tina Marie Campt, "Black Visuality and the Practice of Refusal," *Women & Performance: A Journal of Feminist Theory* 29, no. 1 (2019): 83.

Plate 1. Graffiti in NW Washington, DC. Photo by author.

Plate 2. Busboys and Poets sign. Photo by author.

Plate 3. Asha Santee performing at the Rock and Roll Hotel. Photo by author.

Plate 4. Carolyn Malachi working in the recording studio. Photo by author.

Plate 5. Oh He Dead performing at Busboys and Poets. Photo by author.

Plate 6. Graffiti in LeDroit Park. Photo by author.

Plate 7. Graffiti in NW Washington, DC. Photo by author.

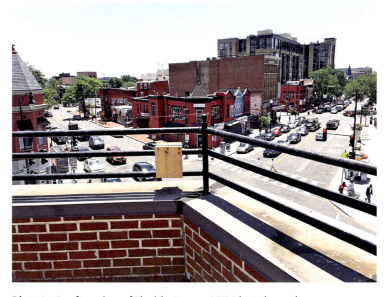

Plate 8. Rooftop view of Florida Avenue NW. Photo by author.

Plate 9. Florist at 7th and Florida NW. Photo by author.

Plate 10. Gospel Spreading Church on Georgia Avenue NW. Photo by author.

Plate 11. Rooftop view 7th and Florida Ave. NW. Photo by author.

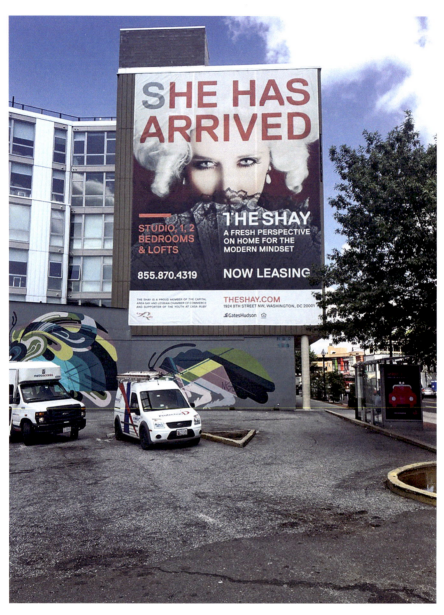

Plate 12. "She Has Arrived" sign at the Shay Apartments. Photo by author.

May: 9:00 a.m. Birds are the star of the show this morning, this recording sounds like spring. Multiple birds like robins or jays are sounding throughout this moment. Nothing harsh the caw of a raven or the squall of a seagull. These birds sound like the beginning of a Disney movie. There is also the never-ending crosswalk, light traffic, and what sounds like early morning men's conversations. Greetings, perhaps, or maybe something deeper. Timbre and shape are audible on the recording, but not specific words.

that moved through the space. Central Communications began to archive their material and make it available for the public via a monthly streaming service that listeners can subscribe to. Not only did advocates for Central Communications refuse to be removed from the intersection, they also ensured a wider reach for the go-go music that they play: through social media, a streaming service, and the continued international press covering the movement.

In the midst of this vibrant space known for its dynamic sounds, one unassuming office has long been perhaps the cornerstone of the entire intersection. Next to the florist, not quite in the intersection but not quite out of it, is the Gospel Spreading Bookstore, operated in conjunction with Gospel Spreading Church a couple blocks north on Georgia Avenue. The church owns not only its own building, but the building on the northwest corner at 7th and Florida as well, that houses a florist on the ground floor and church offices on the upper floors. The church's ownership and stewardship of that building is a key part of the intersections' livelihood, because they are continually getting offers for that real estate and refuse to sell. James Stokes, accountant for Gospel Spreading, described the process of his refusal to me:

> Realtors wanted to talk to people about selling property, and they even came to our church up here, and wanted to buy our church, take over our building, and give us some land out in Maryland to build the church, which was a no-no. They've been asking me about this building here, for years. This first started about 10, 12 years ago, wanting to come in here. We would not listen to them. I'm still getting letters and calls wanting to talk to me, I refuse to have a conversation with any of the realtors. Because one came in one day, and he did meet me. They wanted to take this building, wanted to buy this building, they would demolish this building and put up such is what we have on the back streets. They would give me space for the bookstore in their own building, But the space, they

September: 4:30 p.m. Sometimes the go-go music coming out of Central Communications is louder than the traffic sounds, but in this instance, the traffic is winning. A mid-tempo pocket and some low-pitched melismatic singing is barely audible, and the primary sounds are large engines, some idling and others moving through the space. At the beginning of the recording, as the pocket beat flows through the space, a car horn sounds in rhythm on the second beat. Always hitting the two-and-four.

> really were not interested in having the bookstore here. All of them, everybody that came and wanted to put something in these buildings, it was like a club, a nightclub or something, restaurant, and they also wanted to sell alcohol, and we wouldn't go for it. Now my church owns the church down there plus the restaurant next door. That property. We had so many offers, wanting to take over even the restaurant down there. But we refused to talk to any of them. We had some of the chain restaurants, wanting to take that area, but my thing is, my people own that business. I'm not going to do something to hurt them, as long as we get along, the rent that we're able to charge them. We don't try to charge them a high rent, because my thing is, I want them to be successful, in what they do, and the people here, in this building, are renting from us. They're not high rents, we cover our expense, real estate tax, and all of that. So why not let them be successful? So that's what we're doing.[19]

The process of solicitation that Stokes describes here is not unique to the church. In an interview with Mechelle Baylor of LeDroit park down the street, she talked about the numerous offers she received for her home along with her refusal to sell, insisting that when she leaves the house it will be "feet first."[20] Stokes's refusal, then, is the reason why the northwest corner of the intersection has not been given to commercial food or nightclub space, much like the rest of the neighborhood and the U Street Corridor. The politics of refusal are key here, because although the public narrative of gentrification is one characterized by forced displacement, we must also be willing, indeed excited, to tell those stories of a refusal to move, especially notions of Black refusal. Furthermore, the refusal to sell the building is rooted in a constellation of racial and religious values, in which Stokes is loath to leave the intersection to a nightclub or alcohol but determined to help "my people," in this case Black people. The florist, then, is Black-owned, as well

---

[19] James Stokes, interview with the author, 2018.
[20] Mechelle Baylor, interview with the author, 2018.

July: 4:50 p.m. A nice, open pocket is flowing out the speakers this afternoon. There is a lot of hi-hat that makes the pocket feel big and open. A man and woman's voice float out from the recording; she says "Play it again!" A truck or bus comes through and muffles the sound, but when it leaves, the big open pocket is still playing. About 45 seconds into the recording the pocket closes, not as much cymbal being used, and the man begins to sing. This is a masterclass in go-go music-making, how to hold a consistent pocket but account for timbral and textural variation as the musical situation calls for it. The drummer moved back into a slightly less dominant groove to let the singer take center stage.

as the restaurant, Torries, that he cited in this conversation. Processes of gentrification are full of these refusals, loud and soft alike. People refuse to leave their spaces, refuse to sell them, refuse to go quietly, refuse to change the way that they've been doing things for the sake of new neighbors and businesses. Black refusal is a dynamic thing, from Stokes's decade long refusal to sell the building to every time I refuse to step off the sidewalk for white people walking two and three abreast. Black refusal lingers in the intersection and in Washington, DC, and the language of refusal resonates because it operates in friction with the fiction that Black people have been told over and over again: that life is available to us via compliance. Just turn down the music, just quiet down, just wait for the public housing to be rebuilt fifteen years later or not at all, just put your hands up, just get in the car. The intersection at 7th and Florida sounds like decades, even centuries, of refusal vying to be heard in gentrifying space.

Digital Palimpsest aka "And Now It's Time for a Breakdown"

In addition to approaching the intersection as sonic palimpsest from an ethnographic and historical perspective, I also listened digitally for traces of the intersection's histories and relationship to gentrification through sound analysis.[21] I utilized passive acoustic recording, a methodology that entails long-term recording of a given place or object at particular intervals of time. This

---

[21] The section header is a shout-out to En Vogue. This section details the process and intricacies of passive acoustic recording. All figures in this section can be found at intersectionallistening.com.

July: 6:15 p.m. It was a rainy evening in DC, so the recording is being clipped by rain, but it really only adds to the ambience because the go-go recording here is a cover of Tevin Campbell's "Shh (Break it Down)," a 90s slow jam. Her voice is sultry, yet percussive like many other go-go singers, as she ad-libs the "break it down" lyrics. She adds melisma throughout, voice moving deftly through the lyrics. There is light traffic moving through the space, and the cars and light rain are only adding to the slow, jazz club feeling of the intersection. The recording ends right as she is reaching the climax of her performance, and the drums start to open up to give her room to belt.

method of recording is typically used in a bioacoustic recording context, to hear changes within soundscapes and the living environment. The impetus for using passive acoustic recording comes from soundscape ecology and the burgeoning field of ecomusicology, both of which employ bioacoustic recording that is typically reserved for underwater (listening to whales) or rich rainforest environments (listening to birds, frogs, etc.). Pijanowski et al. define soundscape ecology as all sounds "emanating from a given landscape to create unique acoustical patterns across a variety of spatial and temporal scales."[22] In this way, the recorders are a method of studying the soundscape ecology of 7th and Florida, though most particularly considering the sounds created by human actors. To explore the sonic changes and aural perceptions of the neighborhood, I installed two recorders on rooftops in the intersection that recorded one minute out of every five minutes, all day every day. This resulted in 288 recordings per recorder, per day, one for a six-month period and one for a nine-month period. This difference in recording lengths of time is notable, because it was due to the amount of time it took me to do fieldwork in the intersection. The first recorder, hung from the room of the Florida Avenue Baptist Church, was done so with the permission of the pastor, who I asked about it after our interview in early 2018. I put Recorder 1 up soon after, with installation help from my uncle. Although the data from Recorder 1 was helpful for this project, I knew I needed something slightly closer to the intersection, if possible. I nervously stumbled into the Gospel Spreading Bookstore one day in the spring, asking about the history of the store and

---

[22] Bryan C. Pijanowski et al., "Soundscape Ecology: The Science of Sound in the Landscape," *BioScience* 61, no. 3 (2011): 204.

July: 7:30 p.m. There is a bungle of traffic at the beginning of the recording that makes way for a slow, smooth, jazzy pocket. A go-go band's horn section is playing a tight riff in a minor key while the lead talker speaks to the audience. The beginning of the riff is four ascending staccato notes, which then hit their peak and slide into a long note with a glissando. Engines rev around the horn section, creating the impression of a smoky club environment. Wind clips the edges of the recording, while more traffic bounces through.

if I could potentially interview the owner. The woman working there, Ms. Joyce, patiently took down my information and told me that I could reach out to the owner, James Stokes, whose story is quoted in this and the previous chapter. It was only after being invited into Mr. Stokes's office and conducting a moving interview with him that I realized that his office balcony looked out directly over the intersection at Central Communications. I asked permission, he said yes, and Recorder 2 was installed not soon after. In this way, the progress of the fieldwork, the process of asking questions and permission from real people, influenced every part of the data and recordings that I have analyzed below. One recorder had six months and one had nine months because it took me another three months, give or take, to build up enough relationships to get it installed. That said, using a variety of digital methods and tools, primarily computational sound analysis, I was able to extract some of the key elements in the soundscape, including sirens, buses, car horns, and go-go music. My analysis and interpretation of this soundscape data offers different hearings of the same space, shaping digital tools in service of hearing Black life.

For the duration of the project I utilized two Wildlife Acoustics Song Meter SM4 recorders, described by the manufacturers as "a compact, weatherproof, dual-channel acoustic recorder capable of long-term acoustic monitoring of birds, frogs, insects, and aquatic life."[23] I installed the first recorder in March of 2018, on the rooftop of Florida Avenue Baptist Church, after

---

[23] In my initial curiosity about the potential of these recorders for listening to gentrification, I called Wildlife Acoustics and asked a general question what the recorders would be able to hear. The man I spoke to then asked me what I was trying to hear, and my response of "gentrification" audibly threw him off. He did admit, though, that they can pick up "everything." "Song Meter SM4 Wildlife Audio Recorder," Wildlife Acoustics, https://www.wildlifeacoustics.com/products/song-meter-sm4 (accessed August 26, 2024).

August: 11:10 a.m. The recording starts with a man and a woman's voice trading off, singing "slow jam, slow jam." The man's voice soon fades out completely as the woman riffs on the words "slow jam" for the remainder of the recording. She sings, "slow-ooh-oh-ooh-oh, slow-ooh-oh-ooh-oh, it's a slow jam." Her voice pushes into the intersection, seeming to almost be straining against the speakers. Her singing is punctuated by a very loud truck or bus. Both the sounds of the bus and the woman's voice get progressively louder, each one drowning out the other, until the recording abruptly ends.

receiving permission from their pastor. The rooftop was about five stories off the ground, covered with solar panels. I hung the first recorder, nestled in a wooden arm, off of the western edge of the roof, near the southwestern corner, so as to be directed toward the intersection of 7th street and Florida Avenue. I installed the second recorder in May of 2018 over the balcony of the church office of Gospel Spreading Church, located in the northwest corner of the intersection at 7th and Florida. The final tally of over 100,000 recordings is nearly impossible to listen or analyze manually, and yet the possibilities for the dataset are nearly endless.

Before analysis, I engaged in "data cleaning," that time consuming and nebulous process of preparing a dataset for analysis. This involved any number of processes, from discarding particular parts of the data, to segmenting it for more regimented analysis. This process is a large part of the data analysis process, and yet often remains left out of formal analysis. In my own "cleaning" process, I engaged in several iterations of work, continually returning to both my research questions and the goals of the project. I asked myself, *Does segmenting the data in this particular way help us to hear processes of gentrification? To decriminalize Black sound and amplify Black life? How do I negotiate the ethics of hearing voices on the recorders?* My attention to the data cleaning process here draws from Trevor Muñoz and Katie Rawson's critique of data cleaning as well as Lauren Klein and Catherine D'ignazio's principles of feminist data visualization. Muñoz and Rawson interrogate the language of data cleaning in digital humanities projects, because "is data dirty?"[24] When

---

[24] Catherine D'Ignazio and Lauren F. Klein, *Data Feminism* (Cambridge, MA: The MIT Press, 2020); Katie Rawson and Trevor Muñoz, "Against Cleaning," *Curating Menus* 6, 2016, http://www.curatingmenus.org/articles/against-cleaning/.

September: 2:40 a.m. The intersection is fairly quiet, with the crosswalk pulsing. There is another sound moving in and out of phase with the crosswalk, it sounds like a hiss, or a skitter, or a jump rope hitting the street, every three or four seconds. Sometimes the combination of the crosswalk and the other sound are reminiscent of the beat to a song. And at other points in the recording they sound simply like a quiet intersection in the middle of the night. At the end of the recording, a motorcycle or other small, but loud engine moves quickly through the space, disrupting the quiet.

collecting data that is intertwined with the intricacies of Black life, the language of data as dirty and messy, in need of cleaning and parsing, is problematic. Rather, in considering narrative and the intersection as palimpsest, I have tried to keep the data and my exploration of the intersection as complex as possible, so as not to misrepresent the mosaic of the space itself. There is never just one story moving through that space, but rather many stories constantly passing through. Data cleaning, then, is a way to temporarily focus on one story. Digital work is often presented as magic, and not a continually iterative process that takes many people and skillsets. I spend time with my own data cleaning process in order to emphasize intentionality and the processual nature of this work.

The history of digital humanities data cleaning has largely been a question of text, as the field originated within English departments. Data cleaning of text involves identifying and isolating word patterns, chunks, segmenting sentences, regulating names, place names, and the like. Sound data cleaning can operate similarly, considering the chunking of various sonic markers, such as speech patterns or frequencies. However, as argued by digital humanities scholar Tanya Clement, sound analysis is a question of compromise and an exercise in imagination.[25] For sound, one must contend with extraction of multiple sonic markers that may be sounding simultaneously. Furthermore, sound data is typically converted into a useable spreadsheet via signal processing, where text already exists in a form that can be manipulated via table. In the process of cleaning my data, in addition to questions of segmentation and categorization, I considered carefully the legacy of surveillance that weighs on Black people across the diaspora, where

---

[25] Tanya E. Clement, "Word. Spoken. Articulating the Voice for High-Performance Sound Technologies for Access and Scholarship (HiPSTAS)," in *Digital Sound Studies*, edited by Mary Caton Lingold, Darren Mueller, and Whitney Trettien (Durham, NC: Duke University Press, 2018).

118 Intersectional Listening

September: 5:15 p.m. The recording starts with a pocket beat, the lead talker reigning supreme over the breakdown. There are adlibs, calls of "you ready?" and more. There are sounds of excitement, "ha, ha" and a long call that almost could be compared to a ululation in some way. The pocket goes strong. Sounds of traffic, one loud engine in particular, challenges the go-go music, but ultimately go-go comes out on top here. They move into a cover of a Kanye West's 2005 song "Gold Digger."

Simone Browne reminds us of "surveillance in and of Black life as a fact of Blackness."[26] Specifically, the violence of the United States through the CIA, FBI, and police departments across the country led me to work against repeating the legacies of surveillance, which is why I was determined to ignore potential identifiers in the data. I purposely "cleaned" in such a way that my signal processing would obscure conversation rather than identify it. In fact, the only reason I classified voices at all was just to be able to train the classifier to be able to listen to go-go music, which features spoken vocals from lead talkers.[27]

---

[26] Simone Browne, *Dark Matters: On the Surveillance of Blackness* (Durham, NC: Duke University Press, 2015).

[27] The cleaning process largely involved Kaleidoscope, a software suite built by Wildlife Acoustics in order to visualize and classify bird and bat calls for bioacoustic research. I cleaned the data, working with month-long sets, because my data was already organized in this schema and because I ascended the rooftops monthly to download data and change the batteries on the recorders. In order to train a data set, I first ran a month's worth of data through Kaleidoscope's unsupervised classifier, which allows the algorithm to group the recordings into unnamed clusters based on similarities in frequency and waveform. This classification is conducted through Fast Fourier Transform, an algorithm utilized within typically math and physics to decompose a signal down to its individual parts. With these base classifiers in hand, I then went through manually and "tagged" clips within the clusters I wanted to create, which included the following: car horns, bus hisses, brakes, music, voices, and sirens. I developed this set of clusters through trial and error, and then went through to only tag the best examples of these sounds. After tagging a number of clips of each category, I then reran the classifier with the same data to only include the clips that I tagged. This second file then became the official training set. Finally, I ran a new set of data under a supervised classification, using the training set. This produced a table that clusters the data based on my training set and is reasonably accurate within a set distribution. After solidifying the training set, I was then able to run all nine months of data from both recorders through Kaleidoscope, using my training set. I uploaded the final spreadsheet into Sequel Pro, a database management application used for working with Structured Query Language (SQL) databases. Working with SQL and Indiana University's supercomputing support, I was then able to manipulate the data into visualizations that speak to my research questions. SQL is useful for this kind of analysis because it allows for querying a dataset. For example, the following query pulls all sirens out of the dataset, ordered by date:
SELECT *
FROM ethel_june_dec
WHERE SoundType = "siren"
ORDER BY DATETIME
I wrote queries, for example, to see how sounds differed during different months of the year or even different days of the week.

March: 8:55 a.m. This recording sounds like morning traffic and construction. There is a backup beep beep beep and then what sounds like a garbage truck or some other large vehicle groaning with whale-like sounds as it moves from one place to another. Squeaky brakes and wind compete for the rest of the intersection's attention, until a car horn sounds from far away.

Drawing on this extended cleaning process as well as other methods of sonic representation, I offer a tripartite analysis of the soundscape data here, focused at different levels of scope to engage a variety of aural insights in a gentrifying intersection. I begin with close listenings, because even amid the possibilities of large-scale machine learning, there is still room for and urgency within both traditional and computationally informed close listenings. By computationally informed close listening, I am referring to a kind of deep engagement with and interpretation of a sound source that stems from mediation types other than listening from a standard playback device. In this case, I facilitate close listenings via spectrograms, which are visual representations of sound that mark frequency and amplitude over an x-axis of time.

I include several annotated spectrograms here, detailing some of the most common sounds in the intersection: Metro Buses, go-go music, sirens, car horns, and beeps. All of these sounds present a different visual and sonic profile in the soundscape. Sirens are perhaps the most immediately recognizable. They appear like waves, drawing the attention of the eye and ear as the present as the loudest sounds in the intersection. Less pronounced is go-go music, which appears almost ubiquitous on a spectrogram. Because go-go is an entire soundscape of its own, it easily overlaps and intermingles with the traffic and conversations at 7th and Florida. I use spectrograms here to think about the common claim of go-go as too loud, or of go-go as an interruption to the intersection. On a spectrogram, go-go is perhaps the least noticeable sound in the space, especially as compared to sirens, car horns, and construction. One of the claims of the #DontMuteDC movement was that go-go is a foundational part of the intersection, and should not be turned off because of people that have recently moved in. These annotated spectrograms support that claim, because they illustrate go-go as a part of the fabric of the space, rather than an aberration. While many studies and narratives of gentrification emphasize displacement and loss, these sonic materials assert the enduring presence of Black life in the intersection. I posit here that all of these sounds, from the bus stop to the siren to the go-go music, are "Black sounds." The bus network is an important facet of Black working life and labor in DC, and sirens are closely

April: 7:20 a.m. The recording starts quite loudly, a large vehicle is in the process of coming to a stop or leaving the intersection. It quiets down almost immediately, as though someone had just turned down the volume switch. There is a great deal of traffic moving through the intersection in this recording. Several seconds are dominated by a vehicle reversing and having the signature backup beep. There are birds sounding in the distance, calling out that it indeed morning. Cars drive over steel plates, a horn honks far out into the distance.

connected to the same notions of policing and criminality that frame core conceptions of Blackness.[28] So as these neighborhoods become visually unrecognizable, their soundscapes remain discernible as a space in which Black people exist. As gentrification threatens to erase memories of a Black DC, the sonic footprint of a space on a granular level serves as an important timestamp and a refusal to be overlooked.

My next level of analysis zooms out to focus on particular days rather than minutes, represented by a 24-hour timeline built with Microsoft's Timeline Storyteller (Figure 3.1). Several days are important to the life

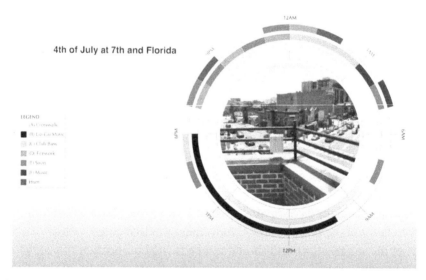

Figure 3.1 Timeline 1
A 24-hour timeline representing various sounds at 7th and Florida

---

[28] Brandi Thompson Summers, *Black in Place: The Spatial Aesthetics of Race in a Post-Chocolate City* (Chapel Hill: University of North Carolina Press, 2019); Jennifer Lynn Stoever, *The Sonic Color Line: Race and the Cultural Politics of Listening* (New York: NYU Press, 2016).

October: 10:40 a.m. A large vehicle is almost completely drowning out the go-go music. It could be a cement truck, a garbage truck, a bus, or something else. Soaring melismatic singing can be heard in the distance, as though it is very far away and not just in the same intersection as the loud vehicle. When the sound moves away, the intersection seems much quieter overall. Just very melodic go-go music and a few horns beeping in the space as punctuation or almost adlibs for the music.

of this intersection, from major holidays to the first day of each month, which is a popular day for many to go to Central Communications to pay their phone bills. Here I offer a 24-hour look at July 4, 2018, which features annotations about the various sounds heard on that day, from sirens to fireworks, which are common within the neighborhood as well as on the National Mall.

In this timeline, hours of the day are represented by rectangular blocks that move clockwise beginning at 12 midnight (the beginning of the day, then, visually, is actually late at night). These hour blocks are delineated in larger groups of three hours that mark time around a standard 24-hour day. In this representation, the only space continuously filled is that of the beeping crosswalk. While crosswalks are known to beep for accessibility purposes, this one in particular sounds throughout the day without prompting, inserting itself as the most consistent sound in the recording process. The consistent beeping of the intersection offers up a glimpse into a broader conversation about sound, gentrification, and accessibility, as the intersection serves a large population of disabled people. Go-go music, as per usual, begins at 10 a.m. when Central Communications opens, ending at 6 p.m. which is earlier than its usual 8 p.m. close but reasonable because of the holiday. Car horns are present throughout the day, as 7th and Florida is a busy vehicular and pedestrian intersection in the city. I offer "music" in the representation here distinct from "go-go music" and "club bass" to encompass the myriad of other types of musical expression that permeate the intersection, from people playing music on their phones as they pass through or the radio that spills out of cars that idle at red lights. Go-go and club bass are relatively stable categories, whereas music more broadly could be any number of sounds or sound sources. For the remainder of the evening and into the night, sirens and fireworks crisscross each other in the timeline, giving the impression of a loud and busy night. Club bass is an interesting swatch in the timeline, present briefly in the late afternoon before asserting a more sustained presence from 12 a.m. to 3 a.m. Bass is more visible here than audible in actual recordings, because of the low frequencies spilling out of the club. Bass is felt, rather than heard, in most instances, and visual

August: 9:40 p.m. The recording opens with the quick hiss of a bus brake releasing. There is steady conversation from what sounds like a woman's voice. The words aren't distinguishable but there are a few key phrases that stand out: "yooo" and "yassss." Affirmation and the "y" sound are audible. More brakes squeak by as the conversation fades out.

representation of such a consistent frequency is helpful here because many noise complaints (whether overtly racialized or not) begin and end with bass being too loud.

The 4th of July is an effective site for analysis because of the frictions between federal and local life in Washington, DC. The 4th of July is the city's most popular tourist holiday, where people flock in to visit national museums by day and enjoy fireworks by night. However, amid national festivities lie a city that is characterized by its lack of statehood, a drastic wealth gap, and a vibrant local cultural life. This timeline provides sonic entry into these tensions, noting how the neighborhood shifts because of the holiday, but also maintains its own character and traditions, in this case the go-go music at Central Communications.

This circle timeline offers a grammar of audibility in the intersection through the unit of a day, a way of hearing the space that acknowledges patterns and routines but does not obscure or leave behind the sonic messiness of the day. Although gentrification is often considered primarily in longitudinal capacities, the unit of the everyday remains an incredibly useful metric of analysis. As Michel de Certeau argued in "Walking in the City," the city is made by those that walk every day, made not from looking down from the empire state building and mapping the urban as city blocks, but instead in the compilation of those steps.[29] There is a hubris in the longitudinal that I use the day to avoid and to disrupt. As Amiri Baraka wrote about tradition, this is the changing same.[30] Much of the gentrification story is not about what changes, but what stays the same. The crosswalk beeps, the music plays, the sirens wail.

My final level of analysis, which is most dependent on that initial data cleaning process, scales back even further to think about gentrification across a series of months in the intersection. Here I consider data over the course of the months long period in which the recorders were installed. Gentrification

---

[29] Michel de Certeau, *The Practice of Everyday Life* (Berkeley, CA: University of California Press, 1984).
[30] Leroi Jones, *Blues People: Negro Music in White America* (New York: Harper Perennial, 1999), 153.

February. A muffled Wale verse is being played from somewhere. I can tell it's the rapper Wale not necessarily because the lyrics are intelligible because they're not quite, but because I know the tone and cadence of Wale's flow; they're very distinctive. His voice rumbles through the space for most of the recording, and then a siren slowly moves into the recording as though someone is slowly turning up a fader.

is, on the surface, a problem of time. If I had wanted to hear gentrification over time in a purely longitudinal way, I would have needed to install the recorders in 2008 or 1998 instead of 2018. But this is a case, perhaps even a call, to lean in to the limitations of a dataset. What can nine months tell us about an intersection? What can this interval of time give us about a space? Does this period function only in anticipation of a longer, future dataset, or is there something to learn in listening to these months as incidents themselves?

I draw on sirens here as an example, which operate as both icon and index of a broader urban imaginary.[31] Sirens, depending on their source, can signal crime, emergencies, crises, danger, impending violence, even terror.[32] Both interviews and informal conversations led me to understand sirens as a powerful indicator of a neighborhoods crime status, with some of my conversation partners sharing that they heard less sirens as the neighborhood around 7th and Florida gentrified. Furthermore, this decrease in sirens was often interpreted as a decrease in criminal activity. I was therefore interested in tracking the presence of sirens across time at 7th and Florida, and offer here a brief representation of that pursuit in Figure 3.2.

This simple line chart shows sirens from July to October of 2018, and displays the frequency of detected sirens every day.[33] A number of insights arise from the chart. The peaks and valleys here are often indicative of the number of people active in the space on any given day. For example, most peaks, where the recorder detected more than twenty sirens, were on weekends, typically Fridays and Saturdays. Days with the least number of sirens often corresponded with difficult weather patterns, typically heavy rain and thunderstorms. Looking across the longer four-month period, from July

---

[31] Alisha Lola Jones, "Stereotypical Images in Film and Media," Global Popular Music Class (Indiana University, 2017).
[32] Ruth M. Stone, "'Ebola in Town': Creating Musical Connections in Liberian Communities During the 2014 Crisis in West Africa," *Africa Today* 63, no. 3 (2017): 79–97.
[33] Because the recorders only recorded one minute out of every five, it's important to note that this is not every siren.

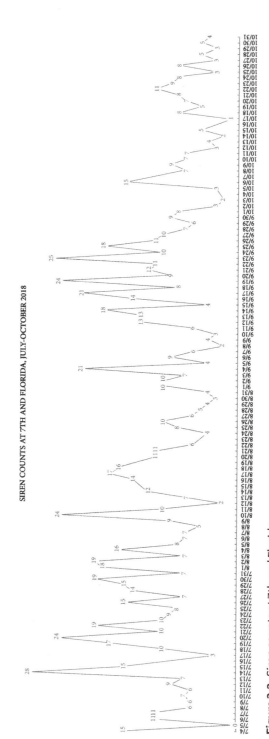

Figure 3.2 Siren counts at 7th and Florida

A line chart detailing how many sirens are heard at 7th and Florida between July and October of 2018

May: 8:10 p.m. The intersection sounds incredibly busy. There is the customary traffic rolling through, engines rumbling while they're stopped for a bit at the light and then moving on, their sounds fading away. At the same time, there is music being played from somewhere that has a quick tempo, around 124 bpm that makes everything sound heightened. You can almost imagine a fast walking upright bassline to go along with it. The music is interacting with the crosswalk, making the crosswalk beep sound like a jazz instrument from a 1920s big band. There are voices talking at the beginning recording, not quite over all the sounds but mixed in. At the end, a siren begins to wail.

to October, there is a noticeable decrease in sirens as the season turns from summer to fall. This decrease is consistent with two narratives of a gentrifying city: The first is that crime levels peak during summer months because summers are hot, in terms of both heat and criminal activity. The second narrative is that crime decreases over time in gentrifying neighborhoods. My intervention lies in the disruption of these narratives, however true they may be. Gentrification is not a linear, gradual process of displacement. Gentrification is a series of jagged interruptions, community meetings, demolitions, protests, contracts, construction projects, and violence.

In carrying connotations of crime and loudness, sirens exist within a nexus of aural indicators of race, criminality, and urban life. Sirens are so closely molded to Black urban life because they are indicative and representative of those forces that have deemed themselves in control of Black life, particularly the police. The chart here details the pattern of sirens in the intersection, offering a visual experience of what it is to exist in a space in which Blackness has been marked as existent and available. I read this pattern as a demonstration of the cycle of potential sonic traumas that come through the intersection every day, sometimes dozens of times a day: of policing, terror, emergency, and health crises. This chart disrupts a visual narrative of gentrification, in which neighborhoods become better and more beautiful looking because it repositions gentrification as a cyclical process of sonic violences, an ebb and flow of sirens.

Futures of 7th and Florida

The futures of 7th and Florida remain uncertain, though there has been a flurry of action since the initial protests in April 2019. The tide of public opinion and organizing forced the hands of T-Mobile. The CEO at the time John Legere tweeted "I've looked into the issue myself and the music should

A go-go band is playing a cover of Chaka Khan and Rufus's "Sweet Thing." The recording is full of melismatic singing, guttural timbres, pushing, and straining. The singer is belting loudly into the intersection, and traffic swirls all around as the band swells to support her. She ad-libs over the band's punctuating phrases: "I'll go crazy, out my mind . . . you're my my my my, my my my my . . . sweet thing."

NOT stop in D.C.! @TMobile and @MetroByTMobile are proud to be part of the Shaw community—the music will go on and our dealer will work with the neighbors to compromise volume." Since then, the music has been returned, albeit at a lower, more consistent volume than was previously customary. The store promotes its music on Instagram, going viral on occasion for a particularly interesting or eclectic dance party. There continue to be rallies and events in support of the #DontMuteDC movement, from programming at the Kennedy Center and Anacostia Arts Center to continued media appearances and fundraisers. Council members Robert White Jr. (At Large), Kenyan McDuffie (Ward 5), and Mayor Muriel Bowser have all tweeted in support, and Ward 1 councilmember Brianne Nadeau wrote a public letter to T-Mobile explaining the importance of keeping go-go playing in the intersection. Councilman McDuffie went so far as to propose legislation to make go-go the official music of Washington, DC, a gesture of public protection. The legislation passed in the council December 2019, with gratitude on behalf of go-go musicians across the DMV, but with questions about the bill's legislative and financial power. Activist and community organizer Tony Lewis organized a photoshoot and music video in the intersection featuring Rare Essence. At the 2019 Folklife Festival, the Smithsonian Institution planned around the "Social Power of Music," featuring Central Communications, Don Campbell, and other go-go legends on the National Mall. These events speak to how #DontMuteDC has reverberated through the city, sparking conversation and debate on what the city owes to Black people and to go-go music.

In addition to the #DontMuteDC petition and subsequent protests, another parallel movement has formed in response to the T-Mobile's temporary shutdown of the go-go music at Central Communications. Moechella is a clever portmanteau of Coachella, the outdoor music festival in California and "moe," the DC slang term used to describe another person or a friend, as in "what's good moe." Moechella is sponsored by an organization called "Long Live Go-Go," which is run by a team of young Black activists, organizers, and artists that have thrown a dozen go-go's of various shapes and sizes since April of 2019. The face of the Moechella movement is Yaddiya, a thirty-two-year-old rapper and activist that has made a name for himself organizing these

November: 3:50 p.m. There is a very loud idling engine in the intersection, potentially stopped at the traffic. The go-go band on the recording is having a soft keyboard solo. It might only sound soft because it's being muffled by the engine. The crosswalk signal beep softly punctuates the piano solo as the lead talker speaks over the music. His voice is muffled but the flow suggests talking, rather than singing or rapping. The band starts a new song as the light changes and everything becomes a bit more harried, both in the music and in the cars that had been idling. A car horn beeps twice.

miraculous parties all over town. When I spoke with him at a pop-up shop in summer 2019, he told me that he was relatively new to activism, saying: "Not even two years of activism. My first stint in activism started last summer. It's just God's plan, God's using me as a vessel. It's not like I chose." He cited his pacing as a primary reason for Moechella's success, where "the way I work when I have a vision I want to do it right then and there, I don't want to be talking about do it next month." In addition to organizing go-go's all over the city, Moechella has been making important and insightful connections between gentrification and Black erasure in DC, throwing their weight behind DC's quest for statehood, one of the most enduring and critical campaigns in the city.

Even amidst this collective action and parallel movements, there is a fragility about the sonic life of the intersection, because legislation could still be passed to silence or police the space. Spaces like Central Communications and even 14th and U Street with its many musical performances are always subject to the threat of complaint, where if enough people with enough legislative capability get upset enough they can shut a space down. Despite this constant threat of being shut down, the work happening in the space is a kind of sonic justice, an enactment of equity through the aural. For example, Moechella, in creating a space for thousands of Black people to fellowship in a neighborhood where many of them cannot afford to live, is indeed an enacting of justice. On the possibility of policed spaces, geographer Margaret Ramirez notes, "the precarity of [the] space also demands creative modes of survival and resistance."[34] The fragility and ephemerality of this sonic justice allows for more possibilities and facilitates a kind of hopeful replication and remediation through the digital. When I finally arrived back at the intersection in 2022, the country was both "post-pandemic" and experiencing its fourth largest surge since the pandemic began in 2020. The music was still on at the intersection,

---

[34] Margaret M. Ramírez, "City as Borderland: Gentrification and the Policing of Black and Latinx Geographies in Oakland," *Environment and Planning D: Society and Space* 38, no. 1 (2020): 14.

playing songs that felt like jazz versions of go-go. Metro buses were still running from the two stops in the intersection, and a bus driver kindly made sure to make eye contact with me twice to ensure he wasn't leaving me off the bus. I wasn't there to travel, rather simply to stand and see what time had wrought. The biggest change to my eyes and ears was the CVS being closed. The closure brings a sense of anticipation about what is to come to the space, and how it will interact with the other businesses in the intersection, especially Central Communications. There was still construction, still no parking, still copious amounts of Black people congregating on street corners to talk and lounge around. The sign for the Shay, which once held a white woman in a Victorian era costume declaring that "she's arrived," has since been replaced by a sign that simply says, "The Shay." The sign is now washed out, no longer part of the new and shiny DC. There was an apartment window in the Shay that features a prominent "Don't Mute DC" sign, a reminder that even if residents of the Shay were the ones to originally submit the complaints to T-Mobile, that does not mean that everyone in the building supported them. Some people, still and always, are advocating for the music to go on.

Chapter 4
Life, Death, and Legacy in Go-Go Music

In 2017, *Complex* Magazine posted the following tweet: "How DC killed go-go: and why Goldlink created its memorial." The tweet, linked to an interview with rising hip-hop artist Goldlink, received a wave of criticism from local DC communities for a number of reasons: First, Goldlink is technically from Northern Virginia, not DC proper. The distinction matters here; the cultural politics of Northern Virginia are different from those of DC, which are different still from those of Maryland. The DMV is not always a useful catchall term. Second, if anybody killed go-go, it wasn't local DC (often used to distinguish from federal Washington). Finally, and most importantly—go-go is not dead, and for a national publication to describe it as such, without nuance, is an act of violence. In such a short tweet, Complex accepted and codified the death and cultural erasure that gentrification promises to Black music genres across the United States.

Indeed, there is a conversation to be had about go-go and death, but it requires more nuance than the aforementioned tweet. In this chapter, I think through the conflicting narratives of go-go's death and dying in a gentrifying DC, drawing on Christina Sharpe's conception of "wake work," which she describes as "that mode of inhabiting and rupturing this episteme with our known lived and un/imaginable lives."[1] By this episteme, Sharpe refers to the unending afterlives of slavery, making "wake work" a mode of understanding how Black lives are lived in and through an unceasing impending death. In DC, go-go is killed in many ways: through policing; through gentrifying forces, where rising rents, changing tastes, and removal of liquor licenses frequently shut down clubs; and through individual death, where members of the community are dying not only from sensationalized violence but also from the violence of poverty and a lack of healthcare. Go-go is killed every day and yet go-go lives—in the clubs that open as quickly as old ones are shut down, in community programs, where bands play in neighborhood parks and local correctional facilities, and on the internet, where online radio shows interact with their audiences in real time, no matter where they are. Go-go is

---

[1] Christina Sharpe, *In the Wake: On Blackness and Being* (Durham, NC: Duke University Press, 2016), 18.

not dead, and yet it lives in the shadow of its own death. In this chapter, I amplify the wake work of the go-go community while simultaneously imagining a soundscape in which go-go is able to live free of its own impending end.

Go-Go 101

Musically, go-go is located within an Afro-diasporic sonic lineage, emphasizing repetition, participatory performance, polyrhythms, and percussive timbres. Although tangentially related to the Smokey Robinson and the Miracles 1969 hit "Going to a Go-Go," the name of the genre is primarily based in the drive to keep people going and going on the dance floor. The genre's origins are most often attributed to the "Godfather" of Go-Go Chuck Brown, a guitarist and singer who moved to DC from Gaston, North Carolina in 1942. Brown and his band, The Soul Searchers, capitalized on a funk-derived style of music predicated on keeping people dancing, with the beat continuing to play between songs.[2] John "JB" Buchanan, the trumpet player for the Soul Searchers, described this musical shift as unintentional:

> Instead of going into the song, though, we started jamming, improvising, until he [Brown] got comfortable with the groove. Prior to that, we'd start the song, and do the song. But this time, we kind of jammed, and something happened that night that I'll never forget, okay. On the break, we took intermission. Somebody came up to me and Chuck and said, "Hey man, what was that song you played before the real song." They didn't understand what we were doing, they didn't know that we were improvising, jamming. So, a lightbulb went off.[3]

The Soul Searchers quickly realized that people enjoyed the "jamming" before and after the "real" songs, which led them to develop a performance style that carried little distinction between the two. As their performance style became popular, more bands across the city adopted go-go, in part because it kept them employed. The band that could rock the crowd best was the band that would be hired back. Audience appeal has always driven go-go music, and is one of the reasons why go-go has remained primarily a live music genre. Go-go functions best with an enthusiastic audience, one that knows what to expect and how to participate. For example, call and response is central to

---

[2] Before joining the Soul Searchers in the early 1970s Brown played in the band Los Latinos. It was with that band that he reportedly developed his Afro-Caribbean rhythmic style.
[3] John "JB" Buchanan, interview with the author, 2016.

go-go, with lead talkers cycling through a well-worn repository of chants that are adjustable based on audience. Many are place based, featuring a version of "Is [neighborhood] in the house?" Some chants are song specific, such as the Junkyard Band's 1986 hit song "Sardines." The chorus of "Sardines" is both antiphony and meal, with the lead talker calling "Sardines!" and waiting for the audience to respond with "Hey, and pork and beans!" Other modes of participation include calling out one's neighborhood, performing a specific dance or gesture, or simply singing and dancing along to the music. Because of their repetition, well-understood expectations, and hyperlocal community focus, these shows have been dubbed "ritual spaces" by journalist and scholar Natalie Hopkinson, spaces that "comfort and reassure the crowd that they exist."[4] In this way, go-go has always been a life-giving institution for its audiences. The ritual space is similar to many others in Afro-diasporic music genres, from gospel to hip-hop. These genres that make Black people feel seen and heard through performance practice are an important part of how we listen to Black life.

The instrumentation of go-go bands differs from band to band, but there is a general unifying structure across the scene. Bands typically consist of a drum set, two sets of congas (typically two small, two large), auxiliary percussion (tambourine, cowbell, etc.), at least one keyboard, an electric bass, a lead guitar, and a few vocalists. Go-go bands always include a lead talker or lead mic, whose function is to lead the band and interact with the audience, which is one of the most important facets of creating this inclusive community. The singers and lead mic are on the frontline of the band, with percussionists and guitarists making up the backline. The most important component in the go-go sound is the beat (or the groove), commonly referred to as "the pocket." Kip Lornell and Charles Stephenson Jr. describe the music's beat:

> characterized by a syncopated, dotted rhythm that consists of a series of quarter and eighth notes (quarter, eighth, quarter, (space/held briefly), quarter, eighth, quarter) . . . which is underscored most dramatically by the bass drum and snare drum, and the hi-hat . . . [and] is ornamented by the other percussion instruments, especially by the conga drums, timbales, and hand-held cowbell.[5]

This pocket beat is featured throughout go-go music, perfected by bands such as EU and Junkyard. Although the pocket remains a crucial element of

---

[4] Natalie Hopkinson, *Go-Go Live: The Musical Life and Death of a Chocolate City* (Durham, NC: Duke University Press, 2012), 45.
[5] Kip Lornell and Charles C. Stephenson, *The Beat! Go-Go Music from Washington, D.C.* (Jackson: University Press of Mississippi, 2009), 12.

go-go music and culture, I have delineated five broad overlapping subgenres in my study of go-go music, characterized both by the type of beats they play as well as the crowd to which they cater.

The first subgenre is "old school," which plays the pocket beat described above, and has fueled the Chocolate City's music for over forty years. This subgenre of go-go music uses the pocket beat, from Chuck Brown and the Soul Searchers to Trouble Funk to Ayre Rayde. Old school go-go draws an older crowd, primarily catering to the audiences that have grown up with them. The age of the crowd also changes the shows in terms of call and response and setlists. Popular old school go-go songs include "Bustin Loose" (1978) by Chuck Brown and the Soul Searchers, "Pump Me Up" (1982) by Trouble Funk, and "Da Butt" (1988) by EU (Experience Unlimited). All of these songs come with their own histories and mythologies. "Bustin Loose" is one of the most famous go-go songs outside of DC, a funk hit in its own right as well as famous for being sampled in Nelly's 2002 hit "Hot in Herre." The song is also somewhat of a hometown anthem and is played every time a player on the Washington Nationals baseball team hits a home run at a home game. Not to be outdone, "Da Butt" was featured in Spike Lee's film *School Daze* and was subsequently nominated for a Grammy in 1989. Between the release of these two songs, Trouble Funk released "Pump Me Up," which is a good example of the relationship between go-go and hip-hop music in the 1980s. Both genres were on the rise and bands frequently collaborated with MCs, as "Pump Me Up" featured Melle Mel of Grandmaster Flash and the Furious 5, most famous for their hit song "The Message." Trouble Funk was, for a time, signed to New York City label Sugarhill Records, which is most famous for having been the home of the Sugarhill Gang and "Rapper's Delight," the first commercially successful rap records. These fragments of go-go music's earlier days offer a glimpse into how influential this genre was and continues to be not only in DC but on a national (and international) stage as well. Go-go is a rare genre that operates relatively self-sufficiently (unlike commercial hip-hop) and still influences the global soundscape of Black music.

After old school comes "crank," developed in the 1990s by bands like Backyard Band and Northeast Groovers. Crank utilizes the pocket as well as a faster, more aggressive version known as the socket. This subgenre carries the influence of gangsta rap, which became a more commercial enterprise in the 1990s with the rise of artists like Ice-T and NWA. Backyard Band, led by lead talker Big G, began their career playing on trashcans, emulating their idols, the Junkyard Band, who also started off on "junk." Over the past twenty-five years, Backyard's sound has developed into one of the most popular on the go-go scene today. Lead talker Big G's famous bass growl combined with singer

Weensey's distinctive tenor has catapulted the band into national recognition, collaborations with rapper Wale, and a trip to perform in Ghana in 2018. Some of the most well-known crank songs come from Backyard Band, with their hits "Pretty Girls," and "Unabomber." In addition to Backyard and Northeast Groovers, some of the original go-go bands developed a more crank based sound in the 1990s, such as Rare Essence and the Junkyard Band. The power of a crank song depends in part on the strength of the lead talker's voice, and Donnell Floyd (formerly of Rare Essence) and Buggs (Junkyard) have always been up to the task. Some of these songs carry their own mythologies as well. For example, the concept of RE's hit "Overnight Scenario" was sampled without permission by rapper Jay-Z on his song "Do it Again (Put Ya Hands Up)." They later won a lawsuit to that effect, which is a somewhat rare example of a smaller music scene being acknowledged and fairly compensated for their labor and musical influence. Shortly afterward, lead talker Donnell Floyd left Rare Essence to form his own bands, first 911 and later Familiar Faces (now known as Team Familiar) Team Familiar was instrumental in ushering in the next subgenre of go-go, "Grown and Sexy."

Arguably the most popular subgenre of go-go today, Grown and Sexy utilizes the pocket beat to transform R&B for a DMV audience. Top grown and sexy bands include Suttle Squad (now known simply as Suttle), Vybe Band, and Be'la Dona, which is one of the only all-women bands in the scene. Grown and Sexy is perhaps the subgenre most open to women creators and musicians because it is the most focused on singing and sensuality. This subgenre features the same instrumentation and pocket beat as old school for the most part (usually fewer horns, if any), but is more contemporary than old school go-go, with less original music and more covers of popular R&B, hip-hop, and pop songs. Go-go musicians across subgenres have the ability to completely transform a song from the radio into something that makes you certain that they were the ones that originally wrote it. For example, Rare Essence, mentioned above, covered Ashlee Simpson's "Pieces of Me" in 2004 and many who grew up in that era still don't know the original song. Suttle has covered Sam Smith, Be'la has covered Kendrick Lamar, and the possibilities for future go-go covers remain endless. But Grown and Sexy has done perhaps the most with covers, using the continuation of the pocket beat between songs to blend similar songs, such as Ed Sheeran's "Thinking Out Loud" and Marvin Gaye's "Let's Get it On."[6] Just as with old school and crank, subgenres in go-go

---

[6] In May 2023, Sheeran stood trial for the similarities between his song "Thinking Out Loud" and Gaye's "Let's Get it On." The lawsuit was originally filed not by Gaye's estate but a company that has the rights to a part of co-writer Ed Townsend's estate. Townsend had two hits of his own in the 1950s but subsequently wrote with and for other singers like Gaye and Jimmy Holiday. In the case versus Sheeran, a jury decided

music are not binding, and bands move freely between them. For example, for as much as Backyard Band cranks, they also produced an incredibly popular cover of Adele's hit song "Hello" in 2016. Grown and Sexy is a subgenre, but it is also a mood, a state of being, and a defense mechanism against the go-go music of the younger generation. Grown and Sexy intentionally draws a "mature crowd," with many of their flyers asking for "25 and older" patrons. The primary assumption here is that people under twenty-five are rowdier and more prone to violence and rowdiness than older crowds. This assumption of rowdiness is one of the explanations for the generational gap that has grown within older iterations of go-go music and its newest subgenre.

Go-go's youngest fans, now in their thirties, have created "bounce beat," a newer evolution of go-go that was established in 2003. Bounce beat is a more percussive, energetic style of music than its predecessors, utilizing a different rhythmic innovation called the "bounce beat" (which has variations of its own, the most popular of which is called the slow bounce). With a slightly different instrumentation than the pocket beat, rototoms rather than congas are highly important to the bounce beat sound, and drive the music along with the drum set. The melodic content of bounce beat is provided primarily by keyboards and vocalists, rather than a horn section or even guitar. The heavily percussive bounce beat is popular among the DMV's youth, and often found at "all ages" go-go's, which allow people under twenty-one to attend. The most popular bounce beat bands, sometimes called "Alphabet Bands," typically consist of three letter acronyms, such as AJA (All Jokes Aside) or CCB (Critical Condition Band). The origins of bounce beat are debated but ultimately conceded to TCB, or Total Control Band, particularly their lead mic Reggie "Polo" Burwell. Celebration of bounce beat's origins has become almost synonymous with a memorialization of Polo, who passed away in 2013. In addition to the bounce beat and its variants, the subgenre has sparked a number of dance movements as well, including "beat ya feet" and "chopping." Beat ya feet is the more popular of the two, with individuals or groups moving their feet in fluid rhythms to the music and giving the appearance of boneless legs. Chopping, a jerkier set of movements involving the entire body, can also lead to a chop train, in which audience members, mostly men, move very quickly in a circle while chanting "chop!" Chop trains are boisterous and rowdy, but also infectious and carry the hype of the moment. While bounce beat does feature its fair share of rapping and spoken lead mic selections, this community also values singing. Bounce beat band New Impressionz has perhaps highlighted

---

in Sheeran's favor, deciding that the "chord progression and harmonic rhythm" were not similar enough to warrant the $100 million in damages sought by the estate.

singing the most, focusing on the presence of lead mic and singer TJ, who has made singing an integral part of the band's work together. Rapper Wale was instrumental early on in popularizing bounce beat beyond Washington, DC, with songs like "Chillin," where the radio version featured Lady Gaga (who was little known at the time), but the bounce beat band XIB did a version that was more popular in the city itself. Bounce Beat also offered its share of covers, with CCB doing Maroon 5's "This Love" and Reaction Band performing Lloyd's "Lay it Down." While Bounce beat has been the target of intergenerational strife, some of the young leaders have been instrumental in protesting the conditions imposed onto go-go within the city. For example, the Juneteenth protest in June of 2020 that led thousands of people downtown featured music by TCB.

One of the biggest criticisms of bounce beat music by earlier generations of go-go musicians and fans is the change in instrumentation: emphasizing rototoms and minimizing or removing the melodic sections of the band, particularly the horn section, takes away some of the musical nuance that go-go fans enjoy and makes it a more percussive experience. This change, though, has been explained as a consequence of the educational shifts in Washington, DC. Simply put, as DC schools close and emphasize a charter model as well as STEM (science, technology, engineering, math), rather than arts education, many students have not been able to learn to play the instruments that would be present in a go-go band. If a student is not in concert band or marching band learning to play the trumpet or saxophone, they would not be able to then take that skillset into a go-go band. Organizations within the city are working on this, particularly Teach the Beat, which is dedicated to teaching students in DC Public Schools the history of go-go music and how to play it as well. Go-go luminaries such as Sweet Cherie, JuJu House, and JB have participated in this program to great success, which helps students to understand that go-go culture is not only alive and well but also available for them to tap into.

The other primary criticism of bounce beat that I have encountered is a kind of local musical respectability politics that chastises bounce beat for its informal nature, and for the stage presence of its band members. I once listened to a veteran musician talk about bounce beat musicians for not having a "show" or choreography as a part of their act. She told the audience, who largely seemed to agree with her, that bands used to be named "band and show" because they gave you music and a show. Bounce beat bands, she said, were missing the "show" part of the performance. They didn't wear matching uniforms, or even uniforms at all. Bounce beat bands often perform in t-shirts and jeans, and over the course of the night, as things get sweatier, can often strip down to just undershirts or no shirts at all for the men performers. Watching this critique, I was struck by this hyperlocal permeation of respectability politics. However, as often is the case with respectability politics and generational amnesia, they are not altogether true. Chuck Brown, the godfather of go-go music, learned how to play the guitar in Lorton Correctional Facility. There has always been criminality, raunchiness, and money tied up in go-go music, and it does us no favors to forget these histories. Filmmaker Ayanna Long skillfully presents these correlations in her film *The Let Out*, which chronicles bounce beat music and its audiences as they leave the club. Long juxtaposes pictures and videos of contemporary dancing to bounce beat music, often called twerking or clapping, with archival footage from the 1980s and 1990s of women go-go audience members doing the same (or more). Although there are indeed generational differences between bounce beat go-go and its predecessors, bounce beat inherited many of its musical and performance practices from the communities that came before.

The final subgenre of go-go is gospel go-go, which operates somewhat outside of the traditional landscape of nightclubs and parties that secular go-go works within. Gospel go-go is defined by its Christian messages, the belief that Jesus died for people's sins, and asking God to help the performers and listeners through the struggles of life in a place like the DMV. Although it is outside of standard performance networks, gospel go-go does not operate outside of the stigmas of go-go music and Black music more broadly. For years, church leaders hesitated about whether to invite gospel go-go bands to perform inside of churches themselves because of the belief that the music would drive youth to violence. They instead preferred to host events offsite, in spaces that were more acceptable to dance in. Gospel go-go bands include Submission Band and Peculiar People, and has the genre has also been adopted by gospel artist Kirk Franklin on songs like "Die For You" and "Melodies from Heaven." Despite the difference in lyrical message from the other subgenres, gospel go-go music favors the same bottom heavy timbral elements as the rest of the go-go music scene, with bass and percussion dominating the soundscape.[7]

With these five flexible and nuanced subgenres (shown in Figure 4.1), accounting for the historical and contemporary iterations of go-go music is a monumental task. Histories and archives of go-go music have been compiled and maintained by a number of eclectic sources over the years. There are many prolific collectors in the scene, some of whom sell copies of their live recordings burned as CDs or as direct downloads. In addition to these

---

[7] Alisha Lola Jones, *Flaming? The Peculiar Theopolitics of Fire and Desire in Black Male Gospel Performance* (New York: Oxford University Press, 2020), 117.

Life, Death, and Legacy in Go-Go Music   137

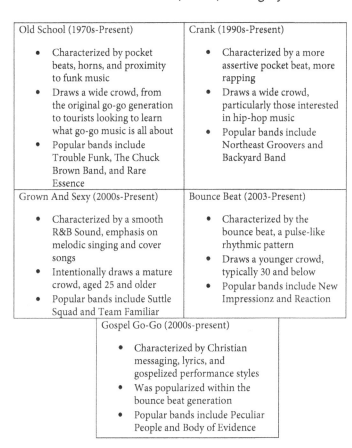

Figure 4.1 Go-go subgenres
Table of go-go music subgenres and their characteristics

collectors, go-go's community participates in robust discourse online as well. In popular Facebook groups like "The Go-Go Report" and online radio stations like "tmottgogo" (Take Me Out to the Go-Go) and "gogoradiolive," members of the community come together to share information, debate rankings, and listen together. Scholarship on go-go music regularly disrupts the boundaries of the academy and what we might understand to be "traditional" scholarship. Kip Lornell and Charles Stephenson Jr., an ethnomusicologist and former manager of EU respectively, are credited with writing the first scholarly book on go-go music, *The Beat: Go-Go Music from Washington, DC*. This book, groundbreaking for its time, explores the cultural and political roots of go-go music, featuring generous input from band members and fans alike. The second academic book on go-go music is *Go-Go Live* by journalist and scholar Natalie Hopkinson, who takes a deep dive into go-go music as it relates to the changing landscape of DC, both racially and politically. In addition to these scholarly monographs, there are also a growing number of autobiographies, exhibition catalogs, and other sources that document go-go music and its histories.[8] As gentrification in DC continues to change and disrupt the spatiality of Black life, these print and digital resources have become more important as repositories, texts, and gathering spaces for the community to participate in the creation and maintaining of their own histories.

Death and Wake Work

Amidst these intricate webs of musical and cultural variety within the go-go scene, rumors of go-go's death have been circulating for at least a decade. In 2013 I interviewed Diamond, a fan who had spent her formative teenage years in the scene. She had the following to say about go-go's death:

> Well, there has been a lot of talk in the city, in the DMV period about how go-go is dead, or go-go is dying. There's a lot of people who are trying to hold on to it, but it's slowly drifting away. I know a couple of years ago, me and my sister we were always at a go-go. We were always dancing, every weekend. The lines were packed. The lines were flooded. But because of them bringing more white people into the city, and they don't like go-go music. When they hear us listening to it, their reactions on the train, they're looking at us like we're crazy. And honestly, a lot of places we used to party at have been shut down, have been closed down. They either knocked them down, the police were called, and came through and shut the place down. So, there's really not a lot of go-go's going on anymore. At least there aren't a lot of go-go's that cater to the youth... if I had to pick a side, I would say go-go is dead.[9]

Diamond covers a wide range of territory, from the intensity of go-go's crowds to the common practice of playing music without headphones on public transportation. She also connects the influx of new white residents to the shutdown of various youth clubs, asserting that the institutions that are unwanted by or disruptive to white people are the same ones that become slated for removal. This consistent cycle of policing, removal, and demolition

---

[8] Lloyd A. Pinchback, *The Soul Searchers 1968–1978: A Decade of Memories* (Largo, MD: Pinchbax Books, 2013); Kato Hammond, *Take Me Out to the Go-Go: The True Story of a Music Culture and the Impact It Made on the Life of One Man* (Scotts Valley, CA: CreateSpace, 2015); Roger Gastman, *Pump Me Up: DC Subculture of the 1980s* (Bethesda, MD: R. Rock Enterprises, 2013).
[9] Diamond, interview with the author, 2013.

of spaces that cater to Black youth leads her to acknowledge that go-go, in the way she wants and knows go-go to be, is indeed dead.

Christina Sharpe describes the space in which Black people are constantly faced with our own death as the wake. The wake of the slave ship, the wake before a funeral, wake as watch, as vigil. But what about the work that is done in the wake? The work that insists that life is here, happening despite the seemingly unceasing loop of Black death around the world? Sharpe articulates this process as "wake work," as "the modalities of Black life lived in, as, under, and despite Black death."[10] In the case of Washington, DC, this is the work that go-go music does, has always done, and listening intersectionally to go-go's wake work is instructive for the study of gentrification, and for the study of Black life. How to we listen to ourselves dying but know that we are not dead?[11] This is about how go-go lives despite and in spite of the forces that attempt to end it every day. Here I explore the parameters of go-go's supposed death, the nuances of its language, the space it leaves and the lives it both creates and ignores. I hear go-go music's continued perseverance as a celebration in the key of Lucille Clifton: "Come celebrate with me that everyday something has tried to kill me and has failed."[12]

Some of go-go music's wake work is about grief, about listening to musicians and audiences process death in its most literal sense. In the opening of Backyard Band's song "The Unabomber," Big G and other members of the band lament "I don't want to die, I don't want to die." Because go-go is primarily a live genre, the song always starts a little differently, and in one particular recording from 2004, Big G says "Put your hands up for all your dead homies." The YouTube comments for that particular recording are filled with names, death dates, and invocations to rest in peace. There is a connection between Backyard and the audience because most of the people there have experienced loss, and do not want to themselves die. In live performance, this involves countless young Black people pressed together in club spaces exclaiming that they don't want to die, and honoring their friends and loved ones who have. This is wake work, acknowledging death's proximity while still holding it at arm's length and refusing its closeness. Go-go music is full of grief and memoriam, in sound, in fashion with the number of RIP t-shirts that proliferate the scene. Natalie Hopkinson understands this grief as a quintessential part of go-go's past and present: "From the RIP T-Shirts worn by fans, to the live

---

[10] Sharpe, *In the Wake*, 20.
[11] I pivot here from a terminology of death to one of dying, because there is a difference between accepting the fact of death and probing the process of dying, or in Diamond's case, "drifting."
[12] Lucille Clifton, *How to Carry Water: Selected Poems of Lucille Clifton* (Rochester, NY: BOA Editions, 2020), 180.

tributes to lost members of the community that form part of some live go-go performances ... go-go is an art form that remembers the dead."[13] These RIP t-shirts are not only worn by fans but brought to shows and held up to the lead talker so that they might more closely see the names of the dead. Audience members also get too hot at go-go's to wear the shirts, so they take them off and dance in only undershirts and tank tops, holding the names and faces of the dead close by.

This remembrance of the dead is combined with a powerful will to live on in their names and is further bolstered by the absolute refusal of narratives that claim that go-go doesn't exist. While conducting fieldwork, I spoke to a community relations member of the Metropolitan Police Department, who informed me that go-go was effectively banned in the city because none of its members were doing anything "positive."[14] This was confusing because a month before our conversation, Mayor Muriel Bowser had declared May 6, 2018 as Rare Essence Day, celebrating the band and their decades of accomplishments. Even earlier than that, in April of 2018, I watched Mayor Bowser celebrate a number of go-go bands at the city's annual Emancipation Day Parade. I left the police station that day baffled about hearing a public official speak confidently about the banning of a genre of music that the city publicly supports. Herein lies the city's fractured approach to go-go: law enforcement officials unaware or unwilling to cast the music as anything other than a violent activity while other public officials support, sponsor, and lean on the go-go community to support their administrations. Law enforcement marks go-go music as death, and the go-go community rejects this categorization. In "summer, somewhere," poet Danez Smith asks for a shift in the name of Black boys killed by police and vigilante violence, "don't call us dead/ call us alive someplace better."[15] This is in part the wake work of the go-go community, who are consistently asking the city and its new residents not to call them death but to call them life someplace better. Go-go speaks life into Black people in DC even as it is called death by those sworn to protect its communities. The #DontMuteDC movement has been perhaps the largest refusal

---

[13] Hopkinson, *Go-Go Live*, 155.
[14] This was one of my more interesting "interviews," although I hesitate to call it an interview proper because the officer in question did not sign a consent form or consent to be recorded. I reached out via email to ask for the interview, telling him that I wanted to know more about the police's role in neighborhood change. He responded asking for me to come to the station because he needed more background information. I went but would have preferred to do the interview elsewhere. Coming of age and entering Black Studies during the age of the Black Lives Matter Movement has made me deeply uncomfortable around the police; every day I learn more about their practices of impunity. During our conversation, I listened as he told me about his work revitalizing relationships between residents and police, about attending community meetings, and being present for people going through traumas.
[15] Danez Smith, *Don't Call Us Dead: Poems* (Minneapolis: Graywolf Press, 2017), 13.

of go-go's death narratives. Through protests and social media campaigns, the go-go community used the shutdown at 7th and Florida in order to reestablish themselves as a life giving and life affirming institution in DC and beyond. In the process, they shifted more than one city's public discourses on gentrification and Black cultural displacement.

In addition to grieving the dead and rewriting narratives of absence, go-go's wake work is also prevalent in the community's commitment to intricacy. Outside of DC, go-go is often characterized as Chuck Brown and the Soul Searcher's "Bustin Loose" and not much else. Within the community, though, there is fierce competition and many different ideas about what should be done for the good of the whole community. There are musical differences, rankings, discussions of virtuosity, grooves, where lead talkers should stand on stage, performance etiquette, and the list goes on. Go-go is an entire universe unto itself and is consistently being made and remade in both online and in person cultural practices. An example: in 2016, I met DJ Black House, a DC native, Morehouse graduate, and veteran of the bounce beat community. He invited me to observe the Bounce Beat Radio Show, a weekly radio show that he hosted along with other go-go musicians and promoters CBO, Juan, Cocky, and Shootaz. The show was hosted out of Iverson Mall, a popular mall in Prince George's County, only minutes away from Southeast DC. During my first visit to the show, after declining to be on the radio, I watched the guys interview "Rockin Rob," their guest for the week and the lead talker of popular bounce beat band HQB. Rob was there to discuss a previous performance, and during the show there was discussion of whether his band had performed better than MTM Flavor Gang, another prominent bounce beat band. During the show, members of MTM repeatedly called into the show to talk to Rob and defend their performances. Members of MTM even showed up at the studio to continue their conversation in person. Eventually, I found myself in the middle of two bands, perhaps five men each, yelling at each other about the quality of their musicians, singers, overall crank factor, and credibility.[16] It was overwhelming at the time because of the vehemence of the conversation but it also served as one of the best examples I can give of life and love in go-go music today. These men drove miles to be in conversation with each other, to defend their music, their homes, and their bandmates. Go-go regularly carries this commitment to intricacy, to the quality of the music itself, even as the genre has been rumored to be at death's door.

---

[16] Crank Factor has a shifting definition, but it can be loosely understood as a band's overall "it" or "X" factor.

Mapping the Abundance of Go-Go Music (Life)

The above stories are but a few examples of go-go's wake work; there are countless others because the community is constantly being pressured to operate within circumstances of precarity. What becomes clear across all of these examples is that a gentrifying city sounds like refusal just as much as it sounds like development. Furthermore, in addition to carrying a commitment to intricacy and depth, go-go music also has an extensive spatial breadth that I attend to here with a series of maps. Mapping go-go's relationships with the city as well as the world contributes to a conversation of critical cartographies and critical GIS, within a valence of Black digital humanities. Both critical cartography and critical GIS speak to the power of maps and mapping practice to address power and inequity, and to enact and imagine equitable representations of space and place.[17] While maps can be useful tools, they are not arbiters of truth, and I approach the practice of cartography critically knowing that these maps are incomplete and only tell partial and positioned truths of go-go's relationship with the world.[18]

The maps here are shaped from two primary spheres of influence regarding cartography and visualization. The first is Candace Fujikane's notion of "mapping abundance," which draws on indigenous cartographies in order to reject the scarcity on which capitalism operates, a way to "show functioning Indigenous economies not premised on the crises of capital."[19] Fujikane presents abundance as a way not of ignoring climate change but as a method of refusing processes of apocalyptic disaster capitalism. Where capitalism requires a narrative of expansion on the brink of catastrophe, mapping abundance posits the "demise of capital."[20] Given gentrification's existence as a consequence of rampant capitalism, it is instructive to think with Fujikane's notion of abundance when thinking of go-go music. What would it mean to map go-go music not only in recession and displacement but in growth, in innovation, and abundance? This is a response to consistent narratives of gentrification as a narrowing reduction of Black sound and Black life when in fact, some sounds are becoming louder and denser.

---

[17] Matthew W. Wilson, *New Lines: Critical GIS and the Trouble of the Map* (Minneapolis: University of Minnesota Press, 2017); Julie Cidell, "Challenging the Contours: Critical Cartography, Local Knowledge, and the Public," *Environment and Planning A: Economy and Space* 40, no. 5 (2008): 1202–18.

[18] Donna Haraway, "Situated Knowledges: The Science Question in Feminism and the Privilege of Partial Perspective," *Feminist Studies* 14, no. 3 (1988): 575–99.

[19] Candace Fujikane, *Mapping Abundance for a Planetary Future: Kanaka Maoli and Critical Settler Cartographies in Hawai'i* (Durham, NC: Duke University Press, 2021), 4.

[20] Fujikane, *Mapping Abundance for a Planetary Future*, 3.

The second sphere of influence is the data visualization practices of W. E. B. DuBois. In 1900, DuBois and a team of researchers created a number of data visualizations to present in the "American Negro" exhibit at the Paris World Fair, intended to contextualize and explain the circumstances of Black people in the post-Reconstruction United States. These visualizations came in two sets, one which featured information about the entire United States, and one that was focused on the state of Georgia, which at that time had the highest population of Black people in the country. For example, one of latter visualizations is titled "Age Distribution of Georgia Negroes Compared with France."[21] The chart shows that Black Georgians had many more children than France, which in turn had higher percentages of adults and elders. In these types of visualizations DuBois makes Georgia the center of his universe, the epicenter of Black life in the United States as he tried to translate Black life to a European audience. Here I ask, how can I depict go-go as the center of the universe?

One answer is to put DuBois's approach to visualizing Black life in conversation with Fujikane's notion of mapping abundance in order to hear go-go music as the center of the city's soundscape, as an intentional move toward abundance rather than scarcity. I am drawing primarily on traditional digital tools for mapmaking such as ArcGIS, Google MyMaps, and Palladio (a mapping tool created by the Research and Design Lab at Stanford University). Even as I focus on work created with these mapping tools, I am ever cognizant of the ways in which maps exist in nontraditional and sonic ways: songs, conversations, and drawings, and constellations are all maps. Go-go performances in particular are cartographic in nature, as lead talkers shout out neighborhoods of the city all night. If the lead talker of the band asks, "Is Southeast in the house tonight?" and a large contingent of people in the middle of the room scream "Hell, yeah!" then the middle of the room becomes, if only for the night, the Southeast quadrant of Washington, DC. Lead talkers, as musicians and griots, make maps out of their audiences and their songs, marking points in space based on the responses that they receive. They are then more likely to continue shouting out Southeast in that kind of performance because they know that the quadrant is well represented.

---

[21] Britt Rusert and Witney Battle-Baptiste, *W. E. B. Du Bois's Data Portraits: Visualizing Black America* (Princeton, NJ: Princeton Architectural Press, 2018).

Mapping the Movement of Go-Go

The first map is a series, "Go-Go Music and Displacement," and engages an essential question: How has gentrification affected go-go music venues in DC? This question has been asked and answered by many in the go-go community and came to a head during the #DontMuteDC movement in 2019. The displacement of DC's Black communities is one of the primary stories told about gentrification, and one of the most prevalent stories told about go-go music in DC, so it makes sense that they would be told together. Go-go has always been a financial endeavor, a way to hustle and make money for bands, promoters, and clubs. DC hardcore punk luminary Ian MacKaye has told stories about playing shows with bands like Trouble Funk in the 1980s. He observed that while his band, Minor Threat, and other punk bands were just there for the experience of the show, the go-go bands like Trouble Funk were always there to get paid and did not typically play shows like that for free. So as venues have closed, reopened, and shifted around the region, it has indeed become harder to make a living playing go-go music.

I began to answer the question of how gentrification affects go-go music by creating a map that overlays a database of music venues with the Black population of the city, two crucial factors in the successful performance of go-go music. Each map features the venues open in that year overlayed with the percentage of Black residents in each census tract.[22] The venues are represented by Black stars, and the Black population of the census tract is represented by shades of gray, where the deeper the gray the higher the Black population in that particular census tract. The result is a set of maps that tell stories of how go-go venues in the city have closed while the Black population in the city decreases (Figures 4.2, 4.3, and 4.4). These maps carry the assumption that gentrification can be, in part, "measured" by tracking the decrease in the Black population percentage in any census tract. As I have considered sound to be a speculative method, so too do I encourage the use of cartography as speculative. This map is not meant to be an "accurate" measurement of gentrification across census tracts, but rather a visual representation of what it means to have venues close as the people that used to frequent those venues disappear.

Within the broader story of go-go's displacement, each of these maps contains countless stories of the venues in that year, and over the course of the twenty-year period. The Howard Theatre, for example, is the only venue that was open in 1990 and 2010, but not 2000. The theater had not yet been restored

---

[22] In the 1990 map, the empty census tract on the eastern side of the city is largely occupied by the United States National Arboretum, and therefore lacks census data for that year.

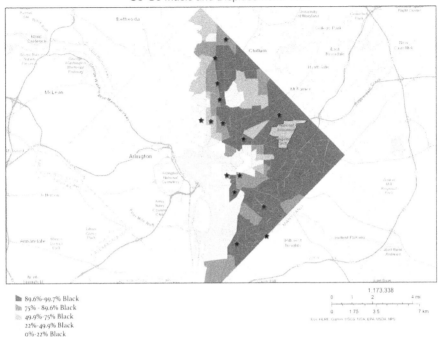

Figure 4.2 Go-go music and displacement: 1990
Map detailing go-go music venues and DC's Black population in 1990

at that point and was reopened after a major restoration by Black developer Chip Ellis. Ellis and his partners had a particular vision for "Progression Place," the block that he redeveloped on 7th Street Northwest between S and T Streets.[23] They secured the United Negro College Fund as the lead tenant, wanting to embrace the neighborhood's African American roots while still making the development more upscale than its previous iteration. This redevelopment was also the site of the city's first Community Benefits Agreement (CBA), an arrangement between a developer and community partners that makes specific amenities or promises to community stakeholders. In this case, the CBA dictated that the rents of local business owners would stay fixed for a number of years.[24] When the Howard reopened in 2012 as a part of this

---

[23] Progression Place is one block over from 7th Street and Florida Avenue, making Ellis's redevelopment and subsequent gentrification of the neighborhood one of the factors influencing the future of Central Communications and the rest of the intersection.

[24] The primary beneficiary of this CBA was Wanda Henderson, a hairstylist who has been struggling to maintain her shop in the area since Shaw began to gentrify. Her story is told more fully in Derek S. Hyra's *Race, Class, and Politics in the Cappuccino City* (Chicago: University of Chicago Press, 2017).

146 Intersectional Listening

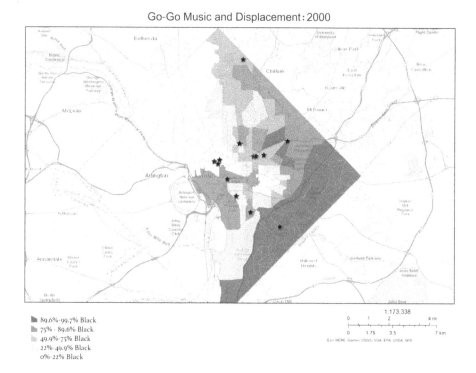

Figure 4.3 Go-go music and displacement: 2000
Map detailing go-go music venues and DC's Black population in 2000

redevelopment project, the venue again became a popular destination for go-go fans and bands. More recently, the venue been in decline because of mismanagement and mysterious tax practices.[25] Now struggling to bring in crowds, the Howard features fewer shows each month. Parking is also notoriously difficult at the venue, which is a crucial concern for those coming in from the suburbs of Maryland and Virginia.

At a DC Public Library panel dedicated to the history of the Howard Theatre, local radio DJ and cultural advocate Rev. Dr. Sandra Butler-Truesdale lamented the reopening of the Howard Theatre, because the management team was brought in from Blue Note, which is based in New York City. She made the following comment on that decision: "I think that was a great mistake Chip made when he brought Blue Note here … because if you're not from Washington, DC, or you haven't been in this area for a long time, you may

---

[25] Tax proceedings at the Howard Theatre are such that the DC Attorney General brought a suit against the organization for violating the Nonprofit Corporations Act (Office of the Attorney General, 2018).

Figure 4.4 Go-go music and displacement: 2010
Map detailing go-go music venues and DC's Black population in 2010

not understand what I mean when I say this is a strange audience here."[26] She compounded this observation by questioning why a local developer would bring in people from New York to manage something in DC. Although the cities are comparable in many senses, they can be drastically different in terms of entertainment. DC's size, lack of statehood, connection the federal government, reputation as a live band town, and its position as *thee* Chocolate City, are what make it a "strange audience," and therefore illegible to management from New York, which is why the Howard Theatre was seemingly in decline. In 2018 a former DC attorney general filed a lawsuit against Howard Theatre Restoration for mismanagement of their board and failing to file tax returns.[27] As of 2022, though, the Howard is being booked through Union State Presents, a larger entertainment company that books for venues such as Union Stage, DC9, and Capital Turnaround.

---

[26] Rev. Dr. Sandra Butler-Truesdale, "DC Legendary Musicians," Washington, DC Public Library, July 30, 2018.
[27] Jonathan O'Connell, "District Suit Alleges Mismanagement at Howard Theatre." *Washington Post*, March 8, 2018. https://www.washingtonpost.com/local/district-suit-alleges-mismanagement-at-howard-theatre/2018/03/07/b9619ab4-224d-11e8-badd-7c9f29a55815_story.html.

Other venues besides the Howard have been reincarnated over the years as well. The Panorama Room was one of the most popular go-go venues of the 1980s and 1990s, located in Southeast DC. When it was not a go-go venue for all ages, playing music well into the night and until dawn, it served as the fellowship hall for Our Lady of Perpetual Help, a Black Catholic church in Anacostia.[28] In the past few years, though, Our Lady of Perpetual Help has reopened its doors to the go-go community, albeit the same generation they originally served, which is now largely in its fifties and sixties. These events are more community fundraiser than moneymaking machine, another way that the go-go's are allowed to exist in this space. Venues close and then they reopen, and there is rebirth after venues die, often negotiated around a problematic ratio of profitability and perceived violence.

In the 2010 map, there is a cluster of venues in the downtown business district, located around K Street NW. At least one of those venues, Capitale, is closed, but during its better days the club hosted the legendary Backyard Band one night a week. I attended Capitale Thursdays once, as they were called, and was fascinated by the number of people that got themselves to downtown K street on a weeknight and paid between $20 and $40 for a band that wasn't even getting warmed up until after midnight. During one of our more informal conversations, I asked go-go community activist Ron Moten why that night was so popular. He told me that go-go music made Capitale more money in one night than any other promotion did for the rest of the week. This has been the story in several interviews, where musicians and promoters cite the importance of selling out a venue, making money for the venue, and making sure that people pay money to drink at the venue's bar. This is not a new system, and during our interview about go-go music's origins, JB explained it to me further:

> Most clubs, their goal is to make money on the bar. So the more breaks you take, the more they're going to sell at the bar. Now I see go-go wants to play for an hour straight or an hour and a half straight. If we do that, that's only one break. You know, so instead of that, they prefer a 45-minute set. That's the standard structure when you go into a club: 45 on, 15 off. That way they can get a lot of people.[29]

Go-go has always been a commercial enterprise, never divorced from the economies of live music or nightlife culture.[30] Another one of those business

---

[28] The church is known not only for the Panorama Room, but for having some of the best views in the entire city, which is also a key reason why Anacostia is currently gentrifying.
[29] Buchanan, interview with the author, 2018.
[30] The city has required artists to "pay to play" for quite some time, even as go-go venues open and close. Pay to play is not just in the go-go community but across more genres in the city, including hip-hop and house music. Regarding hip-hop, artist and promoter 20Bello discussed the difficulties of balancing

district venues was the Meeting Place, a venue I frequented in 2016 and 2017. I was going to shows hosted by DJ Black House, and when we sat down for an interview in 2018, he explained to me how he secured that venue, and the difficulty of doing so. Go-go music, especially the bounce beat generation, is an unattractive crowd for many a venue owner. DJ Black House leveraged his business degree from Morehouse to prove that his parties would be safe and make the venue a significant amount of money, engaging a complex set of respectability politics to secure the space for shows. He essentially had to prove his community safe enough to be profitable, because the violence that once accompanied go-go music is often deemed a financial risk.

Unofficial Venues

Although the displacement map series is useful to consider how gentrification has affected the success of go-go music venues, it does not tell the full story of where go-go is and has been in the city. On the displacement maps there are no go-go venues west of 16th Street, which has served as the unofficial dividing line of racial segregation in DC. However, go-go has indeed been to the upper northwest quadrant of the city—through schools and other public and private events. Private schools in DC, particularly Sidwell Friends, have had go-go's annually for decades. In this map of unofficial venues (Figure 4.5), I consider the informal in addition to the clubs: the parks, house parties, school dances, and streetcorners, in order to create a map that offers a more thorough depiction of where go-go has been in the city. Of course, this representation is still incomplete, as it does not account for the everyday diffusion of go-go, blasting outside of headphones and on city buses and Metro trains. This map, however, strives toward abundance, and attempts to underscore the centrality of go-go music in DC's sonic life.[31]

---

business models between promoters, rappers, the bar, and ticket sales. On the future of rap shows in the city, he said "it goes well. The bar makes the minimum, sometimes more. But I could see as time goes on, that's going to be less and less, you know. Right now under the scene is dry. It's very dry" (interview with the author, 2018). On the house music scene, DJ Tiffany Schoneboom also remarked on the difficulty of getting gigs as a local DJ, where bars are primarily looking to make their minimums (Tiffany Schoneboom, interview with the author, 2018).

[31] A note on digital cartography: Placing 70 + points onto a map and expecting all of their labels to show simultaneously within ArcGIS software proved impossible, because the software resists such a crowded map, only showing a portion of the labeled sites in order to preserve legibility. In thinking toward abundance, though, I circumvented the legibility of the software and labeled the map manually in Adobe Photoshop, making sure that all 70 + points were visible at the same time. The numbered legend is a gesture toward accessibility, a way to offer a legible key to a map that is intentionally crowded and perhaps difficult for those that are not familiar with the places that go-go has been, as well as DC and its various neighborhoods.

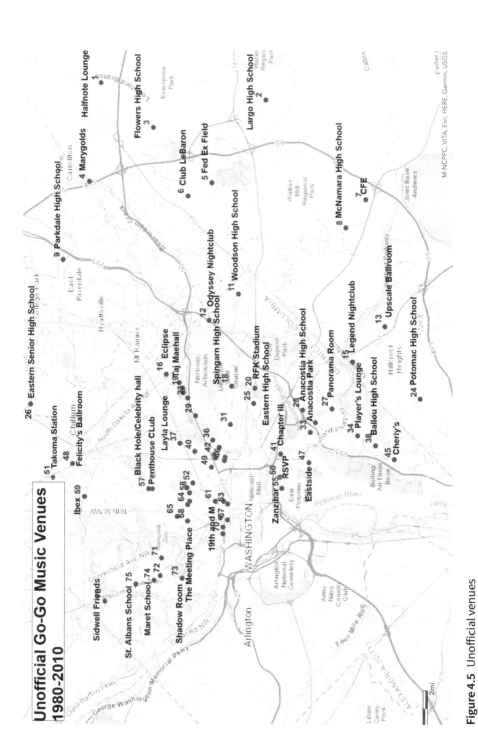

Figure 4.5 Unofficial venues
Map of unofficial venues that have held go-go shows, 1980–2010, with legend

1. Halfnote Lounge
2. Largo High School
3. Flowers High School
4. Marygolds
5. Fed Ex Field
6. Club LeBaron
7. CFE
8. McNamara High School
9. Parkdale High School
10. Tradewinds
11. Woodson High School
12. Odyssey Nightclub
13. Upscale Ballroom
14. Club Elite
15. Legend Nightclub
16. Eclipse
17. Metro Club/Deno's
18. Spingarn High School
19. Taj Maehall
20. RFK Stadium
21. DC Tunnel/DC Star
22. Icebox/De Zulu Cave
23. Aqua Lounge
24. Potomac High School
25. Chuck Brown Memorial Park
26. Eastern Senior High School
27. Del Rio
28. Panorama Room
29. Anacostia High School
30. Love
31. Uniontown Bar & Grill
32. Touche Supper Club
33. Oxon Hill High School
34. Anacostia Park
35. Player's Lounge
36. Martinis
37. Layla Lounge
38. Maverick Room
39. Ballou High School
40. Coliseum
41. McKinley Technology High School
42. Chapter III
43. Ibiza
44. Club XO
45. Fur
46. Cheriy's
47. Gonzaga High School
48. Eastside
49. Felicity's Ballroom
50. Dunbar High School
51. RSVP Club
52. Takoma Station
53. Howard Theatre
54. 9:30 Club
55. Northwood High School
56. Zanzibar
57. Black Hole/Celebrity Hall/Capital City Pavilion
58. Penthouse Club
59. Masonic Temple
60. Ibex
61. Ben's Chili Bowl
62. Capitale
63. Washington Plaza Hotel
64. Pure Lounge
65. Opera Lounge
66. Reeves Center (Club U)
67. Kalorama Skating Rink
68. The Meeting Place
69. Asia DC
70. Kilimanjaro
71. 19th and M
72. Look Lounge
73. Shadow Room
74. Maret School
75. St. Alban's School
76. Paragon II
77. National Cathedral School
78. Sidwell Friends School
79. Georgetown Day School

Figure 4.5 Continued

This map of unofficial spaces is also full of stories: Chelsea Clinton was sighted at the private school go-go's; bounce beat bands play at local correctional facilities as a way of giving back to the community; and more. But one particular set of venues that speaks to the ability of go-go music to thrive outdoors is the public park. Parks and streetcorners are essential to the story of go-go music, where bands have entertained family and friends during the muggy DC summers. Historically, this was in the "Summer in the Parks" program.

Contemporarily, one of the places that has cemented go-go's place as an outdoor activity is the Chuck Brown Memorial Park, dedicated to the late godfather of go-go in 2014, features large images of Brown and his signature guitar in the 42,000-foot space. The park, located in the Northeast quadrant of the city, was originally designed to feature a large amphitheater, but that plan was dissolved after neighbors complained, in part because of the potential noise that the amphitheater would bring.[32] In its current iteration, the park features a monument to Chuck Brown's life and legacy and is home to an annual festival, Chuck Brown Day, that draws thousands for music, fellowship, community programs, and back to school drives. I attended Chuck Brown Day in 2018 and sat for hours with my mother, watching people mill around and enjoy the day and each other's company. There were local booths set up, various city agencies with pamphlets and information about city services. There was some kind of unofficial (or maybe official?) gathering of pit bulls, being paraded around with their gold chains and looking beautifully menacing. There were children running around, playing, folks eating, go-go bands playing one after the other, and a backpack giveaway with school supplies for children about to start school. This annual festival and the crowd that it draws is what I think of every time someone suggests that go-go could possibly be dead.

Go-go music is not only an indoor activity. Junkyard Band started out playing on buckets at 19th and M Streets NW in the 1980s. Many bands have played outside at "the farms," the nickname for the now demolished Barry Farms housing project. Moechella drew thousands to the corner of 14th and U Streets in 2019 to protest the music shutdown at Central Communications, located only seven blocks down the street at 7th Street and Florida Avenue. This is part of the flexibility of go-go music, because as much as it exists in a club setting, the music also lives outside, which is represented in the "Unofficial Venues" map. Go-go travels like air and hip-hop, available to every young person with a lunch table to bang on or the gift of creating a pocket with only their mouth as an instrument. In its outside-ness go-go music presents itself as operating on a proverbial porch, telling stories of the city and its many lives. In a video of Junkyard Band doing their hit song "Sardines" to a dynamic crowd outside of RFK stadium during a campaign event for former mayor Adrian Fenty, lead talker Buggs says "if you don't know this one you don't know yourself." The sound from go-go being performed outside carries, spills from block to neighborhood, and invites the entire family to sing along and learn the story of the music.

---

[32] Mike DeBonis, "No Amphitheater for Chuck Brown Park," *Washington Post*, December 1, 2021, https://www.washingtonpost.com/blogs/mike-debonis/wp/2013/08/07/no-amphitheater-for-chuck-brown-park/.

Go-Go Outside of DC

Part of the work of making go-go music the center of this conceptual universe in a move toward abundance is to illustrate where the music has gone outside of the city (see Figure 4.6). This is also in part a response to a question that I often receive after giving a presentation on go-go music: Why hasn't go-go left DC, and do I think it ever will? This map draws points from Washington, DC to the places where go-go musicians have performed over the years. Some of these performances are close to home, such as Richmond, Virginia, or the yearly "Miami Takeover" that many bands participate in. Some, however, are more indicative of go-go music's global reach. For example, Backyard Band traveled to Ghana in 2018 and held a concert at Cape Coast Castle, near the "Door of No Return." The door of no return is largely understood as the last place enslaved Africans saw before they left their country forever and began the brutal journey across the Atlantic. The site has become an important emotional and symbolic space for cultural heritage and even tourism, as African Americans come to experience the land that they were ripped away from. Backyard Band, in keeping this legacy in mind, positioned this concert as a demonstration of "coming home," a return as well as a way to demonstrate the resilience of Black people and cultural practices. Even having endured the generational brutality of chattel slavery and its afterlives, Backyard was able to make it "home" to share this music that is so clearly influenced by the West African music traditions from which it came, especially the rhythmic practices and the work of the lead talker as griot. In addition to this celebration of return, Backyard's warm welcome in Ghana speaks to go-go's presence on the global popular music scene, alongside with genres such as Afrobeat and reggae. More than a coming home, go-go musicians traveling to Africa speaks to go-go's participation in a larger Afro-diasporic musical community. There is not only return, a one-way transmission. There is a nexus of flows of transmission, that also speak to periods of migration between West Africa and the DC area. Rapper Wale, for example, is Nigerian and freely moves through the sonorities of go-go music and Afrobeat in his work. Tsitsi Jaji reminds us that "when considering the cultural productions of the diaspora, Africa should be understood as a constitutive component of that diaspora, rather than as a point of origin now removed from the contemporary diaspora."[33] Which is to say that although these musicians returned home, they were also moving in one of many possible directions in the global community that is

---

[33] Tsitsi Jaji, *Africa in Stereo: Modernism, Music, and Pan-African Solidarity* (New York: Oxford University Press, 2014), 7.

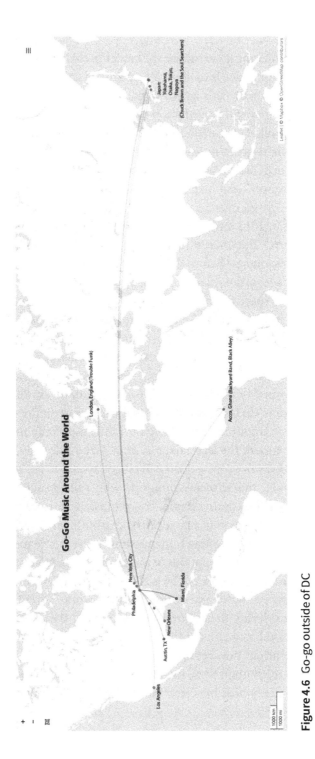

Figure 4.6 Go-go outside of DC
Map of cities that go-go bands have traveled to for performing and recording

Black music, bound together by histories, rhythms, production, patterns, and more. Go-go's international travel is a not recent shift: Trouble Funk recorded a live album in London in the 1980s and Chuck Brown toured extensively in Japan in the 1990s. In combining these performances, this map is intended to consider go-go's global travel alongside its domestic displacement, making it another in a long line of Black music genres that have been accepted and embraced outside of the United States while continuing to fight for recognition at home. This tension is an important part of go-go's spatial relationship with the world: What does it mean to see clubs close all along Georgia Avenue in DC while also seeing the bands travel all over the United States and the world?

Go-Go's Influence on Popular Music

The final map is simply a chart extending the global considerations of the previous by listing countries in which go-go influenced songs have charted (Figure 4.7). This map shows that both go-go beats and full go-go songs have been sampled and interpolated across hip-hop and R&B. Furthermore, some of the biggest hits of the early 2000s were influenced heavily by go-go music. Perhaps the most prominent example of this is Beyoncé's 2003 hit "Crazy in Love." For her first post-Destiny's Child single Beyoncé worked with producer Rich Harrison, originally from DC. "Crazy in Love" leans on the danceability of the go-go pocket in a tightly produced 3-minute-and-56-second package. Timing has always been one of the reasons why go-go musicians have not been featured prominently on radio stations outside of the DC regional market, as their songs are too long and improvised based on the crowd that bands are performing for. Songs like "Crazy in Love" took the infectious nature of the go-go beat but removed the live performance and unpredictability of the songs to make them more palatable for a national and international audience, and the results have been noteworthy, as the song spent eight weeks at number 1 on the Billboard Hot 100. As a part of Beyoncé's many live performances, the song has become part of a different kind of Afro-diasporic musical map. For example, at her historic headlining Coachella performance, "Crazy in Love" was the first song she performed, drawing from her own band as well as the HBCU style marching band she had on full risers behind her. When the beat to the song eventually dropped after the introduction, in addition to the go-go pocket, the beat from Juvenile's 1999 hit "Back that Azz Up" was included as well, which features elements from bounce music, New Orleans's local subgenre of hip-hop. With interpolations such as these, Beyoncé and

156 Intersectional Listening

Artist	Song Name	Country	Year	Chart Position
Beyoncé	Crazy in Love	United States	2003	1
Beyoncé	Crazy in Love	Great Britain	2003	1
Beyoncé	Crazy in Love	Switzerland	2003	3
Beyoncé	Crazy in Love	Germany	2003	6
Nelly	Hot in Herre	United States	2002	1
Nelly	Hot in Herre	Denmark	2002	2
Nelly	Hot in Herre	New Zealand	2002	3
Nelly	Hot in Herre	Great Britain	2002	4
Nelly	Hot in Herre	Norway	2002	5
Nelly	Hot in Herre	Belgium	2002	7
Nelly	Hot in Herre	Germany	2002	8
Nelly	Hot in Herre	Taiwan	2002	9
Nelly	Hot in Herre	Switzerland	2002	10
Nelly	Hot in Herre	Ireland	2002	10
Amerie	1 Thing	United States	2005	1
Amerie	1 Thing	Japan	2005	1
Amerie	1 Thing	Great Britain	2005	4
Amerie	1 Thing	Finland	2005	5
Amerie	1 Thing	Ireland	2005	6
Amerie	1 Thing	Denmark	2005	9
Amerie	1 Thing	Norway	2005	10
Jay-Z	Do It Again (Put Ya Hands Up)	United States	1999	9
DJ Kool	Let Me Clear My Throat	United States	1996	4
Jill Scott	It's Love	Cyprus	2000	20
Jill Scott	It's Love	Cyprus	2017	26
Jill Scott	It's Love	Cyprus	2017	26
Jill Scott	It's Love	Lithuania	2019	77
Grace Jones	Slave to the Rhythm	Germany	1985	4
Grace Jones	Slave to the Rhythm	Switzerland	1985	5
Grace Jones	Slave to the Rhythm	Austria	1985	7
Grace Jones	Slave to the Rhythm	Great Britain	1985	12

Figure 4.7 Go-go's influence on popular music
Chart of songs featuring go-go elements that have reached billboard charts across the world

her collaborators create a connection between the sounds of DC and New Orleans, in a kind of sonic cartography that speaks to the musical connections between these places.

Although less popular than "Crazy in Love," Amerie's 2005 hit "1 Thing" also features a go-go pocket and was produced by Rich Harrison. While not originally from DC, Amerie attended Georgetown University and met Harrison during her time there. The music video for "1 Thing" draws heavily from the go-go scene, featuring Amerie standing in front of a band of over a dozen Black men, one playing drum set and the rest playing a single conga drum. As drum set and congas are the core of go-go music's pocket beat, the lone drum set surrounded by congas is a direct reference to the go-go scene. In the music video and live performances featuring a similar setup, Amerie leans into these references conducting the band and dancing with them. Songs like "Crazy in Love" and "1 Thing," as well as their chart performance, add more dimensions to the story of go-go music, which has traveled all over the world.

Mapping the international chart successes of these and other hit songs, such as Jill Scott's "Long Walk" (which features Rare Essence) and Nelly's "Hot in Herre" (which samples Chuck Brown and the Soul Searchers "Bustin Loose"), serves to visualize go-go's impact around the world as well as its place in the larger diaspora of Black music. These maps detail the tension between abundance and precarity, of how go-go's international presence has troubled and reinvented the terms of hyperlocality and what it means to be of a place. This reinvention has continued throughout the increase in digital content creation the disruption of nightlife all over the world due to the COVID-19 pandemic. What remains is that go-go continues to articulate itself as the center of its own abundant universe, responding to but not limited by the constraints placed onto the genre.

Legacy

If death is engaged and resisted in wake work and life can be visualized as the movement of go-go across the city and across the world, what is legacy? I offer legacy as an in between space, an interstice at the intersection of life and death, a method of crafting the memories of something while that something is still here. What does it mean to create a legacy, something carried over from a previous time or place? Who crafts that which will be carried, and who will do the carrying? Go-go music presents a peculiar exploration of legacy, because it operates somewhere between the "give people their flowers while they're here" sentiment and the creation of legacy as a facet of premature memorialization.[34] Legacies are caught between memory and truths, solidified and canonized in stories, posts, pictures, texts, and ghosts.

---

[34] Giving people their flowers while they're still here is a reference to the notion that people are unable to smell their flower or hear their accolades when they are dead. Instead, it is better to praise and appreciate a person and their contributions while they are still alive to feel that gratitude. This phrase is often invoked in conversations about premature death, where many people do not make it to old age, so they

Just as I considered the city as a sonic palimpsest in Chapter 3, legacy is also a multilayered process, one that begins well before the death of its subject. The construction of go-go music's legacy, whether by musicians, community members, or the larger DC government, is fraught with tension. In some spaces the genre is celebrated as DC's hometown music, but in others it's considered outdated, criticized for its infighting and supposed lack of a successful national business model. These tensions cut across class and gender but can be characterized more broadly as intraracial conflict. That is, Black members of the go-go community critique other Black members of the go-go community because of their business strategies, how much they charge customers, how they present themselves on stage, and their musicianship. Debates on social media often reference the "crabs in a barrel" mentality that describes Black people as crabs climbing on top of each other to get out of a barrel, rather than supporting each other.[35] Listening intersectionally to the construction of go-go's legacy as it unfolds in real time offers an opportunity to better understand what's at stake in the celebration and stigmatization of a local Black music genre.

Regarding local government's involvement with the creation of legacy, the #DontMuteDC movement put go-go in the spotlight, and the DC government's attempts to celebrate go-go publicly have helped somewhat to appease disgruntled residents' claims that Mayor Muriel Bowser caters first to developers and new residents and second (or altogether last) to the Black working class in the city. In 2018, Bowser gave renowned band Rare Essence a Lifetime Achievement Award as well as their own holiday, Rare Essence Day, celebrated on May 6. Furthermore, her Office of Cable Television, Film, and Entertainment (OCTFE) embarked on a go-go documentary project, *Straight Crankin*, that premiered in September 2018 to a packed crowd at the Lincoln Theater. The event was billed as "The Mayor Presents," a very direct signaling of the mayor's support for the go-go community. The premiere was a who's who of the go-go community, featuring the legends like Big G from Backyard Band, Weensey, Killa Cal, Sweet Cherie, and more. The documentary premiere felt like a family affair, with people laughing and clapping every time a new face appeared on the screen. Hosted by DJ Dirty Rico, a staple in the DMV radio circuit, the event solidified a connection between the mayor's

---

need to be celebrated while they're still alive. This sentiment holds true in the go-go community, where many luminaries in the scene, including Anthony "Little Benny" Harley, Quentin "Footz" Davidson, and Reggie "Polo" Burwell, who all died well before old age.

[35] While this metaphor is often employed by Black communities to criticize Black communities, it rarely considers who put the crabs in the barrel in the first place.

office and the go-go community, a kind of intentional "we see you" situation. These celebratory public gestures ensure go-go's place in a larger narrative of cultural life in the city.

Despite the success of these events and the appreciation of the go-go community, this kind of legacy project creates an air of premature memorialization, choosing to celebrate a peak of go-go that has already passed rather than contemporary everyday go-go performances. In his 2017 ethnography of gentrification in Shaw, Derek Hyra explores "Black branding," a kind of marketing strategy that leans on the cultural production and promise of Black life while attracting non-Black buyers to a particular neighborhood. Black branding extends to the mayoral space as well, where if the mayor's office can brand itself as attuned to and supportive of the rich Black musical histories of DC, specifically go-go, they can attract people that are also attracted to that legacy. While #DontMuteDC did result in the naming of go-go as the official music of Washington, DC, the Bowser administration's public embrace of go-go music has not yet translated into policy shifts that dismantle the criminalization of go-go music and of Black sound more broadly.

In the midst of public celebration and day-to-day difficulties both before and during COVID-19, go-go's online communities are having tense and complex conversations about legacy as well, particularly surrounding conversations of ownership. One of the anxieties within the go-go community is that the genre will be co-opted by a white person, or a white band. This anxiety is well founded, drawn from countless instances of white musicians appropriating Black music, from Pat Boone to Elvis Presley to Iggy Azalea. A dramatic 2018 Facebook exchange gave a glimpse into what that appropriation would bring. The trouble began when a Black woman, native to DC, posted a video on Facebook that she had taken at Marvin's, a popular bar, restaurant, and small music venue named after DC native Marvin Gaye. She posted the following as a caption to a video she recorded in the restaurant:

> So, Marvin's on U Street . . . had an ALL WHITE GO-GO BAND appropriating our music last night. Don't believe me, take a look. I have receipts. This is how it starts, in 20 years we'll be arguing whether or not Go-Go started with the Black People who once lived in Chocolate City or the people that currently live there because in 20 years D.C. will pretty much be white. History keeps repeating itself.[36]

---

[36] Due to the intensity of the comments and the fact that they were on social media, comments on this particular post have been anonymized. Anonymous, Facebook comment, June 25, 2018.

Her commentary, attached to a twenty-second video of a dimly lit performance, set off a wave of affirmative responses, citing gentrification, cultural appropriation, and lamenting the death of the neighborhood and of Marvin's. The performance features many of the typical instruments in a go-go band, including drum set, a lead talker on vocals, a guitar, and conga drums. The drummer is playing a pocket beat while the lead talker leads a breakdown that asks the crowd where they're from. The lead talker asks if specific quadrants of the city are present: "Is Northeast in the house tonight? Is Southeast in the house tonight?" After each question, a yelled response can be heard, although it's unclear whether the response is coming from the crowd at Marvin's or from other members of the band. The restaurant looks somewhat full, but the crowd is seated as staff walk around the restaurant fulfilling orders. Many of the initial comments on the video agreed with the woman who posted it, saying things like "I would have grabbed the mike and knocked his ass off the stage. Disrespecting my city and my hood" or "Here they come taking our shit and fucking it up." People were upset that music that they feel a sense of ownership over was being "taken" by outsiders.

In addition to these disparaging comments of folks upset with the performance, people familiar with the band in question began to leave comments, saying that they were not actually an all-white band but instead the "Fusion Band," a band that features a variety of different members and fuses go-go music and other genres of music. The creator and leader of this band is "mixed," a racial descriptor that is often synonymous with having one white parent and one Black parent, because racial formation in the United States is so often focused on only white and Black people. The woman who posted the video refuted these explanations, saying that the Fusion Band, who as pictured on their website are majority Black, was not who *she* saw at Marvin's that night, and not who the video depicts. The comments devolved from there, with many people coming to the bandleader's defense. The bandleader himself stepped in multiple times to defend himself, his bandmates, and the Fusion Band as well. To refute what essentially became an accusation of whiteness, the bandleader cited multiple times his connection with Chuck Brown, whose band he played in for a year before Brown passed in 2012. This connection was offered to legitimize himself in the community, because if Chuck Brown approved of his musical and cultural authenticity, who should doubt him? He also delved into the question of his ethnic ambiguity. In one comment, he named himself as a combination of the following ethnicities: "Here's my heritage to anybody who cares: Indonesian, Yemenese, Swedish, Pakistani." These rhetorical gestures are intended to muddy the waters and to distance himself from the accusation of whiteness, which in Black music spaces (and

Black spaces more broadly) can be career-threatening. No one wants to be the next Rachel Dolezal.[37] He later defended himself by claiming to be born on the city's soil, describing it as sacred. He also mentioned his attendance at the historically Black institution Howard University (another commenter corroborated the connection to Howard University, saying "Small fact, 90% of this band are Howard alum, white boys included").

These defensive gestures were interesting, if contradictory. Citing his birth in the city, relationship to the pioneer of go-go, and education at an HBCU all move him closer in proximity to Blackness. Just as I have seen countless people do in community and neighborhood association meetings, people use their proximity to the city proper to claim authenticity in various ways. To say he was born in DC gives him roots, an anchor in the city that people cannot easily take away. Claims of origin are common in the rest of the go-go scene as well as hip-hop, with people being constantly called out for misrepresenting their origins and homes in order to claim a kind of authenticity or proximity to a harder life than the one they grew up with. Citing his relationship to Chuck Brown gives him direct credibility in the go-go scene that he would not have otherwise. To have played with and carried the approval of Chuck Brown speaks volumes in the go-go community, and is more directly irrefutable because Brown passed away in 2012. Finally, a connection to Howard University offers yet another layer of authenticity, with Howard being one of the most prominent HBCU's in the country and certainly the most prominent in Washington, DC. The bandleader, in every way he could, was saying that he was close to Blackness in place, musical heritage, and educational history. In terms of racial identity, however, listing four "heritages" that do not originate from the continent of Africa serves to move him further away from Blackness, while disrupting the Black-white binary. If he had not listed those nationalities, one could have continued to assume that he had one Black parent and one white.

The hundreds of comments exchanged eventually stopped after one of the band members threatened the woman who posted the video, posting the following comment:

---

[37] Rachel Dolezal became famous (infamous) in 2015 for her claims of Black identity, despite being born and raised by white parentage. She continues to symbolize a profound level of appropriation of Blackness (specifically Black womanhood) because she believes herself to be Black and draws upon hairstyles, tanning practices, and linguistic strategies to do so. Dolezal has also reinvigorated scholarship on the instability of race, from passing to transraciality. See H. Samy Alim, "Who's Afraid of the Transracial Subject? Raciolinguistics and the Political Project of Transracialization," in *Raciolinguistics: How Language Shapes Our Ideas About Race*, edited by H. Samy Alim, John R. Rickford, and Arnetha F. Ball (New York: Oxford University Press, 2016).

You fuckin with the wrong nigga . . . I will fuck you up on sight bitch. Talking bullshit online remember my face. Don't fuck with my family shorty and I'm from DC. Potomac Gardens to be exact you don't want to do that . . . no talking online realshit just wanted to let you know that.[38]

The comment above is from a Black man incensed that a Black woman would publicly discredit his band. The discrediting here comes from an accusation of whiteness, or even a proximity to whiteness. An ethnically ambiguous musician was accused of both looking and sounding white, which had potentially major financial implications for not only him but his band, many of whom are Black men. These implications were being driven by a Black woman who captured, in 20 seconds, a white-looking (and sounding) band, despite the presence of Black drummers and musicians in that space. The financial implications and claims of inauthenticity then led to a threat of violence from a Black man to a Black woman, which no one from the band commented on. She then deleted the entire post shortly thereafter. That comment is an example of Black women becoming eligible for violence when men are upset, and also an example of a model of scarcity, wherein there is not enough to go around, so the threat of physical violence is appropriate to get and keep one's portion. Protecting the reputation of a racially ambiguous band by doing harm to a Black woman thus operates in this case as a sonic dimension of gentrification. Because of the scarcity of resources involved in sustaining a go-go music career in the city, bands cannot afford financially or otherwise to be slandered through accusations of a proximity to whiteness. And because violence against Black women remains tolerated and permitted in so many contexts, particularly social media, the tactic worked to restore authenticity and financial security to the Fusion Band.

The deletion of the video was cited as a win by another Black woman close to the Fusion Band:

When I say it takes a village! A post that falsely put a fellow musician in a bad light was taken down. (Which IMO was a coward's way of no apologizing and admit wrongdoing). Thank you to everyone in my go-go/musicianship (and those who are fans) family who spoke out and for such a talented individual trying to preserve the culture of D.C. through storytelling and music. It is never right to accuse someone or something without all the information. It is also very important that we call out

---

[38] Anonymous, Facebook comment, June 27, 2018.

those individuals (including our own) who feel the need to post or share without having done the research to back up their claims.[39]

This comment is striking, because it celebrates collectivity within Black musician circles while also dismissing the knowledge and experiences of the Black woman that recorded the original video, as well as all the people that agreed with her in the comment section. This comment does indeed cement the claim of whiteness (or in this case, a white band) as an accusation, one that can have a detrimental effect on the success, longevity, and livelihood of the Fusion band and its members. This follows Patricia Hill Collins's claim that Black women's knowledge is subjugated.[40]

The "receipts" offered by the Black woman who posted the video originally were eviscerated by claims of parentage and various proximities to Blackness, and ultimately, violence. What she saw and heard were not enough to support the claims she was making.

Although the deletion of the video and commentary were heralded as a victory for the Fusion Band and their supporters, the deletion was also an act of resistance by the woman that originally posted the video. She was experiencing misogynoir, a term coined by Moya Bailey that "describes the uniquely co-constitutive racialized and sexist violence that befalls Black women as a result of their simultaneous and interlocking oppression at the intersection of racial and gender marginalization."[41] After being threatened and having her footage and opinions dismissed, she chose to remove the video from Facebook, essentially exercising her power as the creator of the narrative. So although the deletion did in some ways benefit the Fusion Band, it also benefited the original poster, because it kept her safe from escalating violence. In her exploration of misogynoir and the digital resistance of Black women, Bailey goes on to outline practices of digital alchemy, or the ways that Black women "transform everyday digital media into valuable social justice media that recode the failed scripts that negatively impact their lives."[42] As it became clear that the violence would only continue as long as the post was up, the original poster chose to stop that narrative, and to stop the escalation in the best way she could, which was to remove the post entirely. This operates as a kind of recoding of a script the was in the process of failing, where violence against Black women, online

---

[39] Anonymous, Facebook comment, June 27, 2018.
[40] Patricia Hill Collins, *Black Feminist Thought: Knowledge, Consciousness, and the Politics of Empowerment* (New York: Routledge, 2002).
[41] Moya Bailey, *Misogynoir Transformed: Black Women's Digital Resistance, Misogynoir Transformed* (New York: NYU Press, 2021), 1.
[42] Bailey, *Misogynoir Transformed*, 24.

and in person, is indeed a failure of both the platform and the people involved. Furthermore, because Black women are not protected on platforms such as Facebook and Twitter, they have to make their own choices about when to remove themselves from conversations that will lead to harm.

The question remaining is that non-Black people are regularly rewarded for successfully performing Blackness, so why not here?[43] What I find particularly generative here is the actual sound coming from the video, which was noted in some of the Facebook commentary:

> "FIRST of all they slummin!"[44]
> "That shit so bad its almost comical, but I get the underlying factors"
> "What kinda adult contemporary smooth jazz kenny g go-go is this?"
> "It doesn't even sound right. He's trying too hard."
> "The vocals suck and that backline ain't hittin on shit"[45]

In the video posted, the bandleader is engaging the audience in a classic go-go call and response chant. In go-go performances, lead talkers will often call something like "wh-wh-wh-where y'all from?" and the audience will respond with however close they can get their neighborhood to two syllables. People respond with quadrants, neighborhoods, streets, neighboring cities, wherever they feel themselves from in that moment. In addition to this chant, the backline of the band is holding up a pocket, and the set player is playing drum fills. According to the comments and the audio, there is something here, beyond the visuals of the band that makes the bandleader "sound" white. Was he not doing the chant right? After multiple listens, it seems that the emphasis is on the wrong syllables in his rendition. It's similar to Lupita N'yongo's character in Jordan Peele's *Us* on rhythm but a little *too* on rhythm when she snaps her fingers to Luniz's "I Got 5 On It."[46] Technically, the bandleader was doing everything he was supposed to do, but Blackness and Black sound are not technical. Just because a person is doing everything that a Black person might do in that moment, does not equate to the soundscape being interpreted as sonically or aesthetically pleasing. Matthew Morrison addresses the emptiness

---

[43] Videos of white people doing "Black" dances or speech patterns often go viral and lead to financial opportunities, such as rappers Iggy Azalea and Bhad Bhabie.
[44] In this case, "slummin" means sounding bad.
[45] Anonymous, Facebook comments, June 25, 2018.
[46] In the movie, N'yongo plays two characters: one is a supposedly "normal" woman (Adelaide) who lives with her husband and two children. The other is Adelaide's "tethered," described in the movie as a kind of demonic clone that every person has. The twist in the movie, however, is that N'yongo's characters actually switched places when they were young children, meaning that the tethered is the one living the "normal" life above-ground. Many on social media pointed to the snapping to "I Got 5 On It" as an early indicator that the roles had been switched, because the tethered was technically snapping "correctly," but not on the

of mimicry and imitation in his theorization of "Blacksound," a framework which, while focused on Blackface, delineates "how the sounds in movements embedded in those [Blackface] scripts become racialized and imagined as authentic or inauthentic, depending upon the body, listener(s), and conditions under which the performance takes place."[47] In that moment, via the mediation of the Facebook video, Fusion Band's bandleader was judged and found wanting, and the repercussions on social media forced him to pull out all the stops to prove his Blackness, musicality, and proximity to an online go-go community that had the power to hurt his career. He needed to shift the imagining of his performance from inauthentic to authentic, recasting how he was seen and heard in the video, although the recorded sound in the video never changed.

This incident is but one glimpse into what the ramifications of cultural appropriation have been and will continue to be in the go-go community. In a community that is being threatened with silencing from all sides, individual bands and musicians cannot afford to be accused of whiteness, going so far as to threaten a Black woman to make that known. This question of legacy amidst scarcity is often a question of control and lies at the complex and evidently dangerous intersections of race, class, gender, and the believability of social media.

Conclusion

In addition to being untrue, the anticipation and pre-emptive declaration of go-go's death makes narratives of gentrification easier to write in the city. Stories of gentrification often rely on a sensationalism that disregards the complexities of gentrifying processes. It is more difficult to write of those fighting for go-go, or those go-go musicians that are thriving, or even those within the go-go community that blame gentrification largely on Black people in the first place.[48] To listen to and amplify these less familiar stories complicates the narrative of gentrification, making it less complete. It is easier to say that

---

beat that followed the more intrinsic groove of the song. In a 4/4 signature, she snaps on the "and" of every beat, rather than the more widely accepted 2 and 4. She does not, however, snap on the shamed 1 and 3. *Us*, directed by Jordan Peele (2019).

[47] Matthew D. Morrison, "Race, Blacksound, and the (Re)Making of Musicological Discourse," *Journal of the American Musicological Society* 72, no. 3 (December 1, 2019), 795.
[48] This story has been told in many different ways but one of the most potent is the notion that Black people were "asleep at the wheel" and therefore allowed to gentrification happen because they were unaware of was happening in the city regarding development practices.

white people move into the city Black people move out, and go-go music has been displaced as a result. It is a more honest endeavor to hold space in the incomplete relationships between go-go music and processes of gentrification in DC, where stories are still being written and songs still sung.

The sensationalizing of go-go's supposed death is cut from the same cloth of the sensationalized deaths of Black people at the hands of the state. With the rise of the Black Lives Matter Movement in 2014, autoplay videos on social media outlets have increased—videos that show explicit violence enacted against Black people, be it through traffic stops or arresting children at a pool party. These videos, a constant fixture on social media platforms, are circulated to raise awareness and call for justice, a kind of grisly amplification of Mamie Till's 1955 decision to hold an open casket funeral for her son. These videos are occasionally "successful": Darnella Frazier's 2020 recording of George Floyd's murder directly refuted the Minneapolis police department's account and led to the conviction of Derek Chauvin. In 2015, Feidin Santana recorded the murder of Walter Scott in South Carolina, capturing Scott being shot in the back and the officer later dropping an object, potentially his own taser, next to Scott's lifeless body. This video was an important piece of evidence leading to the officer being charged with second-degree murder and sentenced to twenty years in prison. Although these videos do become the closest thing to irrefutable proof that exists in a courtroom, they continually raise a question of audience. Who remains unconvinced until they see a Black person die, and what is the cost of auto playing these videos in a never-ending loop of Black death? In a particularly human moment, journalist Wesley Lowery recounted the moments immediately after he watched the death of Philando Castile in the newsroom of the *Washington Post*, broadcasted by his girlfriend Diamond Reynolds on Facebook Live: "I sprang up from my desk and ran to the newsroom bathroom to throw up. Then I began reporting."[49] There is a real physical and psychic cost to the consistent broadcast of Black death, and it takes its toll on us all.

While the constant proclamation of go-go's death is not as explicitly ghastly as the videos of murder that circulate on social media, it still begs the same questions: Who benefits from hearing that go-go is dead, and what toll does the shadow of death take on the community? To speak the narrative of go-go's death as though it was already true works toward the cultural erasure that gentrification promises; however, it also speaks to the exhausting effort to

---

[49] Wesley Lowery, *They Can't Kill Us All: Ferguson, Baltimore, and a New Era in America's Racial Justice Movement* (Boston: Little, Brown, 2016), 225.

fight that erasure. This narrative is spread through multiple channels, from official media to scholarly work to social media, blurred as these lines are. These rumors of go-go's death as well as the death of the chocolate city are based in population data, statistics, but also in the everyday knowledge that neighborhoods are changing hands. In acknowledging the power of these stories and comments I consider the fear that undergirds them, fear that the city will continue to displace its Black residents and in turn, their sonic lives. Despite these challenges, go-go music continues to spread across the city and across the world, due to the dedication of its community members and advocates. As Big G, lead talker of Backyard Band, told *The Atlantic* in 2015, "As long as I have breath in my body, it's [go-go] gonna stay floating."[50]

---

[50] Paul Rosenfeld, "Keeping Go-Go Music Going in a Gentrifying D.C.," *The Atlantic*, November 28, 2015.

Interlude: Sounds of the City

Cities are prideful places. More accurately, the people that create and re-create cities through their daily lives are often quite proud of the spaces they call home. From food to language to sports, people regularly flaunt the talents of their space. As the home of luminaries like Duke Ellington, Marvin Gaye, and Richard Smallwood, Washington, DC's musical pride is well earned, and one of the city's staunchest advocates is Kokayi Issa (known as Kokayi), a Grammy-nominated multihyphenate artist and creator who has traveled the world but still calls DC home. He is particularly passionate about the city's talent: "If you take any of these bands anywhere, they will kill people. Like Black Alley just went to Minnesota and took home the trophy—because we kill people. They killed it all at the club that Prince was in . . . came in first. They killed it. Because you're not going to take a band from here anywhere."[1] In Chapters 2, 3, and 4, I considered the sounds of gentrification from various perspectives: a neighborhood, an intersection, and a genre of music. Here I think through gentrification and sound through the work of Kokayi, who produced four songs for the city's 2016 Funk Parade based on crowdsourced sounds from the public. These four songs, one for each quadrant of the city, offer detailed insights into how the city is perceived sonically, both from the sounds that were submitted to the arrangements that Kokayi made of them. These songs feature the sounds of DC mediated twice over, first through the beliefs and values of those who recorded them and submitted them into the Funk Parade, and then through the prism of an artist that knows the city intimately and is invested in offering counternarratives to the common stories that are told about DC. As these sounds are collected, changed, manipulated, and eventually re-presented in song, they offer an incredibly valuable snapshot of the sounds of the city, and the sounds of gentrification in DC. This continuous process of reflection and refraction facilitates the transition into Chapter 5, which focuses on the sounds of gentrification as interpreted and legislated through legal action.

---

[1] Kokayi Issa, interview with the author, 2018. Black Alley is a band that operates both within and just outside of the go-go scene. They have a crossover appeal that many bands of their generation have failed to cultivate, and as a result, often travel outside of the DMV region to places like Minneapolis to perform.

Kokayi identifies most closely with hip-hop, though he grew up heavily influenced by the go-go culture in the city. Go-go music does indeed take up a large place in the sonic narrative of the city, influencing many a musician that does not specifically make music in the genre but rather in the adjacent spaces of hip-hop, jazz, and R&B. This connection to go-go manifested in the language of "talking" versus "rapping," with talking being a distinctly DC activity. When asked about his early rapping days he would say "oh I don't rap. I talk for the go-go band." In this case the act of rapping was folded into the work of bandleader, into the work of MC, interacting with the crowd. Kokayi has carried this versatility into his career as an artist, offering production, rapping, and other artistic expressions since the 1990s. In 2016, Kokayi was tapped to work with the Funk Parade, an annual festival that takes place in the U Street Corridor. Started in 2013 by Justin Rood and Chris Naoum, the Funk Parade prides itself on amplifying local musicians and sitting deeply in DC's rich legacy of funk musicians. They feature musicians from all over the world, but DC talent is front and center. The festival has made headlines multiple times for its financial troubles, and in 2018 was on the brink of cancellation until Mayor Muriel Bowser stepped in with a funding pledge from her office. While the Funk Parade is intentional in its commitment to local artists, the festivities still exist in the context of a gentrifying Shaw and U Street, and the original leadership by white men has not been overlooked. In 2018, Rood and Naoum passed the Funk Parade to a local arts organization, the MusicianShip, which was founded by Jeffrey Tribble Jr. in 2008. Since the transition, the Funk Parade has been more deeply focused on arts education and local youth. The four commissioned songs, together stylized as "Made In DC/Hecho in DC," take crowdsourced sounds (mostly recorded outside) and filter them into and through the artistic practice of someone that is deeply committed to knowing and cultivating the sounds of Washington, DC. The sounds are diverse, even disparate at times, a fact that Kokayi enjoyed: "People didn't do the typical thing. And I was appreciative of that."

Northwest Gentry and the Ebon Road

Northwest begins with a familiar sound: go-go music being played outside of Central Communications at 7th Street and Florida Avenue. The pocket beat bounces, the cars go by. The combination of go-go and traffic is then distorted, sent from left to right on the headphones a couple of times before it shifts into something slower and more jazz adjacent. After this passage the beat settles in, evoking a combination of house and lo-fi hip-hop fueled by an insistent and steady drum pad. The drum is punctuated by conversation and someone saying "yeah." The vocal being so integral to the beat here is indicative of how intricately the city is made up by conversation, by hustle and bustle, by people in motion and going on about their daily lives. In a new cycle full of government shutdowns and slowdowns and things not getting done, NW provides a sonic sense of how DC moves.

Of the four songs, "Gentry and the Ebon Road" seems to feature the most conversation snippets, which for the most part are muffled and indistinguishable. One of the most telling parts of my conversation with Kokayi about these songs was him revealing that someone sent in sounds labeled "foreigner," which featured a conversation in Spanish. The label of foreign to people speaking Spanish when there are multiple generations of Latinx people in Washington, DC is reminiscent of the white ethnonationalism that has become more violently visible and audible since the election of Trump in 2016. Latinx people have been in the city for centuries, and to label Spanish as "foreign" positions English as "native." Furthermore, the label of Spanish as foreign is part of the common collapse of language and race together, in which "languages are perceived as racially embodied and race is perceived as linguistically intelligible, which results in the overdetermination of racial embodiment and communicative practice."[2] To collapse Spanish into foreignness is to collapse anything vaguely Latinx into the other, the unwanted. Furthermore, as Washington, DC both gentrifies and acts as a beacon for white supremacists because of the actions of the Trump administration as well as the January 6 uprising, Spanish becomes more and more of a catalyst because it signals various ethnic, linguistic, and racialized positions.

Kokayi puts the "foreigners" here in "Gentry and the Ebon Road," claiming the most expensive quadrant in the city for the Spanish language. This is the only decipherable language in the song, where the conversations seemingly in English are muffled, not able to be understood. The song argues that the "foreign" here are the gentry, those who have staked their claim in upper Northwest and reigned as the city's elite for many years. The clearest sounds in the song are the pocket, the conversation in Spanish between perhaps a father and a daughter, and the steady drum pad beat. Many conversations surrounding gentrification are about safety, about displacement, and in many cases, ideas of citizenship and rights. The label of foreigners sits squarely in this realm of conversation, because it draws an intense line on who is and is not welcome in the space. There is a connection between foreignness and

---

[2] Jonathan Rosa, *Looking Like a Language, Sounding Like a Race* (New York: Oxford University Press, 2019), 2.

safety, where the outsider represents a rupture to the everyday. The irony here, which Kokayi draws out well, is that the "foreign" sound is in fact the everyday, where everything else is changing around it being new and "alien."

Northeast Dreams Deterred

"Dreams Deterred" begins with sounds from a mosque and features another insistent drumming rhythm, reminiscent of the drum circle at Malcolm X Park (located in the Northwest quadrant). This track features a great deal of wind a couple minutes in, bringing the "natural" areas of the city to the fore. DC does have an incredible amount of green space, and Kokayi highlighted that here. With traffic sounds come noise that has not been edited out or condensed so that it is inaudible. The drums are removed for a bit, then there is the unmistakable beep of someone scanning their smart trip card to get on the bus, a sonic marker of public transportation. The beat is then built again around the continuous beeping of the smart trip. Public transportation, particularly buses, is incredibly important to Black communities in DC and across the US. As the city gentrifies, key arterial bus routes are being removed and rerouted, leaving people stranded where they are and unable to travel to jobs or family. Brandi Thompson Summers, in writing about the gentrification of the H Street Corridor, has written extensively about how the decimation of bus stops and connections removes people from certain areas of the city.[3] Transportation can be incredibly exclusive, from the New York City highway projects of Robert Moses to the lack of a Metro stop in Georgetown. The removal of Black people from neighborhoods where public transportation has historically served their life needs is part of urban exclusion and confinement practices, in the same lineage as redlining and racial covenants. The blending of wind and public transportation in "Dreams Deterred" does away with the misconception that cities are only concrete spaces that don't allow for outdoor recreation. Perhaps the most compelling part of "Dreams Deterred" is the shifting meaning of the beep. It begins as a smart trip card but over time, within the rhythm of the song, becomes the beep of an EKG monitor. In his description of this song Kokayi speaks to the intention of the beep: "I wanted this song to reflect the resiliency of a neighborhood that [is] intent on peace and making life peaceful. This is reflected in the heart monitor sound and the increase of its rhythm throughout."[4] Moving from the recognition of the smart

---

[3] Brandi Thompson Summers, *Black in Place: The Spatial Aesthetics of Race in a Post-Chocolate City* (Chapel Hill: University of North Carolina Press, 2019).
[4] Kokayi, interview with the author, 2018.

trip card and its ubiquitous signaling of the metro system into a larger conversation of resilience within the same sound is one of the many reasons why this song cycle is so compelling for listening to gentrification. In the years after the release of these songs, the city has faced a wave of shootings. Particular stories have captured the region's attention: teenagers participating in fatal carjackings in 2021, the shooting of ten-year-old Makiyah Wilson in 2018, the list goes on. Despite this unspeakable violence, though, the heartbeat monitor sound in Dreams Deterred reminds us that the city is moving, is ever striving toward the life and peace that the entire community deserves.

Southeast SoawesomE

Kokayi's approach to Southeast is analogous to Black Studies scholar Jayna Brown's formulation of "Black utopias," which she uses "to signal the (im)possibilities for forms of subjectivity outside a recognizable ontological framework, and modes of existence conceived of in unfamiliar epistemes."[5] These are utopias not in the sense of perfection, but utopias in their impossibility. In his description of Southeast's song, Kokayi describes "how SE has always received negative media coverage without people actually knowing the tony estates of Hillcrest." Later in our interview, he said that "the sound of Southeast is not gunshots really. Sound of Southeast most of the times is birds and crickets for real because it's so much wooded area."[6] For many, SE is unrecognizable outside of a framework of violence. In "SoawesomE," Kokayi creates not only a counternarrative to this media coverage and framework, but a utopia out of the found sounds of SE. As Brown describes, this is not a utopia in the sense of perfection, but in the sense that SE, much like Black life, can be anything that Black people make it to be because it is so often devalued as nothing. Kokayi builds a universe that imagines Southeast as a vibrant, wealthy, pleasurable place to be. And given its unfair categorizations as solely crime-ridden, this vibrance is an impossibility to wrap one's mind around. The vibrance, wealth, and pleasure of Southeast are impossible: a Black utopia.

SoawesomE begins with the sound of cars going by and a rich, deep singing voice coming from a speaker. After this dreamy, melodic intro, the song fades almost to silence before the beat comes in, built from drums and church bells. On top of the drum loop, there is a distorted voice repeating "this is a test

---

[5] Jayna Brown, *Black Utopias: Speculative Life and the Music of Other Worlds* (Durham, NC: Duke University Press, 2021), 6.
[6] Kokayi Issa, interview with the author, 2018.

of the city," applicable because Southeast is indeed the most embattled quadrant of the city. Its neighborhoods are divided by the Anacostia River, with the neighborhoods "east of the river," from Anacostia to Congress Heights, bearing the brunt of the negative coverage. Neighborhoods closer to downtown, such as Navy Yard and Capitol Hill, gentrified earlier and are closer to downtown and the federal government, and have such been spared the under resourcing of the communities east of the river. Overcrowding and under resourcing in Southeast began in the 1950s when Southwest was subject to slum removal, and many displaced residents moved to nearby Southeast. This has led to years of distrust and under resourced areas in Southeast, which has begun to change as the quadrants have started to gentrify. Southeast is home to local cultural institutions such as the Anacostia Community Museum, the Big Chair, and the historic home of abolitionist Fredrick Douglass. Southeast also has a rich history of activism, as it was home of the Southeast Settlement house, activists like Etta Mae Horn, and the Band of Angels, a group of women that protested for better housing conditions in Barry Farms. Many of the city's most famous go-go bands are from Southeast, including Junkyard Band and Rare Essence, the former of which got their start playing for the community at Barry Farms, a housing project that was demolished in 2019.

"SoawesomE" also features what sounds like a woman's moan, a sound ubiquitous throughout hip-hop and popular music in general. The moan, coming in the last third of the song, signals that there is pleasure in Southeast. Amidst the tests, the distortions, the church bells, and ever-present boom bap, there is pleasure, and we shouldn't shy away from that. After the moan there is a higher-pitched voice saying "that's awesome." The characterization of southeast as awesome, and as first in the track list, this speaks volumes, SE is a counternarrative of SE that speaks nature, pleasure, and joy into a quadrant that is used as a scapegoat and consistently under resourced in the city, even as it gentrifies. The emphasis on pleasure here is critical, as pleasure is one of the ways that Black people create and exist in new worlds. In *Pleasure Activism*, adrienne maree brown challenges us to think of a framework that is more compelling than suffering in order to live.[7] In this song, Kokayi offers us a framework that is more compelling than the "Southeast is poor, Black, and disadvantaged" narrative that is frequently touted by administrations. While the constant disinvestment in Southeast has indeed led to strenuous living and working conditions, Southeast is also wooded, full of animal life, and a pleasurable place to be, both for those who live there as well as those who

---

[7] adrienne maree brown, *Pleasure Activism: The Politics of Feeling Good* (Stirling, UK: AK Press, 2019).

visit. Sound, and in this case the intentional combination and manipulation of sound, takes us to new worlds.

SW-SolidGold Waterfront

"SolidGold Waterfront" is, to me, about movement. This song features fewer human voices than Southeast, more focused on a looping rhythmic pattern that drives the entire song. The beat in this song is "moombahton," a genre created by DJ Dave Nada in Washington, DC in 2009. The genre combines house elements with reggaeton, and the name combines house track "Moombah" with the -ton suffix from reggaeton. This song sounds like construction, like the sounds that tools make when they're repurposed as instruments. This song sounds like the music of labor and building, as Kokayi ponders what this constant building will do to the city's smallest quadrant, specifically questioning the continued development of the waterfront and the wharf, which has been consistent throughout the 2010s and into the 2020s. The rhythmic consistency in the moombahton rhythm that is comforting as a listener but eerie when I consider that this is the consistency of construction and change in DC. The wharf has indeed become a stable of DC life, with restaurants, condos, and amenities galore. When I visited the area in the summer of 2022 a resident remarked to me that most of the food options in the area were "bland but overpriced," which seems to be an apt description of a recently gentrified area.

One of the constant frequencies in "SolidGoldWaterfront" is reminiscent of a crosswalk beep signal, similar to the one that beeps constantly at 7th Street and Florida Avenue in Northwest near Central Communications. There's also thumping bass, low distorted voices, and a car engine that propel the song forward for almost four minutes of nonstop motion. SW is almost a blur until the end of the song, given that it is under constant construction. From the very beginning, Southwest is moving. There is a high-pitched, almost piercing, car brake at the end of SW, effectively signaling the end of the song. This is the only time where Southwest takes a break. It has long been a quadrant of movement and even upheaval, given the displacement that resulted from eminent domain in the 1950s. Long before eminent domain and slum clearance, though, Southwest was a much larger quadrant, not bound by the river as it is now but rather including the cities of Arlington and Alexandria. DC was a planned city, and included these areas during its inception. But after the Compromise of 1860, with Washington, DC set to end slavery, Virginia required that the land they ceded to create the nation's capital be given back. This is why Southwest remains DC's smallest quadrant. With these long histories of movement, displacement, redrawing of boundaries on stolen land, Kokayi succinctly captures motion with the submitted recordings.

These four songs all carry a richness within them, of the sounds of the city as filtered through a musician's intent on advocating for the city's soundscapes. These songs also show us, again, that sound shows us who we are, and that sound is not exempt from racialization. They are influenced by the specter of go-go on the city but they also speak to notions of safety, of "foreign-ness," and of who belongs in the city. In the next chapter, I consider how belonging plays out through legislation by telling the story of the Amplified Noise Act, of which Kokayi was a part.

Chapter 5
"Plainly Audible"

Before the #DontMuteDC movement rocked the city in 2019, there was the Amplified Noise Act (ANA). In June 2018, three of Washington, DC's thirteen elected city councilmembers quietly introduced the ANA Amendment of 2018. Written to discourage street musicians in DC's Chinatown Gallery Place neighborhood from disturbing local residents and office workers in the area, the bill was an update to noise ordinances already in effect in DC with a few added provisions.[1] The punitive measures proposed in the bill included a $300 fine, up to ten days in jail, and/or the seizing of the offending equipment by the Metropolitan Police Department (MPD). For a month the bill remained relatively uncontroversial, until news of the amendment and a hearing to discuss the changes spread on social media, primarily through Twitter and Facebook. The public hearing, rally, and legislative maneuvering that followed encapsulated the racialized and sonic dimensions of gentrification in Washington, DC, and are a part of the city's long history of imposing legislative and criminal restrictions onto Black sound.

In this chapter, I tell stories of the ANA through council hearing transcripts, interviews, and my own participant observation. Much like previous chapters, my telling of these stories utilizes intersectional listening as a strategy to acknowledge and disrupt the interlocking matrices of power that are sonically articulated during processes of gentrification, producing an analysis that attends to the complexities of sound and power in a changing city. The events surrounding the ANA provide a rich set of circumstances to unpack the sonic dimensions of gentrification, those facets of neighborhood change that directly or indirectly involve a focus on music, sound, and noise. Here, I continue to argue that processes of gentrification include an amplification of tensions surrounding sound, music, and noise in both public and private space, and that these tensions are deeply racialized because of the ways in which Black people have long been deemed sonically unruly and unmanageable. Whether considered too loud, stubbornly silent, dangerously aggressive,

---

[1] The noise regulations already in effect were DC Code 22-1321 (Disorderly Conduct) and 25-725 (Noise from Licensed Premises).

overly sexual, or resistant to categorization altogether, Black sonic creation has been consistently stigmatized and subsequently punished.[2] In discussing the ANA, I am particularly interested in how processes of gentrification are made manifest through law and legal action. In DC, this largely takes place via the city council, the legislative branch of the city's local government.

The regulation of sound-making engages the intersection of race, law, and sound, and is a key site for the facilitation of gentrification, especially in the rich rhetoric of lawmaking. For example, the District of Columbia Code features a number of different laws about noise and sound-making, particularly in "Alcoholic Beverages" and "Disorderly Conduct." For establishments that serve alcohol, the following regulations are in place:

(a) The licensee under an on-premises retailer's license shall not produce any sound, noise, or music of such intensity that it may be heard in any premises other than the licensed establishment by the use of any:
  (1) Mechanical device, machine, apparatus, or instrument for amplification of the human voice or any sound or noise;
  (2) Bell, horn, gong, whistle, drum, or other noise-making article, instrument, or device; or
  (3) Musical instrument.[3]

There are a number of exceptions to these regulations, for circumstances such as "sounds, noises, or music occasioned by normal opening of entrance and exit doors for the purpose of ingress and egress" or "Heating, ventilation, and air conditioning devices."[4] These regulations are an integral part of the logics of noise and sound-making in a city like Washington, DC, because they write into the world what is allowable sound and unallowable sound. They raise a number of questions, though. What about sounds of bass, which are not so much heard as felt? Is somatic hearing included in these regulations? The exception for the "normal" opening and closing of a door brings to mind a night I spend walking around downtown DC with my sister and her friends. We walked past Café Asia on I Street NW, a popular go-go club at the time, and another club next door that was featuring EDM and house music. The door to the EDM club was open, with the music spilling out into the street, whereas the door to Café Asia was only opening when a person went in or out, and

---

[2] Examples of the punishment of Black music include the censorship of gangsta rap and the criminalization of go-go music in Washington, DC.
[3] District of Columbia Code § 25–725. Noise from Licensed Premises. May 3, 2001.
[4] "Noise from Licensed Premises," §25–725.

during that time the familiar pocket of go-go music spilled out of the club. During those moments, in the "normal" opening of the door, the soundscapes co-mingled, where one was breaking the law and another wasn't, but the one following the law was more likely to get scapegoated or blamed for any criminal activity if anything were to happen.

One of the regulations for disorderly conduct states that "(d) It is unlawful for a person to make an unreasonably loud noise between 10:00 p.m. and 7:00 a.m. that is likely to annoy or disturb one or more other persons in their residences."[5] Laws such as the above on disorderly conduct are not written in such a way that they attend to the histories of race and racialization in DC, let alone the United States. Some people are simply annoyed and disturbed by people in different racial categories than them, regardless of the sounds that they make. Not only are they written without considering the entangled histories of race and annoyance; they are also carceral, carrying a fine of up to $500 and up to 90 days in jail. Enforcement of these kinds of laws is another story, especially because part of the conversation about the ANA was that MPD was not enforcing the laws on the books, but even the legal standpoint of a law that allows someone to serve up to 90 days in jail because they disturbed someone in their residence encourages discriminatory listening and enforcement.

Gentrification is a collaborative process. Local and federal governments, residents, and various financial stakeholders engage in placemaking strategies to build particular kinds of cities, repeating histories of disinvestment while drawing on the cultural processes of the communities they're leaving behind in order to attract residents that are more financially secure. Local governments contribute to this process with various legal maneuvers, from supporting or blocking legislation to instituting policies that support the placemaking of capitalist imaginaries. The mayor's office and council of DC have collaborated in gentrification processes for decades, including the New Communities Initiative that began in 2004 with Mayor Anthony Williams, various updates to the city's comprehensive plan in 2021, allegations of biased arts funding distribution, and more.[6] In this way, the council's introduction and initial support for the ANA was not uncharacteristic, as there is indeed a connection between the placemaking strategies of gentrification stakeholders with the criminalization of Black life and sound, especially as discussed in Chapter 2 with the case of Breanna Taylor in Louisville, Kentucky.

---

[5] "Noise from Licensed Premises," §25–725.
[6] The New Communities Initiative approved the demolition of city housing projects on the promise that units would be replaced and each resident would be able to return. These projects take decades to complete and many residents have since moved away or do not want to return.

In addition to supporting policies that facilitate gentrification, legislation and policing in DC have specifically been used to criminalize Black music for centuries, with laws like the Black Codes. In Washington, DC, these laws were passed in 1848 to determine what was to be legal in the lives of Black people both free and enslaved and were just one iteration of codes passed throughout the United States to guarantee state control over Black life. The laws were extensive, ranging from the cruel ("When runaway slaves can be lawfully killed by their pursuers") to the absurd ("Punishment of slaves for flying kites").[7] Within these codes, several are of particular interest to the concept of Black gathering spaces and sound. For example, "The Prohibition of Assemblages of Colored Persons" decreed that all assemblages of Black people, except for religious meetings supervised by white men, were unlawful. Another code operates similarly, outlawing private, secret, and religious meetings past 10 p.m. The second law went further in that it also implicated the police, declaring that if a policeman did not shut these meetings down after gaining knowledge of them, he was liable to be fined. The Black Codes demonstrate how the police operate as a tool of the state, used specifically to track and suppress Black gathering spaces.

The police have been used to track and suppress Black music performances over the years, perhaps most famously with the Metropolitan Police Department's "Go-Go Report," a document circulated in the *Washington City Paper* in 2010 that detailed the weekly go-go parties throughout the city as well as Prince George's County in Maryland.[8] Prince George's County, closely related to the go-go scene, has also had its own troubles with the overpolicing of Black people and Black gathering spaces, from the dancehall law that go-go musicians protested in 2011 to the infamous murder of Prince Jones in 2000.[9] With this history of controlling and suppressing Black gathering spaces and musical efforts, it is no surprise that city lawmakers attempted to further criminalize street musicians, most of whom are of color.

---

[7] Worthington Garrettson Snethen, *The Black Code of the District of Columbia, in Force September 1st, 1848* (A. & F. Anti-Slavery Society, 1848).

[8] Rend Smith, "Exclusive: A Look at MPD's 'Go-Go Report,'" *Washington City Paper*, July 14, 2010, http://washingtoncitypaper.com/article/471073/exclusive-a-look-at-mpds-go-go-report/.

[9] In his book *Between the World and Me*, author and journalist Ta-Nehisi Coates recounts the story of the murder of Prince Jones, who was a close friend of his. Jones was chased by the Prince George's County Police Department across several jurisdictions in the County, DC, and in Fairfax County, Virginia, which is where an undercover officer eventually shot and killed him in what he called a case of mistaken identity. The officer was never charged, and Prince George's County awarded Jones's daughter a 3.7 million dollar settlement for wrongful death in 2006. Ta-Nehisi Coates, *Between the World and Me* (New York: Random House, 2015).

The Hearing

Where laws are often written to discourage sound-making, processes of legislation are also important spaces to hear people advocate for themselves and their right to the city.[10] This advocacy was on display in the open hearing that the city council organized to hear the bill. When the persecution of go-go music gave rise to the #DontMuteDC movement in 2019, it was foregrounded by the organizing around the ANA, some of which began at the council's hearing to listen to public comment about the bill. Washington, DC's status as a federal city rather than a state makes local politics equally fascinating and frustrating. License plates in the city bear the slogan "Taxation without Representation" to protest DC residents' lack of representation in the Senate despite the city's being taxed by the federal government. The city is governed by a mayor and thirteen-member council, while the shadow of congressional approval looms overhead. This combination of mayor and council is relatively recent, implemented after the Home Rule Act of 1974. Prior to home rule, the city was governed by a board of commissioners that was appointed by Congress. Under the current system, when enacting new legislation the council often holds public hearings, where residents and community members may testify in person or in writing, offering their opinions on proposed legislation and its impact. In the case of the ANA, the council held a public hearing on a Monday afternoon in July 2018 at 2 p.m., a time criticized by some to be intentional because many working members of the public could not come to testify. The hearing was for two bills, the first proposing a ban of gas-powered leaf blowers (because of the noise) and the second for the ANA. With more than fifty people scheduled to testify, the hearing lasted over seven hours.

The majority of the people providing testimony were residents, business owners, and office workers in DC's Chinatown-Gallery Place neighborhood, one of the busiest business districts in the city, bustling with downtown workers, tourists, and young adults. Today, Chinatown is home to approximately 300 Chinese American residents, down from 3,000 in the 1990s due to factors such as gentrification and large commercial investments in the neighborhood in the 1990s.[11] Originally, DC's Chinese community was clustered around Pennsylvania Avenue downtown, but residents were displaced and

---

[10] Phil Hubbard and Loretta Lees, "The Right to Community?," *City* 22, no. 1 (2018): 8–25.
[11] Yanan Wang, "D.C.'s Chinatown Has Only 300 Chinese Americans Left, and They're Fighting to Stay," *Washington Post*, July 18, 2015, https://www.washingtonpost.com/lifestyle/style/dcs-chinatown-has-only-300-chinese-americans-left--and-fighting-to-stay/2015/07/16/86d54e84-2191-11e5-bf41-c23f5d3face1_story.html.

moved in the 1930s to make room for the National Gallery of Art, which remains there today. The Chinese population relocated to what is now known as Chinatown or Gallery Place, as it is home to the National Portrait Gallery. Many of the remaining Chinese residents in the neighborhood are fighting to stay in the neighborhood, despite being driven out by rising rents, new condos, and the commercial attraction of the Capital One Center, built in 1997 (formerly known as both the Verizon Center and MCI Center).

The racial demographics of Chinatown have shifted drastically since the neighborhood began to gentrify. In 1990, Chinatown's population was approximately 66% Asian and 20% African American. In the 2010 census, those numbers shifted to 21% Asian and 9% Black. Beyond residency, though, Chinatown, or "Gallery" as it's referred to colloquially, has long been a popular hangout area for Black teenagers, who bounce between McDonalds, Chipotle, and the Gallery Place mall. In the early 2010s, Gallery was home to "Check It," a crew of Black queer youth that were known for their exploits in the area.[12] These histories of working-class Chinese life and later the sounds of Black youth are at odds with the multimillion-dollar investments that continue to pour into the neighborhood, particularly condo developments.

On several of the street corners in the neighborhood, musicians make their living playing music for the tourists and passersby. The music is loud enough to be heard in apartment buildings and restaurants throughout the area, much to the ire of the testifying residents and office workers, many of whom spoke of migraines, lack of sleep and disrupted workdays, as well as disgruntled customers, and other issues the musicians allegedly caused. One resident even compared the situation to terrorism, calling the music a form of "music torture," and noted that such practices are banned by the United Nations.[13] This kind of extreme language was common throughout the hearing; another resident, for example stated that he felt compelled to call Child Protective Services after hearing how loud the music was and seeing a child in the care of the musicians. He felt it his duty to alert the authorities that the child was in danger because of the decibel level of the music. The councilmembers

---

[12] Check It has since transformed their lives with the help and mentorship of activist Ron Moten, and were the subject of a 2016 documentary of the same name by Dana Flor and Tony Oppenheimer.

[13] Several national and international bodies have spoken out against music and sound as torture, including the Society for American Music and Society for Ethnomusicology. In response to reports that the United States military was using American music as part of torture processes, the Society for Ethnomusicology released the following statement in 2007: "The Society for Ethnomusicology calls for full disclosure of U.S. government-sanctioned and funded programs that design the means of delivering music as torture; condemns the use of music as an instrument of torture; and demands that the United States government and its agencies cease using music as an instrument of physical and psychological torture." Society for Ethnomusicology, "Position Statement on Torture," February 2, 2007, https://www.ethnomusicology.org/page/PS_Torture.

present largely seemed to support the plight of those in support of the ANA, with Ward 2 Councilmember Jack Evans stating that the bucket drummers specifically were indeed "awful." Evans was noticeably absent during most of the hearing due to other meetings but remains a key figure and author of the bill behind the scenes because Chinatown lies in Ward 2, and the disgruntled residents were his constituents at the time (Evans has since resigned his council position due to ethics violations).[14]

While very few of the testifying community members spoke to race specifically, especially the racial identities of the offending musicians, the entire hearing was racially coded. Participants used language and musical vocabularies that have been historically connected to particular racialized groups. In other words, one of the key points of debate during the hearing was the designation of amplified or nonamplified. While the bill specifies only amplified music as problematic, several residents complained specifically about brass bands and drum sets, which are not typically amplified instruments. Council Chairman Phil Mendelson, the veteran legislator who oversaw the hearing, pointed out to residents on more than one occasion that if they wanted to ban brass bands and drum sets, they were essentially asking to ban all of the music because amplified plus nonamplified equals all.

The specific and repeated mention of brass bands and drum sets is racially coded language. These instruments are historically a fundamental part of Afro-diasporic musical practices. From the brass bands of New Orleans to the polyrhythmic percussion of go-go music, percussion and brass instruments are crucial to Black music-making. In traditions found throughout the diaspora, percussion and brass instruments are essential, especially regarding the polyrhythms that are so prevalent in Black music-making. This is an example of what Jennifer Stoever calls "the sonic color line," which she describes as "the audible contour" of race.[15] The sonic color line is an effective mechanism for thinking through race as a sonic phenomenon, continually constituted and reconstituted through laws such as the ANA. By characterizing brass bands and drum sets as outside the purview of lawfulness and simultaneously exceedingly offensive, the testifying residents made it clear that these culturally significant instruments were not to be played in Chinatown. This singling out of instruments operates as an example of the criminalization of Black sonic

---

[14] The ANA is not the council's first foray into criminalizing musicians and closing venues. In the early 2000s, Ward 1 Councilmember Jim Graham led the charge to ban go-go from clubs and close down Club U, located in the U Street Corridor. Graham also led the charge toward various noise ordinance and loitering legislation.

[15] Jennifer Lynn Stoever, *The Sonic Color Line: Race and the Cultural Politics of Listening* (New York: NYU Press, 2016), 6.

production, because they have been sonically coded as part of Black life, and subsequently deemed a problem that needs to be solved via police intervention, incarceration, and financial penalty.

For centuries and without avail, Black sound has been policed and silenced with a number of tactics. During the transatlantic slave trade, silencing led to the creation of the invisible church, in which enslaved people found ways to worship away from white eyes and ears because dominant understandings of worship were in many cases antithetical to Black worship practices. To combat Black expressive worship practices, catechisms were written specifically for Black people "as a mode of noise abatement."[16] Understood as a powerful religious and communicative tool, drumming was prohibited throughout slaveholding states, including the famous Congo Square in New Orleans, Louisiana. This prohibition did not stop drumming practices, but rather developed Black uses of body percussion and alternative instrument making. These attempts to control over Black sonic practice has extended well into the twentieth and twenty-first centuries, and law enforcement practices are but one aspect of a larger project to silence Black sonic production, which includes not only the police, but politicians, developers, and everyday actors. Stoever insists that "dominant listening practices discipline us to process white male ways of sounding as default, natural, normal, and desirable . . . they deem alternate ways of listening and sounding aberrant and—depending upon the historical context—as excessively sensitive, strikingly deficient, or impossibly both."[17] Black sounds are therefore controlled through silencing, policing, surveillance, intimidation, and a reliance on discourses of respectability that reproduce and shape ideas of whiteness as appropriate and quiet. In this way, it makes a lot of sense for gentrifying cities to face a great deal of conflict regarding silence. Part of what makes cities attractive to developers and new residents alike are a number of aesthetic choices, and the music in Chinatown had moved past an interesting aesthetic choice for the neighborhood and into a full-blown nuisance, a problem to be taken care of. Sharon Zukin notes that regarding gentrification and the development of urban society, "certainly the prime factors have to do with land, labor, and capital. Yet the production of space depends in turn on decisions about what should be visible and what should not; concepts of order and disorder; and a strategic interplay between aesthetics and function."[18] The legal strategies put to use in the case of the ANA exemplify the not only what should be audible and what

---

[16] Ashon T. Crawley, *Blackpentecostal Breath: The Aesthetics of Possibility* (New York: Fordham University Press, 2016), 164.
[17] Stoever, *The Sonic Color Line*, 12.
[18] Sharon Zukin, *The Cultures of Cities* (Cambridge, MA: Blackwell, 1996), 44.

should not, but also the interplay between aesthetics and function, where the musicians had moved past their function of being entertaining for passersby and began to impede on the sonic aesthetics in the neighborhood.

Having watched and sifted through the entire seven-hour hearing, I highlight two testimonies here, one in favor of the bill and one opposed to it, as they speak directly to the sonic dimensions of gentrification and provide ample opportunity for practicing intersectional listening. Kymone Freeman, an African American activist and director of the local independent radio station We Act Radio, was one of only two people to testify against the ANA. He characterized the bill as racially discriminatory, citing both the historical outlawing of drumming throughout the diaspora and the racial dimensions of gentrification. He also offered the solution of soundproofing the buildings in question so that musicians could continue to play. A portion of Freeman's testimony is below:

> I'm offended by the speed of this emergency legislation, that's not for a retention plan for long term residents or small businesses being displaced out of the city, but for the powerful, and the wealthy, and their comfort. Amplified Noise Amendment Act of 2018 seeks to provide suburban amenities in urban settings by further criminalizing youth and street musicians. With standards that are subjective and not verifiable, with more negative police encounters. The average white family in DC has 81 times the wealth of the average Black family. This speaks to the inherent disparities in the city. The amplification has not increased in the city, it's the number of new residents that have invaded the city and have increased noise complaints. I run We Act Radio storefront studio in Anacostia with a Metro bus stop that often interrupts our recordings. I do not try to shut down Metro.[19]

Freeman's testimony addresses DC's notorious wealth gap head on, citing this difference in wealth as the reason that noise complaints are increasing across the city, especially in Chinatown. DC does indeed have the widest wealth gap in the country: in 2014, white families had an average net worth of $284,000, and Black families had an average net worth of $3,500. Furthermore, Freeman's comparison of street musicians to the Metrobus is shrewd, as it situates musicians as a vital institution in the city, equivalent to and as necessary as public transportation. He repeated the same rhetorical gesture toward the end of his testimony, asking: "Do fire stations have to mute their sirens in residential areas?" This testimony shifted the nature of the hearing, because

---

[19] Kymone Freeman, testimony against the Amplified Noise Act, [John Wilson Building, Washington DC/July 2, 2018].

prior to this, in the room itself, the bill was being presented as a slam dunk. Scores of people lined up to testify, organized and coordinated by a special interest group in the neighborhood, to present the maximum impact on the council. This was not an instance of a number of concerned neighbors randomly coming together to fight for an issue they all believed in, but rather an organized effort. At the time Freeman testified, several hours into the hearing, social media had begun to latch on to the bill, presenting it simply as an issue of being jailed for noise: for cookouts, music, and everyday life.

Although this testimony inspired applause from the musicians in the audience at the hearing, the council did not receive it as positively. Mary Cheh, a white councilwoman for Ward 3, told Freeman that the dichotomy that he raised between white and wealthy residents and working-class Black musicians was "bull." In addition to her own frustration with Freeman's testimony, which resulted in a tense exchange between the two, Cheh specifically invited other community members to respond to him, a kind of "piling on" gesture that could have made the situation even more combative had the other witnesses chosen to respond forcefully. In sum, Cheh took offense to Freeman's assertion that the testifying residents were not victims of loud noise and music, and rejected his suggestion that the largely white population of residents and business owners could afford to soundproof their buildings.

The exchange between Freeman and Cheh provides a valuable site for an intersectional analysis of sonic and verbal aggression. The tone and accusations within his testimony caused Freeman to be heard as aggressive by the council, especially because he interrupted Cheh during their exchange, which I argue is a gendered gesture:

Cheh: Yes, I'm a little bit troubled by the way you're characterizing this because it's not just residences—

Freeman: Let me stop you right there, councilwoman, with all due respect. I'm troubled that we're having this speed of this legislation, when we have yet to address some of the other issues in the city, like displacement. I just want to say that, tit for tat, if you upset I'm upset but please continue. Please go ahead.

Cheh: No no no no, excuse me, I have the mic. You had your opportunity, this is my opportunity. I'm a little bit troubled by your testimony in respect to residences...[20]

Women are consistently interrupted by men in the workplace, so much so that people have developed methods and games to keep track of these

---

[20] From testimony against Amplified Noise Act, July 2, 2018.

disruptions.[21] Furthermore, since the council members pride themselves on creating a "DC for all," they often bristle when directly accused of supporting gentrification and displacing Black residents. In conjunction with her irritation at being accused of supporting displacement, the antagonism that Cheh exhibits is emblematic of the sonic antagonism of white womanhood. From the white woman who falsely accused Emmitt Till to the white woman who intentionally manipulated her voice in order to cause the police to harm Christian Cooper in May of 2020, the vocal exertions of white women often have detrimental consequences for Black people.[22] In the case of Freeman and Cheh, the councilwoman leveraged her power as an elected official to potentially direct vitriol toward Freeman, who, although he interrupted her, had as much right to testify as the rest of the residents who were in favor of the ANA. In the face of a testimony that drew connections between gentrification, displacement, race, and musical histories, Cheh's angry dismissiveness carried deep-seated racial implications, and further crystallized the racist implications of the bill. By considering the racial implications of the bill as something firmly out of her purview, Cheh aligned herself with the testifying residents, whom she considered to be victims of this loud noise. Taking all of this together, the gendered interruption, the tension of the ANA and its potential for criminalizing musicians, and the histories of white women using their voices to direct violence toward Black people, we begin to get a sense of how intersectional listening can lead us toward a kind of necessary complexity. Intersectional listening posits a refusal of single-axis work, of hearing a racially charged interaction as purely that. Including the auralities of gendered interruption and subsequent retaliation gets us closer to an understanding and furthermore, disruption, of matrices of power.[23]

The second testimony I draw attention to came from a white condominium owner in the Chinatown neighborhood, who was there to speak in support of the ANA. His testimony was one of several of the testimonies at the hearing

---

[21] Gendered interruptions have also been studied by researchers at Stanford University and George Washington University. Online games include "Are Men Talking Too Much," which features two buttons, labeled "dude" and "not a dude," calculating the percentage of men's conversation as the buttons are pressed in real time. See "How Often Are Women Interrupted by Men? Here's What the Research Says," advisory.com, July 7, 2017, https://www.advisory.com/daily-briefing/2017/07/07/men-interrupting-women; and Cathy Deng, "Are Men Talking Too Much?," http://arementalkingtoomuch.com/ (accessed August 26, 2024).

[22] In an exchange recorded by Christian Cooper, a Black birder in New York City, Amy Cooper (no relation) becomes increasingly agitated with him because he asked her to leash her dog and began to record her when she would not. She then threatened to call the police and tell them that "an African American man was threatening my life." When she made the call moments later, she modulated her voice up several pitches, in an effort to appear more in distress than she truly was. The video went viral several times over.

[23] Patricia Hill Collins, *Black Feminist Thought: Knowledge, Consciousness, and the Politics of Empowerment* (New York: Routledge, [1990] 2002).

that referenced Chicago as a city with noise ordinances that should be emulated by DC:

> When I visited Chicago about a month ago, I visited Michigan Avenue and talked with five busker groups that were strewn out along this very prestigious area. They had licenses. In the city of Chicago, you have to have a performance license, it's two years and $100, and if you violate the noise ordinance, the license is lifted. Number two, I went with my noise meter, and I did not encounter any levels higher than 65 decibels. As opposed to over 80 in front of my condo. The third thing, one of the buskers told me that if the law is violated, after several warnings, the police will confiscate the instruments. Confiscate the instruments. So, I saw that the buskers in Chicago, very different than the ones here, they're actually afraid of enforcement. They're afraid. They keep within boundaries, and they know what those boundaries are. So, I would be very happy to submit the Chicago Noise Ordinance.[24]

This testimony is compelling for a number of reasons. Although this area in Chicago is popular for tourists (as is Chinatown in DC), the coding of Michigan Avenue as "prestigious" is thinly veiled to describe the area as affluent, and therefore closer to an ideal of whiteness.[25] Furthermore, it was this testimony that then introduced a conversation into the hearing about the potential for confiscating and impounding musical instruments by the Metropolitan Police Department.

The most striking component of this testimony is his proposal of the adoption of Chicago's Noise Ordinance because there, musicians are afraid. He cited fear of enforcement and a fear of the police as a reason to adopt a law from another city. The testifying resident considered street musicians as people (or entities) to be kept in line within boundaries, which is largely what the other supporters of the ANA were asking for, although it was not put so bluntly by all of them. The residents at this hearing, who were primarily white, were asking the council to authorize the police to engage and enforce the noise regulations. As seen from the wide-scale protests in the summer of 2020 and smaller protests years prior, the relationship between Black residents and police officers in DC is often contentious. In fact, in the same month that the battle over the ANA was raging, councilmembers and residents were seeking

---

[24] From testimony against the Amplified Noise Act, July 2, 2018. I have refrained from using this witness's name because although this was a public hearing, I did not speak to or interview this particular witness.

[25] Wealth is often equated to whiteness, as exemplified in one of Joe Biden's 2019 presidential campaign speeches. He said that "poor kids are just as bright as white kids," a gaffe that connects racialization to wealth so tightly that children of color are inconceivable as not being poor. Matt Stevens, "Joe Biden Says 'Poor Kids' are Just as Bright as 'White Kids,'" *New York Times*, 9 August 2019, https://www.nytimes.com/2019/08/09/us/politics/joe-biden-poor-kids.html.

accountability for the activity of the Gun Recovery Unit of the MPD, which utilizes a tactic known as "jumpouts." Videos of officers searching Black men outside of a barbershop drew outrage on social media because it seemed that the officers had planted someone with a BB gun in order to facilitate the other searches. In the midst of these tensions, many community members were wary of the possibility of greater escalation. The testifying resident wanted to reproduce the kind of fear that he saw and heard from musicians in Chicago, just in front of his own condo. He wanted musicians to be quieter because they were afraid of the police. But what we know about Black people and police and fear is that the fear comes from knowing that the police may harass and murder you with impunity.

In addition to listening to individual interactions (such as those between Kymone Freeman and Councilwoman Mary Cheh), part of what intersectional listening offers as an analytical framework is aural attention to interconnected systems of oppression, and what these systems sound like in the everyday life of a gentrifying city. The systems of oppression relevant here, largely policing, have been sounding across time and space for centuries. The resident testifying in support of the ANA heard fear of the police in Chicago and was encouraged that the fear he heard in Chicago would solve his problem in DC. His testimony asked the council to consider the noise ordinance that produced said Chicagoan fear, so that it might be reproduced in a DC context. Listening intersectionally here produces a sonic spatiality that accounts for and is situated within an aural spacetime of policing Black people and fear. Listening speculatively across these histories helps us to understand how deeply the fabric of white supremacy is woven across the US.

Historian Khalil Muhammad, in a biography of Black criminality in the United States, argues that understanding Blackness as criminal has contributed to understandings of what Blackness *is*.[26] Similar gestures have been made in reference to Black sound, because understanding Black sound as too loud, too noisy, and out of place, stabilizes an understanding of what Blackness sounds like. Herein lies one of the ironies of the hearing. Several residents testified that they did not want the music to stop, and that they thought the music brought vibrancy to the neighborhood. At the same time, however, they were asking specifically for the police to be allowed to enforce the noise ordinances, through fines, jail time, and the seizing of equipment. This contradiction is an opportunity for listening intersectionally to the hegemony of policing. People claim that they love the music and want no harm to come to the musicians and

---

[26] Khalil Gibran Muhammad, *The Condemnation of Blackness: Race, Crime, and the Making of Modern Urban America, With a New Preface* (Cambridge, MA: Harvard University Press, 2019).

then still ask for policing. There is a dissonance here, between the willful ignorance about the level of danger that the police pose to people of color as well as a driving need to utilize the tools made available to citizens for their safety and comfort, namely the police. Public opinion is also a factor here, where social media very quickly sided with the musicians, and those testifying in favor of the ANA depicted themselves as "pro-music" so as to resist the label of "gentrifier" that was being thrust upon them.

The Rally

In response to the events of the hearing and the upcoming council vote, local independent radio station We Act Radio held an emergency press conference and rally at the corner of 7th Street and H Street NW, in the heart of DC's Chinatown Gallery Place neighborhood. The rally featured a combination of performances, speeches, chants, and DJ sets, all presented to raise awareness about the ANA and the implications of the legislation on the city's musical community. The event was a who's who of the DC's music community, including representatives from groups such as a One Love Massive, Listen Local First, and Kokayi, acting in his capacity as representative from the local chapter of the Grammys.[27] Although the rally was peaceful, the Metropolitan Police Department displayed a highly visible police presence throughout the duration of the event, and organizers repeatedly asked for demonstrators to keep the sidewalk clear on 7th Street, so that the police would not have a reason to disrupt the event. The combination of police, demonstrators, musicians, teenagers, tourists, the homeless population, and media crews all congregated on one street corner produced a level of energy that was tense, hopeful, angry, and familial all at once.

The rally was hosted by Dior Ashley Brown, an emcee and activist originally from DC who spent her childhood in a military family moving around the United States before eventually returning home for high school and college. Brown has a history of combining art and activism in the city, from her work on the Big Ugly Truck to the founding of "Reformance Art," which is a collective meant to perform and reform.[28] Reformance Art was founded in

---

[27] One Love Massive is a media and creative collective founded in 2001 focused on the cultural underground of the DMV. Their headquarters are in Shaw, Washington, DC, next to the historic Howard Theatre. Listen Local First is a collective that advocates for local musicians in DC, in regard to funding, legislative support, and the like. They took a large role in organizing against the ANA.

[28] Big Ugly Truck is a performance venture that offers live mobile dance parties staged from a large truck with speakers and accompanying performers. Dior Ashley Brown performed as a part of Big Ugly Truck regularly at the corner of 14th and U Streets, an iconic space in DC both for its proximities to go-go music

2016 as a response to the election of 45. During the rally, Brown acted as both emcee and performer, keeping the energy of the crowd up and facilitating between performers and announcements alike. As emcee, Brown was responsible for delivering quick, cogent soundbites about the rally to passersby as well as those participating in the event. She engaged in a meticulous citational practice, shouting out the musicians and DJ who participated throughout the event as well as speakers and sponsors. Brown also served as public safety liaison, cautioning everyone to keep the sidewalks clear, so as to let people get home from work but also so as not to provoke the Metropolitan Police Department. Operating on multiple registers at the same time, she implored people to email their councilmembers immediately, to ask them not to vote for the bill. There was a sense of urgency about the entire event, especially because the bill was put to a vote so quickly, as "emergency legislation." Sonically, Brown as emcee embodied a kind of pedagogical repetition necessary for the rally. Black music, especially hip-hop, is traditionally built on practices of repetition, where lines and phrases are repeated often to develop participation as well as to increase fervor and intensity. Brown drew on this tradition as she managed the crowd, the performers, and also the political expectations and goals of the rally.

During our interview about the ANA, Brown attributed the success of organizing not only to the publicity that the rally drew, but also to the work behind the scenes:

> So, Listen Local First hit up everybody, like send this to your councilmen. And I had just been learning about it, and having conversations about it with this team that I work with called Big Ugly Truck. And we play outside at 14th and U. Kymone (Freeman) comes out and supports us, all that. So, we were talking about how we saw Kymone there representing, saw Malik on there and some other people, I think Kenny Sway was on there too. And with Listen Local First, they sent out an email, a blanket draft email on what you should copy and paste, add your wording, and send it to the councilmembers. So, I did that, and once I did that, I went on my Facebook, and posted it and tagged everybody on it. And I just did that because I'm like I want to fight for my community. It was instant. After that, got a gross amount of shares and follows, and my friends were like I got you Dior. And it's so natural for me, you know what I'm saying? So, we came together for the cause, so somehow one of them started the chain message and they were like yo, Dior, Kymone, Chris Naoum, come down to the Wilson Building, [and] we started whipping votes . . . So we spent

and Black Broadway, but also because of its history as the beginning site of the 1968 rebellions following the assassination of Dr. Martin Luther King Jr.

the entire day before we even got to Chinatown whipping from councilmember to councilmember's office.[29]

Brown's work during the organizing process was crucial, as she used her influence, substantial social media following, and contacts within the city's music and activist scenes to prevent the bill from passing in its original state. Brown is one in a long line of Black women organizers in DC, lending her voice and platform for an issue close to her. Women such as Anna Julia Cooper, Mary Church Terrell, and Etta Mae Horn are all a part of the legacy of Black organizing and intellectualism in the city, and Brown is no exception. In spaces where women's issues are often considered peripheral, Black women consistently take on a lion's share of the organizing labor, which cannot be ignored. The histories of Black women's organizing in Washington, DC, is particularly rich, as described by Treva Lindsey in her work on New Negro Womanhood in the city, where she considers how seemingly disparate groups of women were able to connect and build a legacy of intellect and resistance.[30] In addition to a broader collective of Black women's organizing, Black women have also specifically engaged in political artistic practice in Washington, DC. In this way, gentrification is gendered not only in how it affects different populations, but also in the ways in which organizing against gentrification is gendered. Women are often working for people that are not working for them in return.

In addition to Dior Ashley Brown, the rally comprised other Black musicians and dancers that frequent Chinatown including Vanny, a queer Black woman who performs pop song covers with a guitar and microphone, and Malik the Dope Drummer, a well-known percussionist who has gone on to compete on the national competition *America's Got Talent*. They are regulars on the scene along with a number of bucket drummers, who are a staple outside the Capital One Arena after large events and are closely related to DC's percussion based go-go music scene. Although there were quite a few performances during the rally, including rapping and MCing from Brown herself, the band that received the most attention during the rally was Kill Mo, a punk/metal band made up of four young Black men, who closed out the event. After a brief soundcheck, the lead singer offered the following explanation of the band's name: "We're Kill Mo. If y'all from the city or y'all not from the city, Kill Mo is just another way of confirming, reaffirming, stamping, or betting. So, it's like 'yeah, yeah, yeah? Kill Mo.' We do alternative, punk, metal,

---

[29] Dior Ashley Brown, interview with the author, 2018.
[30] Treva B. Lindsey, *Colored No More: Reinventing Black Womanhood in Washington, D.C.* (Champaign: University of Illinois Press, 2017).

thrash, bounce groove. We just like noise." The embrace of noise here is in direct contrast to some of the organizers' efforts to reject the label of "noise."[31] Kill Mo, in line with their punk and metal roots, reclaimed noise during their performance to argue that yes, they are noisy, and yes, they still should be able to perform on the street. Their performance is an example of Black artists and organizers with different aural philosophies working together against legislation that is harmful to Black people.

Kill Mo performed two songs at the rally, "Hourglass Betrayal" and "400 Years." The first was described by the band as a "party song," with heavy guitar licks and verses that alternated between singing and screamed lyrics, most of which were unintelligible over the sounds of the street. The second song, "400 Years," was described by the lead singer as a little heavier than the first: "This second song is about colonialism and slavery, human zoos and strange fruit."[32] He also began the song by screaming "Kill Mo," the band's namesake. Just like with Hourglass Betrayal, the verses of "400 Years" were screamed, and the guitarist sang the chorus. The bridge of the song, however, had a new element: lyrics spoken in French. The lead singer expressed the following sentiment in French: "It's the same for us, all the Africans and the African Americans. We're the same. What are you gonna do?" This last question was repeated several times before the chorus of the song returned, with some vocal harmony between the lead singer and guitarist. At the end of the song, which ended the set, the lead singer offered some parting words amid screams of "Kill Mo," namely that they were "coming for the chocolate city revival."

Kill Mo's performance was well received by the crowd, with plenty of videographers circling during their songs as well as a couple of people asking when they could see the band perform live. I focus here on the identities that the band members asserted during their performance at the rally. The members of Kill Mo first and foremost asserted their regional identity, as young Washingtonians. They did this through the explanation of their name, their DC accents, and the repeated shouting of "Kill Mo" throughout the performance. Beyond this regional identity, though, they asserted their Blackness as well. The inclusion of French in "400 Years" situated the band within a diasporic struggle for freedom, connecting the ANA to the struggles of Haiti, known across the diaspora as a symbol of freedom fighting because of the Haitian revolution and the imperialist consequences that have continued

---

[31] The embrace and theorization of noise is prevalent in Tricia Rose's *Black Noise: Rap Music and Black Culture in Contemporary America* (Middletown, CT: Wesleyan University Press, 1994).

[32] The strange fruit reference is to the 1939 song made famous by Billie Holiday, which described the chilling sight of lynched Black bodies hanging from poplar trees in the American South.

to the present day.[33] They put themselves in the same space as Haitians and Africans on the continent more broadly, further solidifying the diasporic struggle for freedom.

In addition to regional and diasporic identity, Kill Mo also asserted themselves as punk and metal musicians, which can operate as political act in itself, because it lies outside the more popular and expected Black music genres of hip-hop and R&B. The identities espoused here by Kill Mo, of a global Blackness, a fierce loyalty to Washington, DC, and to punk and metal traditions and aesthetics, are important to a practice of intersectional listening, because they provide opportunities to listen to the multitudes of young Black men. These Black men, who are often assigned dangerous two-dimensional narratives of criminality, heteronormativity, and danger, offered a fuller understanding of themselves at the rally. They invited attendees to listen against the grain with them, to a type of local and diasporic noisemaking that supported organizers working against the ANA. Intersectional listening, as both analytic and practice, considers the fullness of Black life, even as it is continually stifled by the binaries and constraints of the cisheteropatriarchy.

Conclusion

The ANA is a prime example of what gentrification sounds like in Washington, DC: a displacement of local genres of music and musicians (in this case street musicians in Chinatown), as well as increased tensions over sound, noise, and music in "public" space. Residents and workers in Chinatown, tired of the noise levels of the musicians, worked with the council to draft legislation that would allow the police to enforce the noise standards, which officers were seemingly unwilling or unable to do previously. These residents leaned on a combination of legislative and criminal justice aspects of city policies in order to take care of what they considered a problem in their neighborhood. The danger of the ANA is that requesting permission for police to escalate encounters with street musicians is actively endangering the lives of people of color. The organizers of the rally were very clear on this, adamant that this legislation had the potential to get someone killed by the police.

---

[33] Haiti's insurrection in the eighteenth century has led to a long and violent history with the Western world, including a swath of environmental racism that is seen in responses to the 2010 earthquake that devastated the island. For an ethnomusicological perspective on Haitian relationships to the environment, see Rebecca Dirksen's ecomusicological work on the subject in "Haiti's Drums and Trees: Facing Loss of the Sacred," *Ethnomusicology* 63, no. 1 (2019): 43–77.

Gentrification involves a claiming of supposedly public space by incoming populations, and the use of various authorities to maintain the exclusivity of these spaces. The news is consistently riddled with stories of Black people being put out of public spaces, out of private spaces to which they belong, and everything in between. White people call the police on Black people at Starbucks, at neighborhood pools, for selling lemonade, sleeping in university common rooms, standing out of the rain, mowing lawns, for simply existing in "white" spaces. White spaces require a kind of exclusiveness, a kind of private attitude so that Black people can be labeled unwelcome. Gentrification is one of the worst instances of this practice because whiteness then claims a space that was (or still is) inhabited by Black people. In the case of Chinatown, people have claimed that space as one that needs to be quiet, or even silent, at particular times, and they have enlisted the police to aid them in this quest. White spaces, much like whiteness itself, demand an exclusivity related to control and policing. The events of the ANA are in many ways an example of what George Lipsitz calls the "white spatial imaginary," a mechanism that "idealizes 'pure' and homogeneous spaces, controlled environments, and predictable patterns of design and behavior."[34] Enforced noise ordinances capping legal audibility at 75 feet would make Chinatown and its surrounding blocks much more predictable in terms of sonic behavior, but at the cost of enforcing desired behavior through direct engagement with law enforcement and carceral consequences.

Composer R. Murray Schafer notes that "the study of noise legislation is interesting, not because anything is ever really accomplished by it, rather because it provides us with a concrete register of acoustic phobias and nuisances."[35] In the case of this noise legislation, Black noise is treated as both phobia and nuisance, where the music is unbearable for residents of Chinatown, but street musicians themselves are treated as unapproachable and unwilling to compromise. Much like the case of Mr. Stokes refusing to sell any property in the intersection at 7th and Florida, there is also something to be said for Black refusal here. The musicians are loud, they are amplified, and all evidence points to them not turning their music down, or only turning it down at certain times of the day. Without knowing how many times specific musicians or groups were approached before legislation was drafted, what can we say about refusal here, and the idea of "being difficult?" I would say here that immediate and consistent compliance with the demands of business owners and residents in Chinatown is not necessarily the "right" answer. Because once you turn your

---

[34] George Lipsitz, *How Racism Takes Place* (Philadelphia: Temple University Press, 2011), 29.
[35] R. Murray Schafer, *The Tuning of the World* (New York: Knopf, 1977), 111.

music down a little, is that the beginning of the end? If you turn it down once, will they eventually want it turned off? There is something to be respected about refusal even when compliance is being presented as the best, most reasonable path forward. Even if the musicians rejected proposals to turn down their music, they still should not have been treated as a public health crisis or threatened with jail time for playing amplified music on the street.

The fear and dismissal of Black music is happening all over the country, with legislation and arrests happening in cities such as Oakland, California and Austin, Texas.[36] It is important to lay bare the histories of policing and legislating Black sound, and to parse the ways in which language and soundscapes are regimented to dismiss particular racialized sound practices. The events outlined here are only a snapshot in time of a larger process. Although the emergency legislation was withdrawn from the council the day after the rally, another hearing to reintroduce the bill took place in October 2018, and eventually the bill was shelved for revisitation, in part because of the #DontMuteDC movement that began in April 2019. In 2021, Ward 1 Councilmember Brianne Nadeau introduced a bill called "Harmonious Living Amendment Act of 2021," which outlines new soundproofing standards for both residential and mixed-use buildings in areas of the city that feature a great deal of entertainment. The language in the newest bill is directly influenced by the advocacy and organizing of organizations like We Act Radio and Listen Local First, who long argued for soundproofing standards and moving away from calling music from street performers "noise." In addition to the soundproofing standards, the bill also requires the following stipulations: "Bill 24-159 ... would create a grant program for soundproofing entertainment venues and creates a property tax deduction for soundproofing buildings. It also requires the Mayor to publish a report on strategies to accommodate outdoor performances."[37] The bill was introduced in March 2021 and as of April 6, 2021, has been referred to the committee on business and economic development as well as the committee of the whole. The Harmonious Living Amendment Act is a step in the right direction regarding whose responsibility it is to manage sonic expectations in busy city areas, but as long as gentrification continues, conversations about noise, Blackness, and criminality will as well. All throughout the city, cookouts, family gatherings, impromptu protests, and block parties are

---

[36] See Zak Cheney-Rice, "A Black Church in Gentrifying Oakland Faces a $3,529 Fine for Being Too Loud," *Mic*, October 16, 2015, https://www.mic.com/articles/126871/a-black-church-in-gentrifying-oakland-faces-a-3-529-fine-for-being-too-loud; and Kevin Curtin, "Don Pitts Calls It Quits: City Music Manager Resigns Citing Bureaucracy," *Austin Chronicle*, February 14, 2017.

[37] District of Columbia B159: Harmonious Living Amendment Act of 2021, TrackBill, https://trackbill.com/bill/district-of-columbia-bill-159-harmonious-living-amendment-act-of-2021/2089794/ (accessed January 29, 2023).

threatened by a refusal to consider other options to settle differences between residents and business owners besides direct confrontation with the police. My goal in marking the sonorities of the ANA is not to track silences and amplifications neighborhood by gentrifying neighborhood, but rather to utilize intersectional listening to make audible what violences are enacted in the name of a "peaceful" night's sleep.

Coda: Freedom Sounds in the Nation's Capital

Summer 2022. The first time in over two years that I felt even remotely comfortable attending large events in Washington, DC since COVID quarantine began in March of 2020. I was excited to do fieldwork, to reacquaint myself with live music in DC, and see folks that I had not seen since I had done the majority of my fieldwork in 2018. Starting in June of 2022, the mantra was "we outside all summer." My first weekend in the city I went to one event, an open studios party at STABLEArts, a gallery that houses studios for over twenty local artists. The weekend after I graduated to two events, the capital pride parade in downtown DC and a beautiful musical exploration of Black spirituality through a Black queer lens. These events were a warm-up for the following weekend's big event: Pharrell's Something in the Water Festival, a three-day music festival in downtown DC that fell on the weekend of Juneteenth. The premise of the festival was compelling: Something in the Water first took place in 2019 in Virginia Beach, Pharrell's hometown. The next two years were cancelled because of the pandemic, and when it came time to make decisions about the 2022 festival, Pharrell made the decision to remove it from his hometown, because the city of Virginia Beach was more concerned with losing the festival than they were with the police killing his cousin, Donovan Lynch, in March of 2021. The lack of transparency regarding the shooting, combined with the council's continued attention to Something in the Water instead of public safety issues, led to Pharrell's decision to remove the festival from Virginia Beach. Pharrell and his team then proposed relocating the festival to DC, a decision Mayor Muriel Bowser wholeheartedly approved of. The festival raised DC's musical and cultural profile and drew thousands of people downtown. It was scheduled for Juneteenth weekend, only the second weekend that Juneteenth has been mandated a federal holiday since Joe Biden deemed it so in 2021. The freedom symbolism was compounded several times over. DC, the nation's capital, aka chocolate city, on Juneteenth weekend, during Black music month, was hosting the music festival of one of the most influential artists of the past century. This was to be a weekend to solidify the

Intersectional Listening. Allie Martin, Oxford University Press. © Oxford University Press 2025.
DOI: 10.1093/9780197671603.003.0009

city's reputation as a focal point of Black life, especially Black millennial life. It was a win for the city several times over.

Yes, it was a win for the city several times over—but it was expensive. Tickets for the events averaged $400 each, and fees for each ticket type were $50. There were no one-day passes available; you had to go for all three days or you couldn't go. There were mechanisms to offset cost, with specific days for DC and VA locals to buy discounted tickets, and every graduating high school senior in DC being given free passes to the festival. For everyone else, though, the festival costs remained exorbitant. The costs to the festival bothered many local organizers, and groups like Harriet's Wildest Dreams took matters into their own hands by organizing a show elsewhere in the city, at Freedom Plaza. They got go-go bands such as Reaction, Ambition Band, TOB, and local artists like Patience Sings to perform, gave out free water and food, and made it a community event. Moechella also hosted an event in the city on Juneteenth. Circling around these three performance events were countless happy hours, club events, parties, and community programs. It was, perhaps, the most lit weekend in DC the entire summer, and I was excited to be a part of it. This, to me, was what gentrification sounded like in 2022: a Black festival coming to DC, as a part of a partnership between a Black Mayor and a Black artist, for a weekend dedicated to celebrating Black freedom that many working-class and poor Black people were excluded from. Amidst this exclusion, there were the continued sounds of resistance and resilience that collide against the sonorities of Black capitalism that flow freely within the city. Black capitalism, a political system in which Black people to individually and/or collectively benefit from the capitalist system in the Western world through ownership and exploitation of labor, runs rampant through popular music, especially hip-hop.[1] These kinds of disparities reckon with DC as a chocolate city that continues to exclude Black people are what gentrification sounds like in DC, as the city hits the limits of Black capitalism that only serves creative classes and elites rather than all Black people in the city.

I was excited to see the go-go bands on the Something in the Water lineup, with Backyard performing on Saturday and Rare Essence and TOB performing on Sunday. I wanted to see how the crowds interacted with these bands, and how the city swelled with the festival before returning to normal.

---

[1] Rappers like Jay-Z and Sean "Diddy" Combs promote the adoption of Black capitalism through their music and business ventures, encouraging people to buy up their own blocks, own property, hustle, rise and grind, and invest in risky ventures like cryptocurrency. These promotions neglect to explain to people that Jay-Z and Diddy are as rich as they are precisely because their fans are not. Everyone cannot be a billionaire, that would defeat the purpose and destroy the planet (even faster). For more on Black capitalism, see Arthur L. Tolson, "Historical and Modern Trends in Black Capitalism," *The Black Scholar* 6, no. 7 (1975): 8–14.

June 17–19 was going to be an amazing weekend in DC. The rest happened very quickly: on June 13 I got a notification that someone at an event that I attended on June 12 had tested positive for COVID-19. On June 14 I had the dreaded tickle in my throat, and by the next morning I tested positive. Festival dreams dashed, I spent the weekend watching the Amazon Prime livestream of the festival and monitoring the social media hashtags, especially "#sitw." My fieldwork became digital. I include my own COVID-19 story to say that although much of the country has decided to pretend that COVID doesn't exist anymore, it is still very much real. And although masked at all of the events I had attended thus far, I still caught it. This is fieldwork during the pandemic, where your best hopes and preparations are no match for a global pandemic. That said, here is what I can say about Juneteenth 2022 in Washington, DC.

The Profitability of Black Freedom

In the introduction to this book, I recounted the events of DC's Emancipation Day celebration in 2018, where I remarked that Muriel Bowser's performance of freedom was not specifically Black, but rather a kind of harmful inclusivity positioned strategically to include the entire city, especially white newcomers. She leaned toward statehood as a mode freedom for all, rather than specifically addressing the harms of chattel slavery. As I write this conclusion in 2023, freedom performances have changed. In May of 2020, the world watched in horror at a video of police officer Derek Chauvin kneeled on George Floyd's neck and killed him. Due to the murders of Floyd, Breonna Taylor, Tony McDade, and others, the United States erupted in a torrent of uprisings against police brutality and racial injustice. These protests were so widespread and passionate that seemingly every major corporation in the United States felt forced to respond. They issued statement after corporate statement affirming that Black Lives Matter, with some going so far as to invest large amounts of money in efforts for racial justice. Wells Fargo, for example, promised to double Black leadership by 2025, facilitate anti racism training for their staff and leadership, and more. Nike promoted a Black woman, Felicia Mayo, to be their "Diversity Chief," and pledged $140 million dollars over the course of ten years to work toward racial justice with local and national organizations.[2] Although there have been countless diversity

---

[2] Yume Murphy, "One Year after #BlackoutTuesday, What Have Companies Really Done for Racial Justice?," *Vox*, June 2, 2021, https://www.vox.com/the-goods/22463723/Blackout-tuesday-blm-sephora-starbucks-nike-glossier.

officer promotions, hundreds of millions of dollars donated to causes of racial justice, there has been no racial reckoning, no abolition, no consistent defunding of police departments.[3] Police killings have continued, as evidenced by the murder of murder of Tyre Nichols by the Memphis Police Department in January 2023. Companies and institutions have become adept at making statements and pledging dollars, but these remain performances of intervention and racial justice, albeit well-rehearsed.

Governmental officials of Washington, DC have not been exempt from performances of racial justice in 2020. On June 5, 2020, Mayor Bowser authorized a section of 16th Street NW to be painted with the words "Black Lives Matter" in yellow lettering, and the street name was officially changed to Black Lives Matter Plaza. This stretch of 16th Street is directly in front of the White House at 1600 Pennsylvania Avenue NW, and Bowser's authorization of BLM plaza was heralded by many as a bold move for a Black woman mayor, because she challenged one of the most outwardly white supremacist presidents that the United States has seen in the twenty-first century. The city streets have become a powerful symbolic battleground for the republican white house administration and the apparently progressive mayor of a city that is still majority African American. On June 1, 2020, Trump incited violence against people in the city who were protesting the death of George Floyd and others who have been killed by the police. In order to create a photo op at St. John's Episcopal Church, many people were tear gassed, kettled, and physically moved by various law enforcement agencies, from the Metropolitan Police Department to Park Police to Secret Service, to clear the way for him. The violence of that event was decried by many, and Black Lives Matter Plaza was revealed four days later. Downtown DC becomes a symbolic and violent space where people try to stake their claim on the city, who owns the streets, and who owns the right to exist and protest in them.

The plaza has indeed become an important symbol for many, holding protests of those that are both for and against the Black Lives Matter movement. Despite the power and publicity in this challenge, many dismissed the creation of Black Lives Matter Plaza as an empty performance, because it did not come with any significant reform to the Metropolitan Police Department, which killed more people in 2021 than in 2020.[4] In their official statement, Black Lives Matter activist Anthony Lorenzo Green remarked that "the mural

---

[3] Wesley Lowery, "Why There Was No Racial Reckoning," *The Atlantic*, February 8, 2023, https://www.theatlantic.com/ideas/archive/2023/02/tyre-nichols-death-memphis-george-floyd-police-reform/672986.

[4] The violence from MPD is not new either, with the *Washington Post* reporting in 1998 that the department led the United States in shootings. Jeff Leen, Jo Craven, David Jackson, and Sari Horwitz, "District Police Lead Nation in Shootings," *Washington Post*, November 15, 1998.

did not stop the DC Metropolitan Police Department (MPD) from murdering Deon Kay, Karon Hylton-Brown, or Terrance Palmer. It did nothing to stop homicides, jumpouts, police terror or otherwise change the material conditions of Black people in DC."[5] Green's statement speaks to the limits of performativity and the lived conditions of Black people. As mayor, Bowser has the political power to make significant changes to the Metropolitan Police Department and how they operate, but the organizers saw the plaza as only an empty gesture, devoid of any real change to operations. This is a complicated gesture because it is indeed a bold move, as the mayor of a city that is taxed without representation, to stand up to the federal government and paint the slogan of the movement that they have tried to kill since it began in 2012. And yet representation and gesture are not enough, nor have they ever been. Many activists, organizers, and others are done with statements and are more than ready for legislative and financial action from local governments and police departments. For many, there is nothing left but the direct improvement of material conditions for Black people.

Bowser's creation of BLM Plaza is an example of what Olúfẹ́mi O. Táíwò calls "elite capture," where during the 2020 uprisings, "two strategic trends in the response quickly became clear: the elites' tactic of performing symbolic identity politics to pacify protestors without material reforms . . . in a stunningly clear summary of the first trend, the mayor of Washington, DC, had 'Black Lives Matter' painted on streets near the White House, atop which protestors continued to be brutalized."[6] Performances have power, but performances alone do not prevent rents from rising or the city from becoming more exclusive. Since 2018, performances of freedom sounds have changed, become more intense and more focused on Black pain and Black life, but they remain performances. These performances have changed in part because Black freedom and Black freedom sounds are more profitable now than they were when I started this work in 2013. Since the murder of George Floyd, police departments continue to receive more and more funding for "training," rents continue to rise, and companies pour more and more money into saying that Black Lives Matter. Black sound makes money, and the acknowledgment of Black life makes money. This capitalist exploitation of Black Lives Matter and Black death, especially at the hands of the police, is within

---

[5] Anthony Lorenzo Green, "Mayor Bowser Painted Over DC BLM Mural," May 12, 2021. https://www.dcblm.org/in-the-media/official-statement-of-black-lives-matter-dc-on-removal-of-the-mural-from-black-lives-matter-plaza-and-plan-for-permanent-art-installation.

[6] Olúfẹ́mi O. Táíwò, *Elite Capture: How the Powerful Took Over Identity Politics* (Chicago: Haymarket Books, 2022), 3.

the locus of Black branding that facilitates gentrification, as well as the fetishization of Black sound and aesthetics that have facilitated much of American music-making. This is capitalism making money off of Black pain, off of efforts of inclusion. Juneteenth, for example, has become marketed like a Memorial Day sale or Presidents' Day sale, with furniture sales, merchandise, and ice cream flavors. Walmart came under fire for selling products that said "it's the freedom for me," phrasing that appropriates African American Vernacular English.[7] Juneteenth as federal holiday has become another day off for people, rather than a humble commemoration of the duplicity and violence that led to Black people being enslaved for two and a half years beyond the signing of the Emancipation Proclamation.

Something in the Water

Within this soundscape of exploitation and Black capitalism, Something in the Water showed that while gentrification compresses the financial viability and stability of the city for many Black musicians and residents, Washington, DC remains central to a global Black music soundscape. From music to fashion to cultural histories, DC was the right city at the right time for SITW, and in some ways, processes of gentrification are what made the festival possible. The Washington, DC of the 1990s—nicknamed the murder capital of the world—would not have been approached to host a festival like SITW. Listening intersectionally requires that we continue to ask the question, "what does gentrification make possible?" The festival did a fair amount of work to ensure that go-go music and DC cultural practices were well represented at the festival. Many bands had spots on the lineup: Backyard Band, Rare Essence, TOB, and more. More than just performances, these bands were also invited to interviews and podcasts with Pharrell and rapper Pusha T where they discussed their influences, collaboration, and what it means for the DMV region to thrive musically and otherwise. Pharrell's citational practice was a key component of these events, with him remarking often about go-go music and the culture of DC. In his headlining set, he played Nelly's "Hot in Herre," which he (as a part of the production collective The Neptunes) produced in 2002 with a prominent sample of Chuck Brown and the Soul Searcher's 1979

---

[7] Amber Corrine, "Walmart Apologizes For Juneteenth-Themed Ice Cream, Pulls Pints From Shelves." VIBE, May 27, 2022, https://www.vibe.com/news/national/walmart-juneteenth-ice-cream-apology-1234664549/.

hit "Bustin Loose." During the set, "Hot in Herre" faded into "Bustin Loose" as dancers moved around the stage and Pharrell danced around singing along to the classic song. After the song, he explained why he felt the need to play it: "If it wasn't for Chuck Brown and the Soul Searchers, I wouldn't be making beats" and "if it wasn't for DC and go-go and what it did to us down in Virginia Beach, it changed our lives." Pharrell also enlisted DC band Black Alley as a backing band for his set, which earned them praise on social media for their versatility and positive representation of the city. This citational practice refutes the narrowness that is sometimes placed on go-go music. These musicians have a hard time finding venues due to gentrification, liquor licenses, and high insurance and liability costs, but go-go artists exist in spaces of national and international acclaim. In conversations about displacement and dislocation it is crucial to add more dimensions to our listening, because there are emancipatory soundscapes being crafted every day. Rather than only contraction gentrification acts more like an accordion, moving through periods of contraction and expansion.

In addition to Pharrell's set, shout-outs to DC were all over the festival, from the surface level "I see a lot of beautiful ladies in DC" that many artists exclaimed to the more genuine, such as when Chicago rapper Saba mentioned during his set that he had never been to DC before but had really been enjoying himself. The go-go bands themselves were unapologetically representing the city during their sets. Backyard Band put on a set on Saturday afternoon that left social media appreciative of the go-go giants. They went through many of their hits, such as "Pretty Girls," and some of other people's hits that have become their hits, like Adele's "Hello." Backyard Band made no attempt to explain what go-go music was and trusted that people knew their songs (or were unconcerned about the alternative). The #DontMuteDC movement was also on display at Something in the Water, where the band Rare Essence had on #DontMuteDC t-shirts as a part of their signature red and white ensemble that they've been rocking since the 1980s.

Something in the Water brought to life an important truth about gentrification, which is that it opens doors for various opportunities that would not be open otherwise. These opportunities come with a cost, though. I once interviewed a business owner in Shaw that did not want to be identified or on record because he told me that gentrification had actually increased the profits of his business. He knew that this story was not the dominant narrative about gentrification, in scholarship or popular media or otherwise, and did not want to be criticized or penalized for the success that new residents and their finances were bringing him. Something in the Water brought a number of opportunities to local musicians, from Black Alley to Backyard to TOB.

Harriet's Wildest Dreams

In addition to Something in the Water and Moechella, there was another free, community focused event at Freedom Plaza in downtown DC. The event was sponsored by Harriet's Wildest Dreams, an organization that takes their namesake from Harriet Tubman and makes a specific claim on the phrase, "you are your ancestors wildest dreams." The organization is "a Black-led abolitionist community defense hub centering all Black lives most at risk for state-sanctioned violence in the Greater Washington area."[8] The organizers were appalled at the costs of the Something in the Water Festival and lamented the expenses as another facet of gentrification and the city not really caring about working-class and poor Black people. In response, they created their own event, which featured a number of different performers, local and national. There was go-go band TOB, Ayanna Gregory (daughter of comedian and activist Dick Gregory), singer Patience Sings, and more. They advertised the event as the "Juneteenth Chocolate City Jubilee," and one of the event flyers on Instagram was modeled after a "Globe" poster. This is a classic design style in the Washington, DC area, with many go-go posters being designed in the style in the 1980s and 1990s and now various DC based events being designed in that way even after the Globe publishing company has since closed its doors and donated its collection to the Maryland Institute College of Art. Globe posters feature large block lettering and various color palettes, with this event using red, Black, and green, all colors that symbolize Black freedom when used together. The event featured a COVID safety table, a DJ, live music, posters, t-shirts, and more. The crowd at the Jubilee was sparser than that of Moechella or Something in the Water but they were still appreciative of the music, and there were still hundreds of people that came out to show their support. The Juneteenth Chocolate City Jubilee is an example of an emancipatory soundscape, a sonic environment in which Black people are striving toward sounding without subjugation. In considering the most marginalized among us, offering seats, water, resources, and community education, the Jubilee demonstrated what it is to be of the community. Events like these speak to the notion of the "already otherwise" that I discussed in

---

[8] "Mission," Harriet's Wildest Dreams. https://www.harrietsdreams.org/mission (accessed January 9, 2024).

the introduction.[9] The alternative worlds we need are already here and being sounded into existence, conjured and practiced by organizations like Harriet's Wildest Dreams.

Moechella

In addition to Something in the Water, the organizers at Long Live Go-Go also held one of their Moechella events discussed in Chapter 3. This one was a classic, held at 14th and U Street where the original one was held, with Bounce Beat legends TOB and New Impressionz. It was also Father's Day, and a video went viral of a father holding his infant up above the crowd like Simba from the Lion King. It was a beautiful moment, an "everything the light touches is yours" type of moment, with everything being the hundreds of Black people gathered to support go-go and Black life in the city. Unfortunately the event ended in violence, with three people shot and one fifteen-year-old boy named Chase Poole killed. The narrative from city officials immediately, without question, became that the event was unpermitted. This was an untruthful way of scapegoating the organizers because not only had the event been running in various capacities since 2018, it was also in part sponsored by the mayor's office of local creativity, "202 Creates." There is also footage of one of the mayor's deputy mayors promoting the event on the local news days before it occurred. The Metropolitan Police Department was present at the event, they assisted with or at least didn't hinder the streets being blocked for the event. Despite this evidence of official sponsorship, there was still violence, and the city's disavowal of Moechella after the violence occurred is a regular that reminder that governments and police departments lie. The first statement that Minneapolis police released about the murder of George Floyd said that his death was the result of a "medical incident" and made no mention of any knee on any neck.

Even outside of city officials, narratives of the shooting remained conflicted. Big G, lead talker of Backyard Band, ended his set at Something in the Water by saying "tell the youngins put them guns down, they messing up the whole town," and "a little love won't hurt nobody." Only two months after this performance, Big G tragically lost his son Kavon Glover to gun violence in the city, which makes his plea at Something in the Water all the more searing. Social media largely seemed to "side" with Something in the Water over Moechella, questioning why the out-of-town festival was able to happen "peacefully" and

---

[9] Ashon T. Crawley, *Blackpentecostal Breath: The Aesthetics of Possibility* (New York: Fordham University Press, 2016).

Moechella wasn't able to. After the shooting, social media, specifically Twitter and Facebook, were alight with commentary and analyses of the event and the violence that occurred there. A local newscaster, John Gonzalez, tweeted the following: "BREAKING: No arrests have been made in DC after 4 people were shot including a police officer. Sadly, a fifteen-year-old had died. The chaos unfolded during a Juneteenth HBCU event last night." I (somewhat sarcastically) replied to the tweet with "Since when is Moechella an HBCU event?" This question was sarcastic because Moechella is not an HBCU event. HBCU, in this case, is also synonymous with Howard University, which is less than a mile from where Moechella took place at 14th and U Streets NW. The newscaster replied to me with "It was organized with college students celebrating Juneteenth. Heartbreaking for me personally who has a daughter who attends Howard University currently." Again, this information is, from everything I know, incorrect. What is frustrating about a newscaster making these claims is that specificity is important on both sides of the coin. We need to be sure about when an event is only go-go related, and we also need to be sure when an event is not. So often when violence occurs at a go-go, the go-go is blamed, and it is this lack of specificity that has led to the stigmatization of go-go music during nearly all of its history. In a similar vein, eliding Howard University and Moechella insinuates that Howard University is the sponsor and supporter of all pro-Black go-go activity that happens within a mile radius of its campus, and that is simply not true. Specificity about the city, its intracultural conversations, class differences, and social stratification is important to understanding the violence that occurred at Moechella.

This is especially true with the go-go community, where misinformation is common due to the various informal and formal media channels that inform the culture. Chris Richards, pop music critic of the *Washington Post*, noted this difficulty when reporting on go-go in 2013, where "I try to talk to at least five times as many people as actually get into the story . . . you've got to get, especially with go-go, where it's kind of mysterious and there's no central media . . . you've got talk to a whole breadth of people to kind of get a real picture of what's really happening."[10] This remains true in the go-go community but it is a practice and a labor that many journalists and politicians are simply not willing to do. One of the best analyses of the violence at Moechella came from Meagan Jordan writing for *Rolling Stone*. Her piece, "How a Celebration of Go-Go Music Became a Scapegoat for Violence in D.C.," did a brilliant job of outlining how Moechella and its parent organization, Long Live Go-Go, have

---

[10] Chris Richards, interview with the author, 2013.

contributed to the cultural health of DC, and how the shooting that killed fifteen-year-old Chase Poole was the only act of violence documented in the organization's history.[11] Jordan also interviewed Natalie Hopkinson, who continues to be an advocate for the music, who declared simply that "having a permit is not a solution to gun violence." Music journalism is a key part of these conversations, and I am grateful for Jordan's work, which astutely cut through many of the narratives that were being weaved through the city about Moechella and the inevitability of gun violence in the city.

My question here is not one of blame or why one festival was able to exist without gun violence and the other couldn't. The answer to that question largely lies in questions of security, surveillance, and what we mean when we say "peacefully." Something in the Water banned backpacks, only allowed small bags, featured security to get into the festival as well as re-entry after leaving, and cost over $400 to enter. Something in the Water also featured a number of other moments of unsafety, where people passed out regularly from heat and overcrowding and a lack of access to water, among other things. Moechella did not have the same security protocols in place, so guns were more easily brought into the space. Rather than weighing the safety benefits of security and surveillance, I ask why gun violence is so inescapable in the United States, particularly for children and young adults. The shootings at Moechella came after a rash of crime in the city and several mass shootings in the United States, most famously the white supremacist killings in Buffalo, New York and the classroom of schoolchildren killed in Uvalde, Texas. Why is this kind of violence so imaginable in the United States, and how can we listen intersectionally to a freedom weekend to try to imagine more emancipatory, more liberatory soundscapes? What would it sound like to not be under the constant threat of gun violence? Chance the Rapper famously described his hatred of summer in Chicago in "Paranoia": "It just got warm out, this this shit I've been warned about/I hope that it storm in the morning, I hope that it's pouring out/I hate crowded beaches, I hate the sound of fireworks/And I ponder what's worse between knowing it's over and dying first/'Cause everybody dies in the summer." Besides hating the sound of fireworks, Chance denounces the entire season, suggesting that if you need to say goodbye to someone you should tell them during the springtime.

Can Juneteenth freedom celebrations in a gentrifying DC, fraught as they are with violence and exclusivity, help us to hear more liberatory soundscapes,

---

[11] Meagan Jordan, "How a Celebration of Go-Go Music Became a Scapegoat For Violence in D.C.," *Rolling Stone* July 2, 2022, https://www.rollingstone.com/music/music-features/how-a-celebration-of-go-go-music-became-a-scapegoat-for-violence-in-d-c-1372069/.

away from the threats of gun violence, where loud noises are welcome signs of life rather than harbingers of death to come? I imagine an emancipatory soundscape to be such a space in which we are not constantly listening for the threat of gun violence, which colored all of the city's celebrations. Something in the Water responded by limiting items and operating in a space of security and surveillance. Moechella responded by collaborating with the mayor's office as well as the Metropolitan Police Department, but when this collaboration failed to engender the safety that they were hoping, dealt with the fallout and consistent mishearing that happens when violence occurs in Black neighborhoods. They dealt with the fallout of being immediately cast aside and dismissed as unpermitted, unallowed, and unauthorized. Go-go music and Black people move in and out of profitability as DC gentrifies, sometimes a selling point for a music festival, and other times easily dismissed because of the heartbreaking gun violence that upends entire communities.

I began this book with a commitment to listening to how Black people experience gentrification as a racialized, sonic phenomenon. The events of Juneteenth weekend are a beautifully complicated example of such a thing. Countless local Black-owned businesses and vendors, local bands, go-go and non–go-go alike, received national and international recognition for their participation in the Something in the Water festival. Disturbed by the exclusivity of the festival, other organizers put together a free event for those unable or unwilling to attend SITW, offering music and community for free. Less than a mile from these two events, a child was shot and killed, and the organizers of Moechella, a movement that has completely shifted conversations about Black life and sonic preservation DC, was almost unequivocally blamed for the violence as though they alone were responsible for centuries of disinvestment, poverty, and cultures of gun violence, toxic masculinity, and retaliation. These conflicting and overlapping events begin to paint the picture of what it means to be Black in gentrifying space in DC. There is a plethora of opportunities in the city, some closed or open depending on one's financial viability. But even within these parameters of exclusion, there are always soundscapes of resilience sounding out into the city. People are always making it.

I am reminded of a poem by Clint Smith about those who make it and those that don't: "When people say, 'we have made it through worse before,' all I hear is the wind slapping against the gravestones of those that did not make it."[12] Many will remain in DC. Many Black people will make it, will continue to shift and bend and make and remake the city in their likeness.

---

[12] Clint Smith, "When People Say, 'We Have Made It through Worse Before,'" *Wildness*, 2019, https://readwildness.com/19/smith-people.

Many new businesses will be created, bands formed, genres of music composed and performed. Go-go will keep the people going on the dance floor. But many will not. Many will continue to die at the hands of police violence, at the hands of gun violence within their communities, many will leave for more affordable neighborhoods in more affordable cities, many will tire of taxation without representation and the continuing rule of Congress. Listening to gentrification requires that we hear it all: the opportunities, the movement, the losses, and the wind slapping against the gravestones of those lost to neoliberal capitalism, carceral and state violence, and the continued development of Washington, DC.

Bibliography

Aalbers, Manuel B. "Introduction to the Forum: From Third to Fifth-Wave Gentrification." *Journal of Economic and Human Geography* 110, no. 1 (2019): 1–11.

Abu-Lughod, Lila. "Writing Against Culture." In *The Cultural Geography Reader*, edited by Timothy Oakes and Patricia L. Price. New York: Routledge, 2008.

Adeyemi, Kemi. *Feels Right: Black Queer Women and the Politics of Partying in Chicago*. Durham, NC: Duke University Press, 2022.

Agard-Jones, Vanessa. "What the Sands Remember." *GLQ: A Journal of Lesbian and Gay Studies* 18, no. 2–3 (2012): 325–46.

Alexander, Michelle. *The New Jim Crow: Mass Incarceration in the Age of Colorblindness*. New York: The New Press, 2020.

Ali, Abdul. "How Washington, D.C., Turned Its Back on Go-Go, the Music It Invented." *The Atlantic*, July 2, 2012. https://www.theatlantic.com/entertainment/archive/2012/07/how-washington-dc-turned-its-back-on-go-go-the-music-it-invented/259147/.

Alim, H. Samy. "Who's Afraid of the Transracial Subject? Raciolinguistics and the Political Project of Transracialization." In *Raciolinguistics: How Language Shapes Our Ideas About Race*, edited by H. Samy Alim, John R. Rickford, and Arnetha F. Ball. New York: Oxford University Press, 2016.

Anderson, Elijah. *Streetwise: Race, Class, and Change in an Urban Community*. Chicago: University of Chicago Press, 1990.

Asch, Chris Myers, and George Derek Musgrove. *Chocolate City: A History of Race and Democracy in the Nation's Capital*. Chapel Hill: University of North Carolina Press, 2017.

Bailey, Moya. *Misogynoir Transformed: Black Women's Digital Resistance. Misogynoir Transformed*. New York: NYU Press, 2021.

Bailey, Phillip M., and Tessa Duvall, "Breonna Taylor Warrant Connected to Louisville Gentrification Plan, Lawyers Say." *Courier-Journal*, July 5, 2020. https://www.courier-journal.com/story/news/crime/2020/07/05/lawyers-breonna-taylor-case-connected-gentrification-plan/5381352002/.

Barz, Gregory F., and Timothy J. Cooley. *Shadows in the Field: New Perspectives for Fieldwork in Ethnomusicology*. New York: Oxford University Press, 2008.

Bazelon, Emily. "White People Are Noticing Something New: Their Own Whiteness." *New York Times*, June 13, 2018. https://www.nytimes.com/2018/06/13/magazine/white-people-are-noticing-something-new-their-own-whiteness.html.

Bolash-Goza, Tanya. *Before Gentrification: The Creation of DC's Racial Wealth Gap*. Berkeley: University of California Press, 2023.

Boyd, Michelle. "Defensive Development: The Role of Racial Conflict in Gentrification." *Urban Affairs Review* 43, no. 6 (2008): 751–76.

Branigin, Anne. "Exclusive: New Report Shows Gentrifiers Use Police to Terrorize Communities of Color—Without Even Calling 911." *The Root*, January 8, 2019. https://www.theroot.com/exclusive-new-report-shows-gentrifiers-use-police-to-t-1831576262.

brown, adrienne maree. *Pleasure Activism: The Politics of Feeling Good*. Stirling, UK: AK Press, 2019.

Brown, Jayna. *Black Utopias: Speculative Life and the Music of Other Worlds*. Durham, NC: Duke University Press, 2021.

Browne, Simone. *Dark Matters: On the Surveillance of Blackness*. Durham, NC: Duke University Press, 2015.

Burnim, Mellonee. "The Black Gospel Music Tradition: A Complex of Ideology, Aesthetic, and Behavior." In *More than Dancing: Essays on Afro-American Music and Musicians* edited by Irene Jackson, 147–67. Westport, CT: Greenwood Press, 1985.

Burnim, Mellonee. "Culture Bearer and Tradition Bearer: An Ethnomusicologist's Research on Gospel Music." *Ethnomusicology* 29, no. 3 (1985): 432–47.

Burnim, Mellonee V., and Portia K. Maultsby. *African American Music: An Introduction*. New York: Routledge, 2014.

Campt, Tina Marie. "Black Visuality and the Practice of Refusal." *Women & Performance: A Journal of Feminist Theory* 29, no. 1 (2019): 79–87.

Casteneda, Ruben. "What's the Plan?" *Washington City Paper*, March 5, 2020. http://washingtoncitypaper.com/article/176104/whats-the-plan/.

Cebul, Brent. "Tearing Down Black America." *Boston Review*, July 22, 2020.

Cheney-Rice, Zak. "A Black Church in Gentrifying Oakland Faces a $3,529 Fine for Being Too Loud." 2015. *Mic*, October 16, 2015. https://www.mic.com/articles/126871/a-Black-church-in-gentrifying-oakland-faces-a-3-529-fine-for-being-too-loud.

Cheng, William. "Black Noise, White Ears: Resilience, Rap, and the Killing of Jordan Davis." *Current Musicology*, no. 102 (2018): 115–89.

Cho, Sumi, Kimberlé Williams Crenshaw, and Leslie McCall. "Toward a Field of Intersectionality Studies: Theory, Applications, and Praxis." *Signs: Journal of Women in Culture and Society* 38, no. 4 (2013): 785–810.

Cidell, Julie. "Challenging the Contours: Critical Cartography, Local Knowledge, and the Public." *Environment and Planning A: Economy and Space* 40, no. 5 (2008): 1202–18.

Clabaugh, Jeff. "DC-Area Rents Still Rising despite National Trend Lower." *WTOP News*, April 19, 2023. https://wtop.com/business-finance/2023/04/dc-area-rents-still-rising-despite-national-trend-lower/.

Clement, Tanya E. "Word. Spoken. Articulating the Voice for High-Performance Sound Technologies for Access and Scholarship (HiPSTAS)." In *Digital Sound Studies*, edited by Mary Caton Lingold, Darren Mueller, and Whitney Trettien. Durham, NC: Duke University Press, 2018.

Clifton, Lucille. "Won't You Celebrate with Me." In *How to Carry Water: Selected Poems of Lucille Clifton*. Rochester, NY: BOA Editions, 2020.

Coates, Ta-Nehisi. *Between the World and Me*. New York: Random House, 2015.

Coates, Ta-Nehisi, and Natalie Hopkinson. "Launch Go-Go Museum and Café." Facebook Live, June 3, 2020. https://www.facebook.com/watch/live/?ref=external&v=255939005653474

Cochrane, Emily. "For D.C. Statehood Advocates, a Hearing Marks Another Step Forward." *New York Times*, September 19, 2019. https://www.nytimes.com/2019/09/19/us/politics/dc-statehood-hearing.html.

Cole, Teju. *Black Paper: Writing in a Dark Time*. Chicago: University of Chicago Press, 2021.

Collins, Patricia Hill. *Black Feminist Thought: Knowledge, Consciousness, and the Politics of Empowerment*. New York: Routledge, [1990] 2002.

Combahee River Collective. "The Combahee River Collective *Statement*." In *Home Girls: A Black Feminist Anthology*, edited by Barbara Smith. New York: Routledge, 2000.

Cooper, Anna Julia. *A Voice from the South*. Oxford: Oxford University Press, [1892] 1988.

Corrine, Amber. "Walmart Apologizes For Juneteenth-Themed Ice Cream, Pulls Pints From Shelves." *VIBE*, May 27, 2022. https://www.vibe.com/news/national/walmart-juneteenth-ice-cream-apology-1234664549

Cottom, Tressie McMillan. *Thick: And Other Essays*. New York: The New Press, 2018.

Council Office of Racial Equity. "DC Racial Equity Profile." 2021. https://www.dcracialequity.org/dc-racial-equity-profile.

Crawley, Ashon T. *Blackpentecostal Breath: The Aesthetics of Possibility*. New York: Fordham University Press, 2016.

Crenshaw, Kimberlé, Andrea Ritchie, Rachel Anspach, Rachel Gilmer, and Luke Harris. "Say Her Name: Resisting Police Brutality Against Black Women." *African American Policy Forum*, January 1, 2015. https://scholarship.law.columbia.edu/faculty_scholarship/3226.

Cross, Richard. "Towards a Practice of Palimpsestic Listening." *Organised Sound* 26, no. 1 (2021): 145–53.

Curtin, Kevin. "Don Pitts Calls It Quits: City Music Manager Resigns Citing Bureaucracy." *Austin Chronicle*, February 14, 2017.

Dasgupta, Nilanjana, Debbie E. McGhee, Anthony G. Greenwald, and Mahzarin R. Banaji. "Automatic Preference for White Americans: Eliminating the Familiarity Explanation." *Journal of Experimental Social Psychology* 36, no. 3 (2000): 316–28.

DeBonis, Mike. "No Amphitheater for Chuck Brown Park." *Washington Post*, December 1, 2021. https://www.washingtonpost.com/blogs/mike-debonis/wp/2013/08/07/no-amphitheater-for-chuck-brown-park/.

de Certeau, Michel. *The Practice of Everyday Life*. Berkeley, CA: University of California Press, 1984.

Deng, Cathy. "Are Men Talking Too Much?" http://arementalkingtoomuch.com/ (accessed August 26, 2024).

Diamond, Vern. *Of Black America*. Episode 5, "The Heritage of Slavery." Aired August 13, 1968, on CBS News.

D'Ignazio, Catherine, and Lauren F. Klein. *Data Feminism*. Cambridge, MA: The MIT Press, 2020.

D'Ignazio, Catherine, and Lauren F. Klein. 2016. "Feminist Data Visualization." https://dspace.ceid.org.tr/xmlui/handle/1/955.

Dirksen, Rebecca. "Haiti's Drums and Trees: Facing Loss of the Sacred." *Ethnomusicology* 63, no. 1 (2019): 43–77.

District of Columbia B159: Harmonious Living Amendment Act of 2021. TrackBill. https://trackbill.com/bill/district-of-columbia-bill-159-harmonious-living-amendment-act-of-2021/2089794/ (accessed January 29, 2023).

Drake, St. Clair, and Horace R. Cayton. 2015. *Black Metropolis: A Study of Negro Life in a Northern City*. Chicago: University of Chicago Press, [1945] 2015.

Du Bois, William Edward Burghardt, and Isabel Eaton. *The Philadelphia Negro: A Social Study*. Philadelphia: University of Pennsylvania Press, [1899] 1996.

Eidsheim, Nina Sun. 2019. *The Race of Sound: Listening, Timbre, and Vocality in African American Music*. Durham, NC: Duke University Press.

Fischer, Jonathan L. "Need an Art Studio? New Spaces Are Coming to Brookland and the Former Warehouse Loft." *Washington City Paper*, November 16, 2012.

Floyd, Samuel A. Jr. *The Power of Black Music: Interpreting Its History from Africa to the United States*. New York: Oxford University Press, 1996.

Forman, Murray. *The 'Hood Comes First: Race, Space, and Place in Rap and Hip-Hop*. Middletown, CT: Wesleyan University Press, 2002.

Freeman, Lance. *There Goes the Hood: Views of Gentrification from the Ground Up*. Philadelphia: Temple University Press, 2011.

Frey, William H. "The US Will Become 'Minority White' in 2045, Census Projects." *Brookings* (blog), March 14, 2018. https://www.brookings.edu/blog/the-avenue/2018/03/14/the-us-will-become-minority-white-in-2045-census-projects.

Fujikane, Candace. *Mapping Abundance for a Planetary Future: Kanaka Maoli and Critical Settler Cartographies in Hawai'i*. Durham, NC: Duke University Press, 2021.

Gastman, Roger. *Pump Me Up: DC Subculture of the 1980s*. Bethesda, MD: R. Rock Enterprises, 2013.

Gautier, Ana María Ochoa. *Aurality: Listening and Knowledge in Nineteenth-Century Colombia.* Durham, NC: Duke University Press, 2015.

Glass, Ruth. *London: Aspects of Change.* London: MacGibbon & Kee, 1964.

Golash-Boza, Tanya Maria. *Before Gentrification: The Creation of DC's Racial Wealth Gap.* Berkeley: University of California Press, 2023.

Gomez, Amanda Michelle. "Ward 7 Lacks Maternity Care Services. Mamatoto Village Wants to Change That." *DCist* (blog), June 7, 2022. https://dcist.com/story/22/06/07/dc-ward-7-mamatoto-village-new-location/.

Green, Anthony Lorenzo. "Mayor Bowser Painted Over DC BLM Mural." https://www.dcblm.org/in-the-media/official-statement-of-black-lives-matter-dc-on-removal-of-the-mural-from-black-lives-matter-plaza-and-plan-for-permanent-art-installation.

Gumbs, Alexis Pauline. *Dub: Finding Ceremony.* Durham, NC: Duke University Press, 2020.

Hackworth, Jason, and Neil Smith. "The Changing State of Gentrification." *Journal of Human and Economic Geography* 92, no. 4 (2001): 464–77.

Hadley, Fredara Mareva. "In Defense of Loud, Black Summers." *REVOLT*, July 30, 2016. https://www.revolt.tv/article/2016-07-30/18627/in-defense-of-loud-black-summers.

Hall, Stuart. "What Is This 'Black' in Black Popular Culture?" *Social Justice* 20, no. 1/2 (1993): 104–14.

Hammond, Kato. *Take Me Out to the Go-Go: The True Story of a Music Culture and the Impact It Made on the Life of One Man.* Scotts Valley, CA: CreateSpace, 2015.

Hannerz, Ulf. *Soulside: Inquiries Into Ghetto Culture and Community.* New York: Columbia University Press, 1969.

Haraway, Donna. "Situated Knowledges: The Science Question in Feminism and the Privilege of Partial Perspective." *Feminist Studies* 14, no. 3 (1988): 575–99.

Harvey, David. "The Right to the City." *New Left Review* no. 53 (2008): 23–40.

Haynesworth, Shellée. "Black Broadway on U: A Transmedia Project." 2014. https://Blackbroadwayonu.com/.

Headlee, Celeste. *We Need to Talk: How to Have Conversations That Matter.* New York: HarperCollins, 2017.

hooks, bell. 2014. *Teaching To Transgress.* Routledge, [1994], 2014.

Hopkinson, Natalie. *Go-Go Live: The Musical Life and Death of a Chocolate City.* Durham, NC: Duke University Press, 2012.

"How Often Are Women Interrupted by Men? Here's What the Research Says." *Advisory*, July 7, 2017. https://www.advisory.com/daily-briefing/2017/07/07/men-interrupting-women.

Hsu, W. F. Umi. "Digital Ethnography Toward Augmented Empiricism: A New Methodological Framework." *Journal of Digital Humanities* 3, no. 1 (2014): 43–61.

Hubbard, Phil, and Loretta Lees. "The Right to Community?" *City* 22, no. 1 (2018): 8–25.

Hughes, Langston. *The Big Sea: An Autobiography.* New York: Knopf, 1945.

Hunter, Marcus Anthony, Mary Pattillo, Zandria F. Robinson, and Keeanga-Yamahtta Taylor. "Black Placemaking: Celebration, Play, and Poetry." *Theory, Culture & Society* 33, no. 7–8 (2016): 31–56.

Hurston, Zora Neale. *Mules and Men.* New York: Amistad, [1935] 2008.

Hyra, Derek S. *Race, Class, and Politics in the Cappuccino City.* Chicago: University of Chicago Press, 2017.

Jackson, John L. Jr. *Thin Description: Ethnography and the African Hebrew Israelites of Jerusalem.* Cambridge, MA: Harvard University Press, 2013.

Jackson, Travis A. *Blowin' the Blues Away: Performance and Meaning on the New York Jazz Scene.* Berkeley: University of California Press, 2012.

Jaji, Tsitsi. 2014. *Africa in Stereo: Modernism, Music, and Pan-African Solidarity.* New York: Oxford University Press.

James, Cordilia. "D.C. Has Had the Most Gentrifying Neighborhoods in the Country, Study Finds." *DCist* (blog), March 19, 2019. https://dcist.com/story/19/03/19/d-c-has-had-the-most-gentrifying-neighborhoods-in-the-country-study-finds/.

Jemisin, N. K. *The City We Became*. Boston: Orbit Books, 2020.

Johnson, Azeezat, Remi Joseph-Salisbury, and Beth Kamunge. *The Fire Now: Anti-Racist Scholarship in Times of Explicit Racial Violence*. London: Bloomsbury Publishing, 2018.

Johnson, Gaye Theresa. *Spaces of Conflict, Sounds of Solidarity: Music, Race, and Spatial Entitlement in Los Angeles*. Berkeley: University of California Press, 2013.

Jokinen, Johanna Carolina, and Martina Angela Caretta. "When Bodies Do Not Fit: An Analysis of Postgraduate Fieldwork." *Gender, Place & Culture* 23, no. 12 (2016): 1665–76.

Jones, Alisha Lola. *Flaming? The Peculiar Theopolitics of Fire and Desire in Black Male Gospel Performance*. New York: Oxford University Press, 2020.

Jones, Leroi. *Blues People: Negro Music in White America*. New York: Harper Perennial, 1999.

Jordan, Meagan. "How a Celebration of Go-Go Music Became a Scapegoat for Violence in D.C." *Rolling Stone*, July 2, 2022. https://www.rollingstone.com/music/music-features/how-a-celebration-of-go-go-music-became-a-scapegoat-for-violence-in-d-c-1372069/.

Kapchan, Deborah. *Theorizing Sound Writing*. Middletown, CT: Wesleyan University Press, 2017.

Keeling, Kara. *Queer Times, Black Futures*. New York: NYU Press. 2019.

King, Deborah K. "Multiple Jeopardy, Multiple Consciousness: The Context of a Black Feminist Ideology." *Signs* 14, no. 1 (1988): 42–72.

Kubota, Samantha, Jesse Burkett-Hall, and Josh Bernstein. "DC 'Most Dangerous Place to Give Birth in the US' for Black Women." *WUSA 9*, October 17, 2018.

Lang, Marissa J. "'A Different Kind of Cellphone Store': Business Was a D.C. Staple Long before Go-Go's Brief Silence." *Washington Post*, April 12, 2019. https://www.washingtonpost.com/local/a-different-kind-of-cellphone-store-business-was-a-dc-staple-long-before-go-gos-brief-silence/2019/04/12/735a7498-5d23-11e9-a00e-050dc7b82693_story.html.

Lazo, Luz. "Violating D.C. Traffic Laws Could Soon Cost You More." *Washington Post*, September 26, 2018. https://www.washingtonpost.com/transportation/2018/09/26/violating-dc-traffic-laws-could-soon-cost-you-more/.

Leen, Jeff, Jo Craven, David Jackson, and Sari Horwitz. "District Police Lead Nation in Shootings." *Washington Post*, November 15, 1998.

Lees, Loretta, Hyun Bang Shin, and Ernesto López-Morales. *Planetary Gentrification*. New York: Wiley, 2016.

Levin, Sam. "Guards for North Dakota Pipeline Could Be Charged for Using Dogs on Activists." *The Guardian*, October 26, 2016. https://www.theguardian.com/us-news/2016/oct/26/north-dakota-pipeline-protest-guard-dogs-charges.

Liebow, Elliot. *Tally's Corner; A Study of Negro Streetcorner Men. With a Foreword by Hylan Lewis*. Boston: Little, Brown, 1967.

Lindsey, Treva B. *Colored No More: Reinventing Black Womanhood in Washington, D.C.* Champaign: University of Illinois Press, 2017.

Lingold, Mary Caton, Darren Mueller, and Whitney Trettien. *Digital Sound Studies*. Durham, NC: Duke University Press, 2018.

Lipsitz, George. *How Racism Takes Place*. Philadelphia: Temple University Press, 2011.

Lock, Margaret M., and Judith Farquhar. *Beyond the Body Proper: Reading the Anthropology of Material Life*. Durham, NC: Duke University Press, 2007.

Lockhart, P. R. "'A Multibillion-Dollar Toll': How Cash Bail Hits Poor People of Color the Hardest." *Vox*, December 6, 2017. https://www.vox.com/identities/2017/12/6/16739622/ucla-report-bail-low-income-race.

Lomax, Tamura. *Jezebel Unhinged: Loosing the Black Female Body in Religion and Culture*. Durham, NC: Duke University Press, 2018.

Lornell, Kip, and Charles C. Stephenson. *The Beat! Go-Go Music from Washington, D.C.* Jackson: University Press of Mississippi, 2009.

Lowery, Wesley. *They Can't Kill Us All: Ferguson, Baltimore, and a New Era in America's Racial Justice Movement.* Boston: Little, Brown, 2016.

Lowery, Wesley. "Why There Was No Racial Reckoning." *The Atlantic*, February 8, 2023. https://www.theatlantic.com/ideas/archive/2023/02/tyre-nichols-death-memphis-george-floyd-police-reform/672986/.

Makalintal, Bettina. "A Deep Dive Into the 'Gentrification Font.'" *Vice*, September 9, 2020. https://www.vice.com/en/article/ep499w/gentrification-font-meme-neutraface.

Martinez, Natalia. "City Buys Home Rented by Breonna Taylor's Ex-Boyfriend for $1 as New Allegations Arise." *WAVE*, July 6, 2020. https://www.wave3.com/2020/07/06/city-buys-home-rented-by-breonna-taylors-ex-boyfriend-new-allegations-arise/

May, Vivian M. *Pursuing Intersectionality, Unsettling Dominant Imaginaries.* New York: Routledge, 2015.

McKittrick, Katherine. *Dear Science and Other Stories.* Durham, NC: Duke University Press, 2021.

"Mission." Harriet's Wildest Dreams. https://www.harrietsdreams.org/mission (accessed January 9, 2024).

Modan, Gabriella Gahlia. *Turf Wars: Discourse, Diversity, and the Politics of Place.* Wiley, 2008.

Morrison, Matthew D. "Race, Blacksound, and the (Re)Making of Musicological Discourse." *Journal of the American Musicological Society* 72 no. 3 (2019): 781–823.

Moskowitz, P. E. 2017. *How to Kill a City: Gentrification, Inequality, and the Fight for the Neighborhood.* New York: Bold Type Books.

Muhammad, Khalil Gibran. *The Condemnation of Blackness: Race, Crime, and the Making of Modern Urban America, With a New Preface.* Cambridge, MA: Harvard University Press, 2019.

Muñoz, José Esteban. *Cruising Utopia: The Then and There of Queer Futurity.* New York: NYU Press, 2009.

Murphy, Yume. "One Year After #BlackoutTuesday, What Have Companies Really Done for Racial Justice?" *Vox*, June 2, 2021. https://www.vox.com/the-goods/22463723/Blackout-tuesday-blm-sephora-starbucks-nike-glossier.

Nash, Jennifer C. *Black Feminism Reimagined: After Intersectionality.* Durham, NC: Duke University Press, 2019.

Naveed, Minahil. "Income Inequality in DC Highest in the Country." *DC Fiscal Policy Institute*, December 15, 2017. https://www.dcfpi.org/all/income-inequality-dc-highest-country/.

O'Connell, Jonathan. "District Suit Alleges Mismanagement at Howard Theatre." *Washington Post*, March 8, 2018. https://www.washingtonpost.com/local/district-suit-alleges-mismanagement-at-howard-theatre/2018/03/07/b9619ab4-224d-11e8-badd-7c9f29a55815_story.html.

Ortiz, Erik. "New NFL Policy Will Fine Teams If Players Kneel during National Anthem." *NBC News*, May 24, 2018. https://www.nbcnews.com/news/us-news/nfl-announces-new-national-anthem-policy-fines-teams-if-players-n876816.

Parham, Marisa. "break.dance," *Sx Archipelagos*, no. 3 (2019). https://archipelagosjournal.org/issue03/parham/parham.html.

Pattillo, Mary. *Black Picket Fences: Privilege & Peril among the Black Middle Class.* Chicago: University of Chicago Press, 2013.

Pedersen, Morten Axel, Kristoffer Albris, and Nick Seaver. "The Political Economy of Attention." *Annual Review of Anthropology* 50, no. 1 (2021): 309–25.

Perry, Imani. *May We Forever Stand: A History of the Black National Anthem.* Chapel Hill: University of North Carolina Press, 2018.

Pijanowski, Bryan C., Luis J. Villanueva-Rivera, Sarah L. Dumyahn, Almo Farina, Bernie L. Krause, Brian M. Napoletano, Stuart H. Gage, and Nadia Pieretti. "Soundscape Ecology: The Science of Sound in the Landscape." *BioScience* 61, no. 3 (2011): 203–16.

Pinchback, Lloyd A. *The Soul Searchers 1968–1978: A Decade of Memories*. Largo, MD: Pinchbax Books, 2013.

Platon, Adelle. "Bruno Mars 'Latina' Cover Story: Details from the Interview." *Billboard*, January 31, 2017.

Prince, Sabiyha. *African Americans and Gentrification in Washington, D.C.: Race, Class and Social Justice in the Nation's Capital*. Farnham, UK: Ashgate Publishing, 2014.

Quashie, Kevin. *The Sovereignty of Quiet: Beyond Resistance in Black Culture*. New Brunswick, NJ: Rutgers University Press, 2012.

Quintero, Michael Birenbaum. "Loudness, Excess, Power: A Political Liminology of a Global City of the South." In *Remapping Sound Studies*, edited by Jim Sykes and Gavin Steingo, 135–55. Durham, NC: Duke University Press, 2019.

Ramírez, Margaret M. "City as Borderland: Gentrification and the Policing of Black and Latinx Geographies in Oakland." *Environment and Planning D: Society and Space* 38, no. 1 (2020): 147–66.

Rankine, Claudia. *Citizen: An American Lyric*. Minneapolis: Graywolf Press, 2014.

Rawson, Katie, and Trevor Muñoz. "Against Cleaning." *Curating Menus* 6, 2016. http://www.curatingmenus.org/articles/against-cleaning/.

Raymond, Elora Lee, Ben Miller, Michaela McKinney, and Jonathan Braun. "Gentrifying Atlanta: Investor Purchases of Rental Housing, Evictions, and the Displacement of Black Residents." *Housing Policy Debate* 31, no. 3–5 (2021): 818–34.

Reese, Ashanté M. *Black Food Geographies: Race, Self-Reliance, and Food Access in Washington, D.C.* Chapel Hill: University of North Carolina Press, 2019.

Rosa, Jonathan. *Looking Like a Language, Sounding Like a Race*. New York: Oxford University Press, 2019.

Rose, Tricia. *Black Noise: Rap Music and Black Culture in Contemporary America*. Middletown, CT: Wesleyan University Press, 1994.

Rosenfeld, Paul. "Keeping Go-Go Music Going in a Gentrifying D.C." *The Atlantic*, November 28, 2015. https://www.theatlantic.com/video/index/417780/keeping-go-go-going-in-a-gentrifying-dc/.

Roy, Ananya. "Racial Banishment." *Keywords in Radical Geography: Antipode at 50* (2019): 227–30.

Ruble, Blair A. *Washington's U Street: A Biography*. Baltimore: Johns Hopkins University Press, 2012.

Rusert, Britt, and Witney Battle-Baptiste. *W. E. B. Du Bois's Data Portraits: Visualizing Black America*. Princeton, NJ: Princeton Architectural Press, 2018.

Schafer, R. Murray. *The Tuning of the World*. New York: Knopf, 1977.

Shabazz, Rashad. *Spatializing Blackness: Architectures of Confinement and Black Masculinity in Chicago*. Champaign: University of Illinois Press, 2015.

Shange, Savannah. "Black Girl Ordinary: Flesh, Carcerality, and the Refusal of Ethnography." *Transforming Anthropology* 27, no. 1 (2019): 3–21.

Sharpe, Christina. *In the Wake: On Blackness and Being*. Durham, NC: Duke University Press, 2016.

Shaver, Katherine. "D.C. Has the Highest 'Intensity' of Gentrification of Any U.S. City, Study Says." *Washington Post*, March 3, 2019. https://www.washingtonpost.com/transportation/2019/03/19/study-dc-has-had-highest-intensity-gentrification-any-us-city/.

Silva, Denise Ferreira da. "To Be Announced: Radical Praxis or Knowing (at) the Limits of Justice." *Social Text* 31, no. 1 (2013): 43–62.

Smith, Clint. "When People Say, 'We Have Made It through Worse Before.'" *Wildness*, May 2019. https://readwildness.com/19/smith-people.
Smith, Danez. *Don't Call Us Dead: Poems*. Minneapolis: Graywolf Press, 2017.
Smith, Max. "DC Dangerous Intersections 2018." *WTOP*, February 27, 2019. https://wtop.com/dc/2019/02/the-most-dangerous-d-c-intersections-of-2018/.
Smith, Neil. *The New Urban Frontier: Gentrification and the Revanchist City*. New York: Routledge, 1996.
Smith, Rend. "Exclusive: A Look at MPD's 'Go-Go Report.'" *Washington City Paper*, July 14, 2010. http://washingtoncitypaper.com/article/471073/exclusive-a-look-at-mpds-go-go-report/.
Smith, Suzanne. "Tuning Into the 'Happy Am I' Preacher: Researching the Radio Career of Elder Lightfoot Solomon Michaux." *Sounding Out* (blog), March 5, 2015. https://soundstudiesblog.com/2015/03/05/tuning-into-the-happy-am-i-preacher-researching-the-radio-career-of-elder-lightfoot-solomon-michaux/.
Society for Ethnomusicology. "Position Statement on Torture." February 2, 2007. https://www.ethnomusicology.org/page/PS_Torture.
"Song Meter SM4 Wildlife Audio Recorder." Wildlife Acoustics. https://www.wildlifeacoustics.com/products/song-meter-sm4 (accessed August 26, 2024).
Southern, Eileen. *The Music of Black Americans: A History*, 3rd ed. New York: Norton [1972], 1997.
Southern, Eileen, ed. *Readings in Black American Music*. 2nd edition. New York: Norton, 1983.
Spillers, Hortense J. "Mama's Baby, Papa's Maybe: An American Grammar Book." *Diacritics* 17, no. 2 (1987): 65–81.
Stein, Perry. "Why Are Bike Lanes Such Heated Symbols Of Gentrification?" *Washington Post*, November 12, 2015. https://www.washingtonpost.com/news/local/wp/2015/11/12/why-are-bike-lanes-such-heated-symbols-of-gentrification/.
Stein, Perry. "Net Worth of White Households in D.C. Region Is 81 Times That of Black Households." *Washington Post*, November 2, 2016. https://www.washingtonpost.com/news/local/wp/2016/11/02/net-worth-of-white-households-in-d-c-region-is-81-times-greater-than-black-households/.
Sterne, Jonathan. *The Audible Past: Cultural Origins of Sound Reproduction*. Durham, NC: Duke University Press, 2003.
Sterne, Jonathan. *The Sound Studies Reader*. New York: Routledge, 2012.
Stevens, Matt. 2019. "Joe Biden Says 'Poor Kids' Are Just as Bright as 'White Kids.'" *New York Times*, August 9, 2019. https://www.nytimes.com/2019/08/09/us/politics/joe-biden-poor-kids.html.
Stock, Jonathan, and Chou Chiener. "Fieldwork at Home: European and Asian Perspectives." In *Shadows in the Field: New Perspectives for Fieldwork in Ethnomusicology*, edited by Gregory Barz and Timothy Cooley. New York: Oxford University Press, 2008.
Stoever, Jennifer Lynn. *The Sonic Color Line: Race and the Cultural Politics of Listening*. New York: NYU Press, 2016.
Stone, Ruth M. "'Ebola in Town': Creating Musical Connections in Liberian Communities During the 2014 Crisis in West Africa." *Africa Today* 63, no. 3 (2017): 79–97.
Summers, Brandi Thompson. *Black in Place: The Spatial Aesthetics of Race in a Post-Chocolate City*. Chapel Hill: University of North Carolina Press, 2019.
Taber, Jake. "Q+A: Stephan Pennington Talks Music History, Cultural Appropriation." *The Tufts Daily* (blog), April 16, 2015. https://tuftsdaily.com/features/2015/04/16/qa-stephan-pennington-talks-music-history-cultural-appropriation/.
Táíwò, Olúfẹ́mi O. *Elite Capture: How the Powerful Took Over Identity Politics*. Chicago: Haymarket Books, 2022.

Bibliography 219

"The Right to Community?" https://www.tandfonline.com/doi/epdf/10.1080/13604813.2018.1432178?needAccess = true&role = button (accessed February 19, 2023).

Tolson, Arthur L. "Historical and Modern Trends in Black Capitalism." *The Black Scholar* 6, no. 7 (1975): 8–14.

Tuan, Yi-Fu. *Space and Place: The Perspective of Experience*. Minneapolis: University of Minnesota Press, 1977.

Turino, Thomas. *Music as Social Life: The Politics of Participation*. Chicago: University of Chicago Press, 2008.

Walcott, Rinaldo. *The Long Emancipation: Moving toward Black Freedom*. Durham, NC: Duke University Press Books, 2021.

Wang, Tricia. 2016. "Why Big Data Needs Thick Data." *Ethnography Matters*, December 5, 2016. https://medium.com/ethnography-matters/why-big-data-needs-thick-data-b4b3e75e3d7.

Wartofsky, Alona. "The Mother Who Gave Go-Go Its First Big Push." *Washington Post*, February 1, 2003. https://www.washingtonpost.com/archive/lifestyle/2003/02/01/the-mother-who-gave-go-go-its-first-big-push/15cc724b-b1b1-40bb-a3a3-ec3690dda78d/.

Wartofsky, Alona. "The Success of Moechella and #DontMuteDC Is Galvanizing Go-Go." *Washington City Paper*, May 16, 2019. https://washingtoncitypaper.com/article/180244/moechella-is-just-the-beginning/.

"Wells Fargo CEO: 'A Watershed Moment.'" Wells Fargo Stories, June 19, 2020. https://stories.wf.com/wells-fargo-ceo-a-watershed-moment/.

Weheliye, Alexander. *Phonographies: Grooves in Sonic Afro-Modernity*. Durham, NC: Duke University Press, 2005.

Wheeler, Linda. 2000. "D.C. Slave Emancipation Day Declared a Holiday." *Washington Post*, March 30, 2000. https://www.washingtonpost.com/archive/local/2000/03/30/dc-slave-emancipation-day-declared-a-holiday/1c0fa519-c076-4745-8f0e-683908b94b88/.

Williams, Brett. *Upscaling Downtown: Stalled Gentrification in Washington, D.C*. Ithaca, NY: Cornell University Press, 1988.

Wilson, Matthew W. *New Lines: Critical GIS and the Trouble of the Map*. Minneapolis: University of Minnesota Press, 2017.

Wong, Deborah. "Moving: From Performance to Performative Ethnography and Back Again." In *Shadows in the Field: New Perspectives for Fieldwork in Ethnomusicology*, edited by Gregory Barz and Timothy Cooley. New York: Oxford University Press, 2008.

Worthington, Garrettson Snethen. *The Black Code of the District of Columbia, in Force September 1st, 1848*. A. & F. Anti-Slavery Society, 1848.

Wang, Yanan. "D.C.'s Chinatown Has Only 300 Chinese Americans Left, and They're Fighting to Stay." *Washington Post*, July 18, 2015. https://www.washingtonpost.com/lifestyle/style/dcs-chinatown-has-only-300-chinese-americans-left--and-fighting-to-stay/2015/07/16/86d54e84-2191-11e5-bf41-c23f5d3face1_story.html.

Zukin, Sharon. *The Cultures of Cities*. Cambridge, MA: Blackwell, 1996.

Index

For the benefit of digital users, indexed terms that span two pages (e.g., 52–53) may, on occasion, appear on only one of those pages.

Figures are indicated by an italic *f* following the page number.

"1 Thing" (song), 156*f*, 156–57
4th of July, 77
7th Street and Florida Avenue Northwest, DC, 12–13, 24–25, 27–28, 29–30, 93–94, 95–128, 140–41, 152, 169–70, 174–75, 194–95
"9, The" (show), 51–52
9:30 Club, 49, 78–79, 150*f*
20Bello, 148–49n.30
24K Magic (album), 23–24
"400 Years" (song), 192–93
911 (band), 132–33

Aalbers, Manuel B., 5–6n.12
ableism, 77–78n.36, 121–22
abolitionism, 172–73, 199–200, 204–5
  abolitionist anthropology, 59–60
Abu-Lughod, Lila, 99–100, 99n.7
abundance, 75–76, 142–43, 149, 149n.31, 153–55, 157
accents, 2n.5, 105–6, 192–93
accessibility, 88, 121, 149n.31
accountability, 45, 73, 187–88
activism, 30, 38, 41, 44–45, 126–27, 148, 184, 199–201
  and Black women, 15, 28–29, 44–45
  and music, 73–75, 140–41, 189–93
  See also Black Lives Matter Movement; #DontMuteDC
Adele, 19–20, 78, 133–34, 203
Adeyemi, Kemi, 33, 67–68, 70–71
adlibs, 45–46, 110, 118, 121
AdMo neighborhood, 51
Advisory Neighborhood Commissions (ANCs), 27–28, 87–89, 91
affirmations, 4, 42–43, 47–48, 93–94, 122
affordability, 6–7, 41–42, 77, 88, 208–9
  and musicians, 34–36, 37–38
  See also economics; finances

African American Vernacular English, 201–2
African diaspora, 3n.8, 16–17, 67–68, 70–71, 93–94, 117–18
  and music, 22–23, 45, 130–31, 153–56, 157, 192–93, 195–96
Afrobeat, 103, 153–55
Agard-Jones, Vanessa, 11–12
agency, 13–14, 14n.37
aggression, 30–31, 80, 90, 132–33, 176–77, 185
Aguilera, Christina, 19–20
Airbnb, 71
Alabama Shakes, 54
alcohol, 87–88, 111–12, 129–30, 177–78, 202–3
Ali, Abdul, 105
Allen, William Francis, 3–4
All Jokes Aside (AJA), 134–35
Allure Band, the, 23–24
All Woman Everything (AWE), 42–48
Alphabet Bands, 134–35
Ambition Band, 198
amenities, 8, 51, 82, 88, 89–90, 93, 144–46, 174, 184
Americanness, 20–21, 24, 38–42
America's Got Talent, 191–92
"America the Beautiful" (song), 38–39
Amerie, 156*f*
amplification, 10–11, 15–16, 81
Amplified Noise Act (ANA), 6, 30–31, 175, 176–96, 182n.14, 182n.14, 187n.24, 189n.27
Anacostia, 148, 148n.28, 184
Anacostia Arts Center, 36–37, 126
Anacostia Community Museum, 172–73
Anacostia Park, 1, 150*f*
Anacostia River, 44, 172–73
Anderson, Elijah, 7–8, 9–10
anger, 185–86, 189

anthropology, 9–10, 11–12, 25, 25n.59, 65n.7, 69–70, 71–72, 74–75, 99–100
abolitionist, 59–60
anti-Blackness, 20–21, 33, 46–47, 59–60, 93
antiphony, 22–23, 84, 130–31
See also call and response
apathy, 34–35, 35n.10, 37, 49
appropriation, 5–6, 14–15, 159–61, 161n.37, 162–64, 165
ArcGIS, 143, 149n.31
Area Median Income (AMI), 35
Arie, India, 29n.68
Arts Walk, 42n.22
Asch, Chris Meyers, 9–10
audiences, 4, 49, 51–52, 78–79, 79n.38, 131, 155–56, 166
and Black music, 22–23, 35, 54, 78
and Black queer women's music, 41, 50–51
and go-go, 130–31, 139–40
auralities, 11–12, 15, 66–67, 68, 69–70, 82, 185–86
Austin, Texas, 195–96
authenticity, 77, 84–85, 160–61, 162, 164–65
Ayre Rayde, 132
Azalea, Iggy, 159

"Back that Azz Up" (song), 155–56
Backyard Band, 104, 132–34, 137f, 139–40, 148, 153–55, 158–59, 166–67, 202–3, 205
Bailey, Moya, 163–64
Bailey, Pearl, 72
ballads, 19–20, 78
Band of Angels, 172–73
Baraka, Amiri, 122
Barry, Marion, 9, 17–18
Barry Farms housing project, 44–45, 152, 172–73
Baylor, Mechelle, 112–13
"Beauty" (song), 50
Beauty Island, 103
bebop music, 85
beeping, 171–72, 174–75
and 7th and Florida, 96, 99, 100, 103, 106, 119–21, 122, 125, 127
"Before I Let Go" (song), 100
Be'la Dona, 101, 133–34
belting, 19–20, 114, 126
BET Awards, 108n.17
Beverly, Frankie, 100

Beyoncé, 20, 155–56, 156f
bicycles, 72, 89–90, 90n.56
Biden, Joe, 187n.25, 197–98
big band music, 85, 125
Big Chair, the, 172–73
Big G, 132–33, 139–40, 158–59, 166–67, 205
Big Ugly Truck, 189–91, 189–90n.28
"Big Yellow Taxi" (song), 92
Black Alley, 168, 168n.1, 202–3
Black branding, 159, 201–2
Black Broadway, 71–72, 73–74, 85, 87, 93–94, 189n.27
Black Church, 18–19, 24–25, 73–74, 76n.34, 86
Black Codes, 179
Blackface, 92n.58, 164–65
Black feminism, 14–15, 29, 57–63, 64n.2
Black freedom movements, 13–14, 17–19, 20–21, 21n.51, 22–24
Black gathering spaces, 31, 136–38, 179
Black life, listening to, 2–5, 9–10, 11–12, 15–16, 16n.40, 24, 29–30, 115, 116–17, 119–20, 130–31
Black Lives Matter Movement, 140n.14, 166, 199–202
Black Lives Matter Plaza, 200–2
Black men, 15, 47–48, 74–75, 162, 191–92, 193
Black middle class, 7–8, 15, 105
Black music genres, 83–87, 129
See also go-go music
Black music month, 197–98
Black national anthem ("Lift Every Voice and Sing'), 18–19, 20–21
Black neighborhoods, 66–70
See also 7th Street and Florida Avenue Northwest, DC; Shaw neighborhood
Blackness, 26–27, 57–58, 117–18, 161, 161n.37, 163
and gentrification, 8–10
and music, 106, 107, 108, 120, 192–93
and sound, 11–12, 15, 80–81, 83, 84–85, 125, 164–65, 188–89, 195–96
and space, 12–13, 71, 74–75
Black placemaking, 67–68
Black political power, 8
Black religious studies, 59–60
Black residents, 4–5, 34n.8, 35, 200–1, 202–3
and 7th and Florida, 102, 126
and ANA, 185–86, 187–88
and gentrification, 73–74, 89, 184–85

Black sound, 10, 11–12, 15, 20–21, 23–24, 29–30, 31, 80, 84–85, 93–94, 109, 116–17, 119–20, 142, 159, 164–65, 176, 183–84, 188–89, 195–96, 201–2
Black Studies, 9–10, 62–63, 66, 140n.14, 172
Black utopias, 172
Black vocal traditions, 19–20
Blackwell, Michelle, 45–46
Black women, 13–14, 26–27, 32, 33, 42–43, 74–75, 162
  and activism, 15, 191
  and knowledge, 29, 62, 163
  liberation of, 32
  musicians, 28–29, 33–56, 133–34
  and soundwalks, 57–63
  violence against, 47–48, 64–65, 64nn.1–2, 163–64, 165
Black working class, 2n.5, 3n.8, 30, 44–46, 74–75, 104, 158–59, 198, 204–5
Black youth, 4–5, 138–39, 140–41, 166, 181
Bland, Sandra, 64–65
Bloombars, 50, 51–52
Blue Note, 146–47
blues music, 78, 85
Body of Evidence, 137*f*
body percussion, 4, 183–84
Bohemian Caverns, 72, 87
Bolash- Goza, Tanya, 9n.24
Boomscat, 56
"Boomscat" (song), 50–51
Boone, Pat, 159
bounce beat go-go, 98, 134–35, 137*f*, 141, 148–49, 151–52, 205
Bounce Beat Radio Show, 141
Bowser, Muriel, 21, 22, 36–37n.14, 126, 140–41, 158–59, 169, 197–98, 199–201
Boyd, Michelle, 5–6
Boyer, Nate, 20–21
Brandy, 23–24
brass bands, 182–83
Broadway Theatre, 78–79
Brookland neighborhood, 42–43, 42n.22
Broomfield, Julien, 97, 98, 101–2
brown, adrienne marie, 38, 173–74
Brown, Anthony, 88–89
Brown, Chuck, 1, 130, 132, 135–36, 137*f*, 141, 153–55, 157, 160–61, 202–3
Brown, Dior Ashley, 37–38, 189–92
Brown, James, 4, 72
Brown, Jayna, 172
Brown, Mike, 65

Browne, Simone, 62–63, 117–18
Buchanan, John "JB," 130, 148
Buenaventura, Columbia, 82n.45
Buffalo, New York, 207
Buggs, 132–33, 152
Burnim, Mellonee, 22n.55, 26–27
Burwell, Reggie "Polo," 134–35
Busboys and Poets, 42
buses, 98–99, 104, 115, 119–20, 127–28
Bush, Billy, 47–48
businesses, 25–26, 36, 48, 144–46, 180–81, 185, 203, 208–9
  and ANA, 194–96
  Black-owned, 52n.31, 86, 112–13, 208
"Bustin Loose" (song), 132, 141, 157, 202–3
"But Anyway" (song), 52–54
Butler-Truesdale, Sandra, 36–37, 146–47
buzz, 83, 84–85
"By Her Side" (song), 49–50
Byrd, Donald and the Blackbyrds, 34

Café Asia, 177–78
California, 126
  Los Angeles, 52–53, 65, 67–68, 70–71, 78
  Oakland, 70–71, 195–96
  San Francisco, California, 78
call and response, 4, 22–23, 84, 130–31, 132, 160, 164–65
  See also antiphony
Campbell, Don, 95–96, 97, 126
Campt, Tina, 109, 110
Cape Coast Castle, 153–55
Capitale, 148, 150*f*
capitalism, 34n.9, 51, 178, 201–2, 208–9
  Black, 198, 198n.1, 202–3
  disaster, 142
  racial, 17–18
Capital One Arena, 191–92
Capital One Center, 180–81
Capital Turnaround, 146–47
Capitol building, the, 7–8
Capitol Hill neighborhood, 172–73
carceral interstice, 12–13
carcerality, 9n.24, 10–11, 12–13, 62–63, 64n.2, 135–36, 151–52, 178, 182–83, 184–85, 208–9
  and sound, 5, 194–95
Caribbean carnival, 72
Carter, Darrais, 66
Castile, Philando, 166
catcalling, 57–58, 61

Catholicism, 42n.22, 148
CBO, 141
Cebul, Brent, 65
Central Communications, 95–96, 95n.1, 97, 98–99, 100–1, 103, 106–7, 108, 110, 112, 114–15, 120–21, 126, 127–28, 152, 169–70, 174–75
Chance the Rapper, 207
chants, 22–23, 93, 130–31, 134–35, 164–65, 189
Chauvin, Derek, 166, 199–200
Che, Mary, 185–86, 188
Check It, 181, 181n.12
Cheng, Will, 4
Cherry Blossom parade, 17–18
Chicago, Illinois, 12–13, 67–68, 69, 70–71, 186–88
Child Protective Services, 181–82
children, sounds of, 60–62, 99
"Chillin" (song), 134–35
Chinatown-Gallery Place neighborhood, 9, 98–99, 176, 180–82, 183–85, 189, 190–91, 193–95
Chinatown neighborhood, DC, 30–31
Chinese American residents, 180–81
Cho, Sumi, 14–15
chocolate cities, 7–8, 8n.21, 45, 56, 132, 146–47, 159, 166–67, 192, 197–205
Christianity, 136, 137*f*
  See also Black Church; Catholicism; churches
Chuck Brown Memorial Park, 151–52
churches, 7–8, 18–19, 71, 76n.33, 111–12
  and activism, 73–74
  and dynamics, 76–77
  Episcopal, 1
  FABC, 24–25
  and gentrification, 2, 5, 86–87
  and music, 68–69, 136, 148
church members, 25–26
cisheteropatriarcgy, 193
citational practice, 95n.1, 189–90, 202–3
cities, concept of, 32–33, 45–46
City Winery, 47–48
civic associations, 87–88
civil rights movement, 73–74, 87–88
civil unrest, 40–41
Civil War, 7–8, 38, 71–72
Clasically Dope, 23–24
class, 7–8, 15, 47–48, 67–68, 158, 165
  See also upper class; working class

Clement, Tanya, 117–18
Clifton, Lucille, 139
Clinton, Chelsea, 151–52
club bass, 121–22
Club Benghazi, 72
clubs, 5, 67–68, 71, 72, 82, 112–13, 129–30, 152, 168
  and go-go, 108, 135–36, 139–40, 144, 148–55, 177–78
Club U, 182n.14
Coachella, 126, 155–56
Coates, Ta-Nehisi, 105, 179n.9
Cocky, 141
Cole, Teju, 46–47
collaboration, 178, 207–8
  musical, 28–29, 45–46, 49, 51–52, 56, 132–33, 155–56, 202–3
Collins, Patricia Hill, 58n.3, 62, 163
Collins, Sam, 79, 80
colonialism, 22–23, 62, 97, 192
colorblindness, 20–21, 22
Combahee River Collective, 13–14, 32
Combs, Sean "Diddy," 198n.1
commercialization, 106, 132–33, 148–49
Community Benefits Agreement (CBA), 144–46, 145n.24
community-building, 42
  and go-go, 130–31, 141, 148, 151–52, 158–59, 198
  and musicians, 35, 51
  and sound, 82, 82n.45, 85
Comprehensive Plan, the, 91–92
Compromise of 1860, 174–75
conga drums, 110, 131, 134–35, 156–57, 160
Congo Square, New Orleans, 183–84
Congress Heights neighborhood, 172–73
Constitution Avenue, DC, 17–18
construction, sounds of, 61–62, 119, 127–28, 174–75
Cooper, Amy, 186n.22
Cooper, Anna Julia, 13–14, 191
Cooper, Christian, 185–86, 186n.22
Cosby Show, The (tv show), 43n.23
Cottom, Tressie McMillam, 32
covers, song, 50, 54, 78, 133–34, 137*f*, 138–39, 191–92
COVID-19 pandemic, 36–37, 62, 72, 127–28, 157, 159, 197–99, 204–5
crank factor, 141, 141n.16
crank go-go, 132–34, 137*f*
Crawley, Ashon, 16n.40

"Crazy in Love" (song), 155–57, 156f
Crenshaw, Kimberlé, 13–14
criminalization, 10–11, 80–81, 84–85, 85n.49, 116–17, 120, 125, 159, 172
  and music, 177n.2, 177–78, 182n.14, 182–83, 184, 185–86, 193
  and sound, 123, 125, 176, 178, 188–89, 193, 195–96
critical cartography, 142
Critical Condition Band (CCB), 134–35
critical GIS, 142
Cross, Richard, 101
crosswalks, 96, 99, 103, 104, 105, 106, 110, 117, 121, 122, 125, 127, 174–75
crowdsourced sounds, 30, 168–69
cultural appropriation, 5–6, 19–20, 23–24, 85–86, 159–60, 161n.37, 201–2
Cyrus, Miley, 23–24

"Da Butt" (song), 108n.17, 132
dancing, 8, 53–54, 67–68, 82, 95–96, 191–92, 202–3, 208–9
  and go-go, 130, 134–35, 155–56
da Silva, Denise Ferreira, 43
data cleaning, 116–19, 118n.27, 122–23
data visualization, 116–17, 143
Davis, Jordan, 4, 5
Davis, Miles, 72
DC9, 146–47
DC City Council, 17–18, 18n.46, 27–28, 36–37n.14, 91–92, 105–6, 184–88, 189–91, 193, 195–96
  and ANA, 30–31, 176–77, 178, 180, 181–82, 182n.14
  See also local government
DC Commission on the Arts and Humanities, 36–37n.14, 36–37
DC Grassroots Planning Coalition, 91–92
DC Legendary Musicians, 36–37
DC Public Libraries, 146–47
DC Studies, 9–10, 33n.3
death and dying, 157–58n.34, 207–8
  and Black people, 165–67
  and go-go, 129–30, 138–41, 139n.11, 157
de Certeau, Michel, 58, 58n.4, 122
dehumanization, 4, 5, 53–54
demographics, 6–8, 26n.63, 52–53, 65, 88, 181
  and music, 144, 145–47f, 166–67
demolition, 6–8, 15, 64–65, 67–68, 111–12, 125, 133–34n.6, 138–39, 152, 172–73

Destiny's Child, 155–56
developers, 2, 37–38, 42n.22, 43, 77, 79n.38, 91–92, 138–39, 158, 183–84
  Black, 86, 144–47
development, 2–3, 5–6, 9, 12–13, 17–18, 24, 25–26, 102–3
  and local government, 88–89
  and music scenes, 33, 45, 86
  and policing, 64–65
Devoe, Bel Biv, 2
Diamond, 138–39
"Die for You" (song), 136
Different World, A (tv show), 43n.23
digital humanities, 25, 62, 116–18
  Black, 29–30, 142
D'ignazio, Catherine, 116–17
disenfranchisement, 32–33
disinvestment, 9, 9n.24, 84–85, 88, 99–100, 173–74, 178, 208
disorderly conduct, 177, 178
displacement, 5–6, 12–13, 30, 51–52, 53–54, 55, 66, 74–75, 93–94, 112–13, 119–20, 125
  and Black women, 32, 37, 46–48
  and gentrification, 172–73, 185–86
  and music, 140–41, 142, 144–49, 145–47f, 153–55, 165–66, 170–71, 174–75
  and sound, 80–81, 93–94, 202–3
District Department of Transportation (DDOT), 89–90
District of Columbia Code, 177
DJ Black House, 141, 148–49
DJ Dave Nada, 174
DJ Dirty Rico, 158–59
DJ Rico, 23–24
DJs, 2, 23–24, 42–43, 189–90, 204–5
DJ Tiffany Schoneboom, 148–49n.30
DMV (DC, Maryland, Virginia), 2, 23–24, 42, 126, 129, 136, 138, 158–59, 168n.1, 189n.27, 202–3
dog parks, 8
dogs, 53–54, 79
"Do it Again (Put Ya Hands Up)" (song), 132–33
Dolezal, Rachel, 160–61, 161n.37
"Don't Mind" (song), 109
"Don't Mute DC" (song), 110
#DontMuteDC, 31, 93–94, 97, 98, 100–1, 102, 108n.17, 140–41, 144, 158–59, 176, 180, 195–96, 203
  movement, 6, 97, 98, 109, 110, 126, 127–28

Dorsey, Thomas A., 69
Douglass, Fredrick, 172–73
"Dreams Deterred" (song), 171–72
drug crises, 84–85
drums, 191–92
    and Black queerness, 38, 50, 51–52, 54
    and go-go, 131, 134–35, 156–57, 160, 162, 164–65, 169–73
    and noise, 177, 181–84
    public, 101, 110, 113, 114
drunken noise, 83, 84–85
DuBois, W.E.B., 4, 9–10, 68–69, 70–71, 143
Duke Ellington, 168
Dunbar Hotel, 72
Dunn, Michael, 4, 5
Durant, Guy, 92, 92n.58
dynamics, 75–82, 91, 93–94, 126

East Capital Street and Benning Road, DC, 12
economics, 9–10, 22–23, 44–45, 52–53, 71–72, 73–76, 102, 195–96
    See also capitalism
EDM music, 177–78
education, 7–8, 17n.44, 29, 135, 149, 169
    See also HBCUs; Howard University
Eidsheim, Nina, 3n.7
Ellington, Duke, 71, 78–79
Ellis, Chip, 86, 144–47
Emancipation Day, 17–24, 18n.46, 21n.52, 140–41, 199–200
Emancipation Proclamation, 17–18, 201–2
emancipatory soundscapes, 24, 202–3, 204–5, 207–8
Empower DC, 77
Episcopal church, 1
epistemology, 129–30, 172
equity, 2, 110, 127, 142
erasure, 80, 98, 126–27, 129, 166–67
Ethiopia, 3n.8
Ethiopian residents, 71
ethnography, 14–15, 24–25, 26–28, 31, 105
    and neighborhoods, 68–71, 74–75, 77–78n.36
    of the particular, 99–100, 99n.7
    See also fieldwork
ethnomusicology, 9–10, 14–15, 16–17, 22n.55, 26–27, 49, 136–38
Evans, Jack, 181–82
eviction, 6, 67–68, 80, 104
exclusion, 14–15, 67–68, 171–72, 198, 208

exclusivity, 78–79, 89, 171–72, 194, 201–2, 207–8
Experience Unlimited (EU), 107–8, 108n.17, 131–32, 136–38
exploitation, 15–16, 45, 181, 198, 201–3

Facebook, 27–28, 136–38, 159, 163–65, 166, 190–91, 205–6
fashion, 8, 67–68, 110–11, 202–3
father, author's, 2
Father's Day, 205
Fauntroy, Walter, 73–74
federal government, 41, 146–47, 172–73, 178, 180, 200–1
Fenty, Adrian, 152
Ferguson, Missouri, 65
festivals, 126, 198–99, 202–8
    music, 151–52, 188–89, 197–99
fieldwork, 12, 24–27, 25–26n.61, 29–30, 52–53, 62–63, 140–41, 198–99
    See also ethnography
filmmakers, 35, 37–38, 72–73, 135–36
finances, 46–47, 86, 178, 208
    and music, 144, 148–49, 158, 162, 182–83, 202–3
    See also affordability; capitalism; economics
Finland, 62–63
fireworks, 121–22
Fitzgerald, Ella, 71
Flor, Dana, 181n.12
Florida, 69–70, 76n.32, 76
Florida Avenue Baptist Church (FABC), 24–25, 83, 86–87, 114–16
Floyd, Donnell, 132–33
Floyd, George, 166, 199–200, 201–2, 205
Folklife Festival, 126
Ford, Christine Blasey, 47–48
foreignness, 170–71, 175
Forman, Murray, 12
Franklin, Kirk, 136
Frazier, Darnella, 166
Frazier, Franklin E., 102–3
freedom, 13–14, 93–94, 110, 192–93, 197–98, 199–200, 201–3, 204–5, 207–8
    struggle for, 17–19, 20–21, 21n.51, 22–24
Freedom Plaza, 17–19, 198, 204–5
Freeman, Kymone, 184, 185–86, 188, 190–91
French language, 192
Fujikane, Candace, 142, 143

funding, 36–37, 48, 189n.27
　and racism, 5, 36–37n.14, 178
　See also DC City Council; local government
funk music, 4, 10, 12, 30, 45–46, 85–86, 169
　and 7th and Florida, 95–96
　and go-go, 130, 132, 137f
Funk Parade, 30, 86, 168–69
Fusion Band, 160–61, 162–65
futurities, 15–16, 24, 31, 56, 204–5

Gallery Place, 9, 176, 180–81, 189
Gallery Place mall, 181
gangsta rap, 132–33
Gaston, North Carolina, 130
Gautier, Ana María Ochoa, 16–17
Gaye, Marvin, 133–34, 159, 168
"Gay Sex" (song), 37–42
Geertz, Clifford, 25
gender, 44, 67–68, 158, 165
　and gentrification, 47–48, 191
　and listening, 14–15, 185–86, 186n.21
　and racialization, 13–15, 163–64
　and sound, 15, 75–76
　See also Black men; Black women; white women
genocide, 38–39
gentrification, definitions of, 2–3, 5–6
gentrifiers, 8, 53–54, 82, 89, 93, 110, 188–89
"Gentry on the Ebon Road" (song), 170–71
geography (discipline), 12–13, 71–72
Georgetown neighborhood, 55, 171–72
Georgetown punks, 55
Georgetown University, 156–57
Georgia, 7–8, 69, 143
　Atlanta, 34, 34n.9, 70–71
Georgia Avenue Day, 72
Georgia Avenue neighborhood, 36, 76, 153–55
Ghana, 132–33, 153–55
ghetto culture, 7–8, 74–75
Glass, Ruth, 2–3, 5–6, 9–10
Glover, Kavon, 205
go-go music, 1, 10, 12, 21, 22–24, 27–28, 29–30, 129–41, 172–73, 189n.27, 191–92, 208–9
　and 7th and Florida, 95–96, 98, 100–42
　and festivals, 198–99, 202–3, 204–8
　and legacy, 157–67, 157–58n.34
　and local scenes, 45–48
　mapping, 142–55, 145–50f

and neighborhood sounds, 62–63
and policing, 179, 182n.14
and pop music, 153–57
See also hip-hop music
Go-Go Report, 179
"Going to a Go-Go" (song), 130
"Gold Differ" (song), 118
Goldlink, 129
Gonzalez, John, 205–6
Google MyMaps, 143
gospel go-go, 136, 137f
gospel music, 19–21, 22–23, 22n.55, 26–27, 87, 105n.13, 130–31
　and neighborhoods, 68–69, 73–74, 78
Gospel Spreading Bookstore, 111, 114–15
Gospel Spreading Church, 76, 76n.33, 77, 111, 115–16
Graham, Jim, 182n.14
Grammy awards, 23–24, 132, 168, 189
Grande, Ariana, 19–20
Grandmaster Flash and the Furious 5, 132
grandmother, author's, 1, 12
Great Migration, 7–8
Green, Anthony Lorenzo, 200–1
green space, 34, 92, 171–72
Gregory, Ayanna, 204–5
grief, 70–71, 139–40, 141
Grim, Valerie, 62–63
grit, 83, 84–85
grooves, 130, 131, 141, 164–65n.46, 191–92
Grown and Sexy go-go, 108, 132–34, 137f
Gumbs, Alexis Pauline, 33
Gun Recovery Unit, MPD, 187–88

Haiti, 192–93, 193n.33
Halfsmoke, 27–28, 104
Hall, Regina, 21n.52
Hall, Stuart, 17n.44
Hannerz, Ulf, 74–75
Harmonious Living Amendment Act of 2021, 195–96
Harriet's Wildest Dreams, 198, 204–5
Harrison, Rich, 155–57
Haynesworth, Shelleé, 33n.3, 72–73, 85, 86, 87, 93–94
HBCUs, 102–3, 108n.17, 155–56, 161, 205–6
　See also Howard University
"Hello" (song), 133–34, 203
Henderson, Wanda, 145n.24
heterogeneous sound ideal, 83, 84
heteronormativity, 14–15, 50, 193

high-rise buildings, 76–77
Hill, Dru, 50
Hillman College, 42–43, 43n.23
Hilson, Keri, 95–96
Hine, Darlene Cark, 66n.8
hip-hop music, 10, 23–24, 96n.2, 130–31, 148–49n.30, 161, 169–70, 189–90, 193, 198
and go-go, 132, 152, 155–56, 170n.2
historically Black colleges, 42–43, 43n.23
holidays, 17–19, 77, 120–21, 122, 197–98
homelessness, 62–63, 77, 189
homeownership, 7–8, 10–11, 36, 44–45
Home Rule Act (1973), 12–13, 12–13n.33, 87–88, 180
homophobia, 41
hooks, bell, 63n.10
Hopkinson, Natalie, 8, 9–10, 12n.30, 98, 100–1, 104, 105, 130–31, 136–38, 139–40, 206–7
Horn, Etta Mae, 44–45, 172–73, 191
horns, car, 60–61, 100, 106, 107, 112, 115, 119–20, 121–22, 127
"Hot in Herre" (song), 132, 156f, 202–3
"Hourglass Betrayal" (song), 192
house music, 10, 148–49n.30, 169–70, 177–78
housing, 71, 77, 152, 172–73
affordable, 35, 41–42, 77, 88
and musicians, 34nn.8–9, 35–37, 41–42
Houston, Whitney, 19–20
Howard Theatre, 71, 72, 78–79, 86, 87, 96n.2, 144–48, 146n.25, 150f, 189n.27
Howard University, 36, 95–96, 97, 98–99, 102, 103–4, 105n.13, 105–6, 109, 160–61, 205–6
Howard University Hospital, 86, 98–99
Howar University, 105
HQB, 141
H Street Corridor, 33n.3, 52–53, 52n.31, 60–61, 171–72
Hsu, W.F., 25
Hughes, Langston, 42, 102–3
Hunter, Marcus Anthony, 67–68
Hurston, Zora Neale, 9–10, 69–71
hybridity, 69
Hylton-Brown, Karon, 200–1
hyperlocality, 130–31, 135–36, 157
Hyra, Derek, 9–10, 74–75, 76n.34, 159

Ice-T, 132–33
identities, 10–11, 63n.10, 66–67, 192–93, 201–2
author's, 25–27
Black queer women's, 51–52, 104
Black women's, 57–58, 59
and intersectionality, 11–12, 13–15
and local government, 89–90
"I Got 5 On It" (song), 164–65, 164–65n.46
improvisation, 35, 47–48, 130, 155–56
inclusivity, 131, 199–200, 201–2
income disparities, 35, 41–42, 44–45
Independence Avenue, DC, 35n.10
indie folk pop, 78
indie soul music, 54
Indigenous cartographies, 142
innovation, 28, 46–47, 67–69, 134–35, 142
Instagram, 204–5
instrumentation, 131, 133–35, 160
interdisciplinarity, 11–12
interiority, 16–17, 69–70, 80–81
interludes, 29, 29n.68, 30
intersectionality, definition, 13–15, 14n.37, 66n.8
intersectional listening, definition, 13–15
intersections, 11–17, 29–30
interviews, 1–2, 25–26, 25–26n.61, 66, 70–71
intimacies, 50, 51–52, 78–79
intraracial conflict, 158
intricacies, 29–30, 141–42
Iverson Mall, 141
Ivy City neighborhood, 47–48

Jackson, John, 25n.59
Jackson, Travis, 84–85
Jaji, Tsitsi, 153–55
Jay-Z, 132–33, 156f, 198n.1
jazz music, 5, 36–37, 45–46, 71, 114, 125, 127–28, 169–70
smooth jazz, 15–16, 29, 34, 64–94, 164
JB, 135
Jemisin, N. K., 32
Jim Crow, 22
joggers, 79–80
John F. Kennedy Center, 41–42
Johnson, Cynthia (CJ), 54–56
Johnson, Gaye Theresa, 67–68
Johnson, James Weldon, 18–19
Jones, Kent, 109
Jones, Prince, 179, 179n.9

Jonson, John Rosamond, 18–19
Jordan, Meagan, 206–7
joy, 41, 67–68, 70–71, 75–76, 173–74
Juan, 141
Jubilee Day, 18n.46
JuJu House, 135
juke joints, 68–69
June, Tarica, 52–56
Juneteenth, 134–35, 197–98, 201–2, 204–6, 207
Junkyard Band, 104, 105, 130–33, 152, 172–73
justice, 14–15, 31, 45, 64n.2, 127–28, 163–64, 166, 199–200
    ephemeral, 43–45, 47–48

Kaepernick, Colin, 20–21
Kapchan, Deborah, 15–16
Karis, 101
Kavanaugh, Brett, 47–48
Kay, Deon, 200–1
Keeling, Kara, 29n.68
Kennedy Center, 126
Khan, Chaka, 126
Killa Cal, 158–59
Kill Mo, 191–93
King, Deborah, 13–14
King, Martin Luther, Jr., 33n.3, 72–74, 189n.27
King Willow, 78
Kirk, Roland, 72
Klein, Lauren, 116–17
knowledge production, 29, 41–42, 58–59, 62, 163
Kokayi, 30, 168–75, 189
Kokayi (Issa), 168
Kwanzaa, 105

Lady Gaga, 134–35
Lamar, Kendrick, 133–34
landlords, 104
languages, 168, 170–71, 192, 201–2
Latinx communities, 65, 170
"Lay it Down," 134–35
lead talkers, 130–31, 132–33, 139–41, 143, 152–55, 160, 164–65, 166–67, 169, 205–6
    and soundscapes, 118
LeDroit neighborhood, 83
LeDroit Park, 60–61, 89–90, 102, 112–13

Lee, Spike, 132
Lees, Loretta, 5–6
Lefebvre, Henri, 12–13
legacies, 36–37, 157–65
Legere, John, 125–26
"Lemon" (song), 100
L'Enfant, Pierre, 7–8
"Let's Get it On," 133–34
Lewis, Ramsey, 72
Lewis, Tony, 126
Liebow, Elliot, 74–75
"Lift Every Voice and Sing" (song), 18–19, 20–21
Lincoln, Abraham, 17–18
Lindsey, Treva, 191
Lipsitz, George, 194
liquor licenses, 87–88, 129–30, 202–3
listening logics, 108, 110
    and intersections, 11–17
    and local government, 90
    and racism, 183–84
    and soundwalks, 58–59
    and violence, 4–5
Listen Local First, 189, 190–91, 195–96
live music, 36–37, 41, 96–97, 127, 130–31, 148–49, 197–98, 204–5
Lloyd, 134–35
local government, 12n.30, 18, 87–93, 158–59, 169, 178, 205
    and racial justice, 199–201
    See also DC City Council
Locke, Alain, 102–3
Logan Circle neighborhood, 83
Lomax, Tamura, 59–60
London, England, 2–3, 77, 153–55
"Lonely Sometimes" (song), 55
Long, Ayanna, 135–36
Long Live Go-Go, 126, 205, 206–7
"Long Walk" (song), 156*f*, 157
looping, 35, 38–39, 49–50, 51–52, 172–73, 174
Lornell, Kip, 131, 136–38
Lorton Correctional Facility, 135–36
Los Angeles Police Department, 65
loss, 46–47, 51–52, 139–40, 208–9
loudness, 4, 5, 10–11, 27–28, 30–31, 37, 75–85, 93–94, 142
    and legislation, 185–86, 194–95
    public, 96, 106, 107, 108, 110–11, 119–20, 121–22

Index

Louisville, Kentucky, 64–65, 178
love, 37–38, 39, 40
Lowery, Wesley, 166
low-income residents, 5, 6–7
Lynch, Donovan, 197–98

MacKay, Ian, 144
Mackey, Stevie, 78
"Made In DC/Hecho in DC" (song set), 169
Malachi, Carolyn, 28–29, 42–48, 56
Malcolm X Park, 1, 171–72
Malik the Dope Drummer, 191–92
Mamatoto Village, 44–45
mapping, 142–57, 145–54f, 149n.31
marching bands, 155–56
marginalization, 14–15, 41–42, 67–68
Maroon 5, 134–35
Mars, Bruno, 23–24
Martin, Trayvon, 76n.32
Marvin's, 159–60
Maryland, 4–5, 25–26, 76, 76n.34, 111–12, 129
  Prince George's County, 2, 26–27, 179
  suburbs, 10, 25–26, 76, 76n.34, 144–46
Maryland Institute College of Art, 204–5
mass incarceration, 9n.24, 22
May, Vivian, 15
Mayes, Stanley, 35, 36, 71–72, 82, 93–94
Mayo, Felicia, 199–200
mayors, DC, 12–13n.33, 64–65, 105–6, 159, 178, 180, 195–96, 198, 201–2, 205, 207–8
Maze, 100
McDade, Tony, 199–200
McDonalds, 181
McDuffie, Kenyan, 126
MCI Center, 9
McKittrick, Katherine, 1n.1, 95n.1
McNeill, Gregory, 96n.2, 100–1, 107
MCs, 132, 169
media coverage, 172, 189, 203, 205–6
  and music, 129, 166–67, 179, 206–7
  and police violence, 64–65, 93, 200n.4
Meeting Place, 148–49, 150f
Meghelli, Samir, 2n.4
Mel, Melle, 132
melismas, 19–21, 78, 102, 112, 114, 121, 126
"Melodies from Heaven" (song), 136
Memorial Day, 201–2
memorialization, 134–35, 157, 159
memory, 1, 72–73, 89, 120, 139–41, 157

Memphis Police Department, 199–200
Mendelson, Phil, 36–37n.14, 182
"Message, The" (song), 132
metaphors, 11–12, 34, 83, 85, 87, 158n.35
methodology of book, 15–16, 23–28, 29–30, 113–15
Metropolitan Baptist Church, 76n.34
Metropolitan Police Department (MPD), 1, 140–41, 176, 178, 179, 187–88, 189–90, 200–1, 205, 207–8
Metro System, 9, 11–13, 51n.30, 149, 171–72, 184
  buses, 98–99, 104, 115, 119–20, 127–28
Miami Takeover, 153–55
"MICCO Theme Song" (song), 73–74
"Michael Row Your Boat Ashore" (song), 73–74
Micheaux, Solomon Lightfoot, 76, 76n.33
middle-class people, 2, 5–6
  Black, 7–8, 15, 105
military, the, 20–21, 38, 76, 189–90
Minneapolis, Minnesota, 168, 168n.1
Minneapolis police department, 166
minoritization, 32, 40, 67–68
Minor Threat, 144
misogynoir, 163–64
Mitchell, Joni, 92, 92n.58
moans, 19–20, 173–74
Modan, Gabriella, 89
Model Inner City Community Organization (MICCO), 73–74, 87
Moechella, 31, 126–27, 152, 198, 204–6, 207–8
"Moombah" (song), 174
Morehouse College, 141, 148–49
Morgan, Adams, 51n.30
Morrison, Matthew, 164–65
Morton, Mary, 73–74
Moses, Robert, 171–72
Mosley, Nicole (aka DJ Heat), 42–43, 44–45, 56
Moten, Ron, 8, 98, 110, 148, 181n.12
Moulden, Dominic, 2n.4
Mount Pleasant neighborhood, 89
movement, 8, 16–17, 59, 84, 174–75
MTM Flavor Gang, 141
Muhammad, Khalil, 188–89
multiple jeopardy, 13–14
Mumford, Lewis, 32
Muñoz, Trevor, 116–17
Muscato, Danielle, 60

Musgrove, George Derek, 9–10
musicians, 25–26
    and ANA, 184–85, 187–88, 191–93, 194–95
    Black, 68, 202–3
    and go-go, 133–36, 139–41, 143, 148, 153–56, 158, 159, 163–66
    queer Black women, 28–29, 33–56
    in Shaw, 77–78
    street, 181–84, 187, 193, 194–96
MusicianShip, 169
music production, 35, 38, 50, 153–55, 169, 202–3
music scenes, 8, 10–11, 28–29, 132–33, 136, 148–49n.30, 153–55, 179, 191–92
    local, 45–48, 55, 130–31, 135–36
music schools, 68–69
Mýa, 56

Nadeau, Brianne, 126, 195–96
Naoum, Chris, 169, 190–91
Nash, Jennifer, 14–15, 14n.37
Nashville, Tennessee, 78
Nathan, Syd, 4
national anthems, 18–21
National Football League (NFL), 19–21
National Gallery of Art, 180–81
National Mall, 120–21, 126
National Park Service, 1
National Symphony Orchestra, 41
nature, 110, 115–16, 172–74
Navy Yard neighborhood, 172–73
neighborhood associations, 10–11, 25–26, 161
    See also community-building
Nelly, 132, 156*f*, 202–3
neoliberalism, 208–9
neo-soul music, 29n.68, 35
Neptunes, The, 202–3
N.E.R.D., 100
New Bethel Baptist Church, 73–74
newcomers, 97, 158–59, 194, 199–200, 203
    and local government, 89, 140–41
    and musicians, 49, 53–54
    and sound, 79, 82, 184
New Impressionz, 134–35, 137*f*, 205
New Negro Womanhood, 191
New Orleans, Louisiana, 155–56, 183–84
Newseum, 35n.10
New York City, 2n.5, 32, 77, 132, 171–72, 186n.22

Nichols, Tyre, 199–200
Nigeria, 153–55
nightlife cultures, 33, 82, 98, 136, 148–49, 157
Nike, 199–200
noise, 3–4, 5, 10–11, 15–16, 24, 30–31
    complaints, 96, 97–98, 102, 110–11, 121–22, 127–28
    and neighborhoods, 77, 79, 82–83, 85, 86, 91, 96
    See also Amplified Noise Act (ANA)
NoMa neighborhood, 51, 51n.30
nonbinary people, 44, 47–48, 64n.2
Nonprofit Corporations Act, 146n.25
Northeast DC neighborhoods, 2, 12, 52–53, 151–52
Northeast Groovers, 132–33, 137*f*
nostalgia, 53–54, 105–6
NPR Tiny Desk Concerts, 55
NWA, 132–33
N'yongo, Lupita, 164–65, 164–65n.46

Ocean, Frank, 29n.68
Office of Cable Television, Film, and Entertainment (OCTFE), 158–59
Oh He Dead, 52–53, 54–56
older generations, 132, 133–34, 137*f*, 148
One Love Massive, 189, 189n.27
ontology, 172
open mics, 2, 42–45, 47–48, 50, 56
openness, 49–52
Open Streets DC, 72
Oppenheimer, Tony, 181n.12
oppression, 13–15, 16–17, 67–68, 93–94, 163–64, 188
    and Black women, 32, 33
Orange, Vincent, 18n.46
Organizing Neighborhood Equity, 77
origins, claims of, 160–61, 164–65, 170–71, 192–93
Our Lady of Perpetual Help, 148
"Overnight Scenario," 132–33
Oxford, Mississippi, 57–58

Page, Cara, 38
palimpsests, 95n.1, 100–2, 113–14, 117, 158
Palladio, 143
Palmer, Terrance, 200–1
Panorama Room, 148, 148n.28, 150*f*
parades, 17–18, 24, 140–41
parenthood, 90, 90n.57
Parham, Marisa, 95n.1

Paris World Fair, 143
parking, 54, 65, 76n.34, 86, 92, 144–46
parks, 1, 34, 34nn.7–8, 60–61, 89–90, 102, 112–13, 129–30, 149–52
Parliament Funkadelic, 8n.21
participant observation, 25, 27–28, 66, 176–77
passive acoustic recording, 25, 27–28, 29–30, 113–14, 113n.21
Patience Sings, 198, 204–5
patriotism, 20–21, 37–39, 40
Pattillo, Mary, 66–67
Peculiar People, 136, 137*f*
Peele, Jordan, 164–65
Pennington, Stephan, 19–20
percussive performance, 84, 130, 134–35
performance practices
  and Black pop, 19–21
  and DJs, 42–43
  and go-go, 45–46, 130–31, 135
  gospel, 22n.55
  and Sofar, 78
Perry, Katy, 23–24
Perry Imani, 18–19
Petworth neighborhood, 75–76, 98–99
Pharrell, 197–98, 202–3
Philadelphia, Pennsylvania, 68, 70–71
"Pieces of Me" (song), 133–34
place, concept of, 12, 15–17, 142, 178
Place Based Investigations Squad, 64–65
Plan, The, 6–7
planetary gentrification, 5–6
pleasure, 67–68, 172, 173–74
  queer, 38, 39, 40, 41–42
pocket beats, 45–47, 131–35, 137*f*, 156–57, 160, 169–70
  and 7th and Florida, 100, 109, 110, 112, 113, 115, 118
policing, 1, 10–11, 20–21, 43, 47–48, 125, 127, 189
  and Blackness, 58–59, 64–65, 140–41, 166, 179n.9, 187–88, 197–98, 199–200
  and gentrification, 51–52, 53–54, 65–66, 75–76
  and music, 30–31, 129–30, 138–39, 140–41, 140n.14, 184, 187–89
  and sound, 79–82, 176, 178, 179, 183–84, 193, 195–96
  and whiteness, 185–86, 186n.22, 194
  See also surveillance
polyrhythms, 130, 182–83

Poole, Chase, 205, 206–7
pop music, 19–20, 78–79, 155–57, 198
population growth, 77, 79
poverty, 7–8, 65, 74–75, 102, 129–30, 173–74, 208
  and gentrification, 5, 77, 204–5
President's Day, 201–2
Presley, Elvis, 159
"Pretty Girl Rock" (song), 95–96
"Pretty Girls" (song), 132–33, 203
pride, 75–76, 168, 185–86, 197–98
Prince, 168
Prince, Sabiyha, 9–10, 44–45
Prince George's County, Maryland, 2, 26–27, 141, 179, 179n.9
Process, The (album), 49–50
Progression Place, 144–46, 145n.23
promoters, 141, 144, 148, 148–49n.30
protests, 20–21, 27–28, 31, 40, 44–45, 93, 134–35, 140–41, 152, 187–88, 189–93, 195–96, 199–200, 201–2
  #DontMuteDC, 125, 126
"Prototype" (song), 102
public housing, 7–8, 15
"Pump Me Up" (song), 132
punk music, 55, 144, 191–92, 193
Pusha T, 202–3

Quadrangle, 103
Quashie, Kevin, 80–81
Queer Love Songs (album), 28–29, 37–38, 56
queerness, 67–68, 191–92
  Black, 33, 37–42, 49–52, 59–60, 197–98
quiet, 75–76, 78–82, 85, 93–94, 105, 117, 194
Quintero, Michael Birenbaum, 82n.45

racial capitalism, 17–18
racialization, 5–6, 26–27, 165, 170
  and 7th and Florida, 100–1, 105–6, 112–13
  and ANA, 176–77, 178, 182, 184, 185–86, 187n.25, 193
  and financial stress, 46–47, 86
  and gender, 13–15, 57–58, 163–64
  and gentrification, 2–3, 8, 10, 25–26, 31, 47–48, 89, 208
  and local government, 36–37n.14, 87–88
  and music, 18–19, 83–87, 92n.58, 136–38
  and Shaw, 73–76
  and sound, 4, 15, 16–17, 23–24, 29, 66–67, 80–81, 93, 125, 164–65, 181, 195–96
  and space, 12–13, 187, 194

racism, 34n.8, 57–58, 170, 171–72, 194
 and Black residents, 4–5, 7–8
 and neighborhoods, 67–68, 74–75
 and policing, 20–21, 199–200
 and song, 19, 20–21, 38–39
radio, 133–34, 158–59
 shows, 2, 27–28, 67–68, 76n.33, 141
 stations, 2, 84–85, 138, 155–56, 184, 189
Ramirez, Margaret, 127
Rankine, Claudia, 53–54, 80–81
rap music, 4, 5, 100, 134–35, 137*f*, 169
rappers, 37, 51–53, 123, 126–27, 132–35, 148–49n.30, 153–55, 164n.43, 198n.1, 202–3, 207
"Rapper's Delight" (song), 132
Rare Essence, 23–24, 126, 132–33, 137*f*, 157, 158–59, 172–73, 198–99, 202–3
Rare Essence Day, 140–41, 158–59
Rawson, Katie, 116–17
R&B music, 10, 23–24, 29n.68, 85, 96n.2, 169, 193
 and Black women, 51–52, 56, 108
 and go-go, 137*f*, 155–56
 style of, 78, 84–85, 133–34
Reaction Band, 134–35, 137*f*, 198
redevelopment, 9, 65–66, 144–46, 148
Reese, Ashanté, 9–10
Reeves Center, 9
Reformance Art, 189–90
refusal, 62–63, 142, 194–96
 Black, 109–10, 111–13, 120
reggae, 153–55
reggaeton, 174
removal, 29, 55, 66, 106, 110
rent gap theory, 5–6
rent prices, 8, 31, 41–42, 43, 51–52, 111–12, 129–30, 144–46, 180–81, 201–2
repetition, 12, 22–23, 49–50, 130–31, 189–90
reproductive health, 44, 44n.25, 47–48, 58–59
Research and Design Lab, Stanford University, 143
resilience, 45–46, 55, 153–55, 171–72, 198, 208
resistance, 41–42, 69–70, 73–74, 80–81, 191, 198
respectability politics, 135–36, 148–49, 183–84
responsibility, 45–47, 195–96
restaurants, 8, 12, 27–28, 42, 96–97, 98–99, 174, 181–82

Reynolds, Diamond, 166
RFK stadium, 152
rhythmic complexity, 83–84, 85, 86, 130, 182–83
Richards, Chris, 206–7
Riley, Amber, 78
riots of 1968, 9, 12–13, 33, 33n.3, 52n.31, 72–73, 84–85
Rock Creek Park, 34, 34nn.7–8
Rockin Rob, 141
Rock & Roll Hotel, 51–53, 54
Rogers, Jake Wesley, 78
Rood, Justin, 169
Rowe, Patience, 50–51
Roy, Ananya, 5–6
Rufus, 126

Saba, 203
safety, 60–61, 106, 107, 170–71, 175, 207
Sankofa bookstore, 36
Santana, Feidin, 166
Santee, Asha, 28–29, 48–52, 55–56
"Sardines" (song), 130–31, 152
#SayHerName, 47–48, 58–59, 64–65, 64n.2
scarcity, 142, 143, 162, 165
Schafer, R. Murray, 58, 194–95
Scott, Jill, 156*f*, 157
Scott, Walter, 166
screaming, 4, 6, 61–62, 65–66, 81, 143
Seaver, Nick, 95n.1
security, 207–8
segregation, 32, 34n.8, 67–68
 and Black music, 68–69, 71–72, 149
sexual assault, 47–48
sexuality, 15, 47–48, 107
sexualization, 30–31, 176–77
Shabazz, Rashad, 12–13, 62–63
Shange, Savannah, 59–60
Sharpe, Christina, 30, 129–30, 139
Shaw, Robert Gould, 71–72
Shaw neighborhood, 9, 29, 33n.3, 52n.31, 60–61, 62–63, 66–67, 70–94, 125–26, 189n.27
 and DontMuteDC, 98
 and Funk Parade, 169
Shay apartment complex, 96–97, 127–28
Sheeran, Ed, 133–34
Shootaz, 141
shout-outs, 113n.21, 203
Shrimp Boat, 12
Sidwell Friends School, 149, 150*f*

silencing, 10–11, 15, 29–31, 80–81, 93–94, 110, 113, 127, 176–77
　and gentrification, 194, 195–96
　and local government, 90, 93
　and music, 165, 183–84
Simpson, Ashlee, 133–34
sirens, 29–30, 60–61, 83, 84–85
　and 7th and Florida, 96, 99, 104, 107, 115, 119–20, 121–22, 123–25
Siri, 100
slavery, 3–4, 7–8, 16–19, 20–23, 21n.51, 153–55, 174–75, 199–200
　and music, 39n.17, 139, 179, 183–84, 192
　and Shaw, 71–72, 76n.34
Smallwood, Richard, 168
Smith, Clint, 208
Smith, Danez, 140–41
Smith, Neil, 5–6
Smith, Sam, 19–20, 78, 133–34
Smithsonian Anacostia Community Museum, 100
Smithsonian Institution, 2, 25–26, 126
Smokey Robinson and the Miracles, 130
smooth jazz, 15–16, 34, 83, 84–85, 87, 164
"SoawesomE" (song), 172–74
social media, 9, 27–28, 53–54, 110, 160–61, 162–65, 166–67, 205
　and activism, 126, 140–41, 184–85, 190–91
　and music, 158, 159, 198–99, 202–3, 204–5
Society for American Music, 181n.13
Society for Ethnomusicology, 181n.13
sociology, 9–10, 9n.24, 69–70, 71–72, 74–75
solidarity, 3n.8, 66n.8, 73–74, 93–94
"SolidGold Waterfront," 174–75
Something in the Water Festival, 197–99, 202–5, 207–8
Songs from a Room (Sofar), 77–79, 77–78n.36
sonic color line, 4, 182–83
soul music, 19–20, 29n.68, 54
　pop-, 78
Soul Searchers, 130–31, 132, 141, 157, 202–3
sound analysis, 113–25
soundproofing, 43, 184, 185, 195–96
soundscape ecologies, 58, 114–15
soundscapes, 29–30, 78, 84, 175
　and 7th and Florida, 95n.1, 98–99, 100–1, 110, 113–25
　Black, 17–18, 20–21, 23–24, 25, 28, 49–51, 70–71, 132, 195–96, 202–3
　conservative, 34–35, 37
　emancipatory, 204–5, 207–8

　of local government, 89–93
　and music, 48, 143, 177–78
　and soundwalks, 58–59, 62
sound studies, 9–10, 58
soundwalks, 29, 34, 34n.6, 57–63, 63n.10
South Carolina, 166
Southeast DC neighborhoods, 2, 141, 148, 172–74
Southeast Settlement house, 172–73
Southern Foodways Alliance, 57–58
Southwest DC neighborhoods, 9, 73–74
space, concept of, 12–13, 15–17, 29–30, 142
　and Black sound, 83–85, 183–84
　and whiteness, 187, 194
Spanish language, 170–71
spatial entitlement, 67–68
spectograms, 119–20
speculative methodologies, 15–16, 23–24, 43–44, 58, 144
speeches, 21–24, 187n.25, 189
Spillers, Hortense, 57–58, 62
spirituals, 4, 68–70, 73–74, 197–98
sponsorship, 126, 140–41, 189–90, 204–7
sports, 2, 9, 19–21, 42–43, 84–85, 168
STABLEArts, 197–98
staccato, 83, 84, 85, 115
Starbucks, 2, 8, 194
"Star-Spangled Banner" (song), 19, 20–21
state, the, 2–3, 5–6, 65, 66, 93
　See also DC City Council; local government
statehood, DC's, 17–18, 21–23, 22n.53, 122, 126–27, 146–47, 199–200
static, 85–86, 87, 93–94
Steadwell, Be, 28–29, 34–35, 36–42, 56
Stephenson, Charles, Jr., 131, 136–38
Sterne, Jonathan, 16–17
stigmatization, 30–31, 158, 176–77
St. John's Episcopal Church, 200
St. Lenox, 95n.1
Stoever, Jennifer, 4, 183–84
Stokes, James, 76–77, 111, 112–13, 114–15, 194–95
Stone, Angie, 23–24
storytelling, 1, 1n.1, 14–15, 29n.68, 57–58, 69–70, 93–94, 157, 162–63, 165–67, 168, 176–77
Straight Crankin (documentary), 158–59
streetcorner men, 74–75
street musicians, 181–84, 187, 193, 194–96
Submission Band, 136
suffering, 38, 51–52, 173–74

Sugar Bear, 107–8
Sugarhill Gang, 132
Sugarhill Records, 132
Summer in the Parks, 1, 151–52
Summers, Brandi Thompson, 9–10, 100–1, 171–72
Superbowl, 19–20
surveillance, 10–11, 60–61, 62–63, 117–18, 183–84, 207–8
Suttle Squad, 133–34, 137f
Sway, Kenny, 190–91
Sweet Cherie, 135, 158–59
"Sweet Thing," 126
syncopation, 83, 85, 131
Sza, 29n.68

Taco Tuesday, 78
Táíwò, Olúfémi O., 201–2
taxation, 22–23, 180
　property, 7–8, 35–37, 41–42, 43
tax rates, 8
Taylor, Breanna, 29, 64–66, 80, 93, 178, 199–200
Teach the Beat, 135
Team Familiar (aka Familiar Faces), 132–33, 137f
Terrell, Mary Church, 102–3, 191
textuality, 17n.44
"That's What I Like" (song), 23–24
thick data, 25, 30
thick descriptions, 74–75
"Thinking Out Loud" (song), 133–34
"This Love" (song), 134–35
"Thurgood Marshall" (song), 95n.1
Till, Emmitt, 4
Till, Mamie, 166
Tillman, Drew, 18–21, 22–23
timbre, 45–46, 84, 105–6, 113, 126, 130, 136
timelines, 120–21, 122–23
TJ, 134–35
T-Mobile, 96, 125–26, 127–28
TOB, 198–99, 202–3, 204–5
torture, 177n.3, 181–82
Total Control Band (TCB), 134–35
tourism, 9, 99, 137f, 153–55, 180–82, 187
toxic masculinity, 208
traffic, 29–30, 60–62, 71, 89–90, 118, 169–70, 171–72
　and 7th and Florida, 95–96, 100, 101, 102, 103, 107, 108, 110, 115, 116, 117, 119, 121–22, 125, 127
trap beats, 19–20, 23–24

trendiness, 71
Trent, Earl, Jr., 83–85, 86–87
Tribble, Jeffrey, Jr., 169
Trouble Funk, 132, 137f, 144, 153–55
Trump, Donald, 38–39, 41, 47–48, 170, 200
Tuan, Yi-Fu, 16–17
Tubman, Harriet, 204–5
Tucker, Sterling, 87–88
Turino, Thomas, 79n.38
Twitter, 27–28, 60, 97, 98, 126, 129–30, 163–64, 205–6

"Unabomber" (song), 132–33, 139–40
Union Stage, 146–47
Union State Presents, 146–47
United Negro College Fund, 144–46
University of California, Los Angeles, 65
University of Mississippi, 57–58
upper class, 105
Upper Northwest DC neighborhoods, 34
urban planning, 2, 58n.4, 99–100
urban renewal projects, 9, 55, 73–74
urban sociology, 7–8
US Congress, 22, 180, 208–9
US Senate, 22
U Street Corridor, 9, 33n.3, 49, 52n.31, 60–61, 71, 72–73, 93–94, 98–99, 112–13, 127, 169, 182n.14
utopias, 8, 24, 172–73

Valenti, Andy, 54–56
"Valerie" (song), 54
Vandross, Luther, 67–68
Vandross, Luther (impersonator), 23–24
Vanny, 191–92
venues, 10, 71, 76n.34, 87–88, 145f, 182n.14
　and gentrification, 78–79
　and go-go, 144–52
　and musicians, 47–48, 49
Vermont Avenue Baptist Church, 83
violence, 17–18, 20–21, 41–42, 46–47, 70–71, 123, 133–34, 207–9
　against Black men, 76n.32, 179n.9, 197–98, 199–200, 200n.4
　against Black people, 117–18, 166, 170, 185–86, 193, 201–2, 204–5
　against Black women, 47–48, 57–59, 64–65, 64nn.1–2, 163–64, 165
　against Black youth, 140–41, 171–72, 205–7
　and discourse, 30, 129
　and gentrification, 5–6, 65–67, 70–71, 74–75, 93, 125

violence (*cont.*)
   and listening logics, 4–5
   and music, 140–41, 148–49, 162, 163
   and sound, 80, 93–94, 107, 195–96
Virginia, 2
   Northern, 129
   Alexandria, 174–75
   Arlington, 174–75
   Fairfax County, 179n.9
   Richmond, 153–55
   suburbs, 10, 144–46
   Virginia Beach, 197–98, 202–3
virtuosity, 78, 141
visuality, 6, 9–10, 16–17, 58, 143
vulgarity, 106, 107, 108–9
Vybe Band, 102, 133–34

wake work, 30, 129–30, 139–42, 157
Walcott, Rinaldo, 21n.51
Wale, 123, 132–33, 134–35, 153–55
Walmart, 201–2
War, Sunny, 54
Wartofsky, Alona, 100–1
Washington, Walter, 12–13n.33
Washington Capitals, 9
Washington Mystics, 42–43
Washington National Opera, 41
Washington Nationals, 132
Washington Wizards, 9, 42–43
waves, gentrification, 5–6, 5–6n.12
We Act Radio, 184, 189, 195–96
wealth, 97, 102–3, 172
   and gentrification, 2, 5, 6–7, 8, 44–45, 184–85
Weensey, 132–33, 158–59
"We Like Money" (song), 45–48
Wells Fargo, 199–200
West, Kanye, 118
West African music, 153–55
Westerkamp, Hildegard, 58
Western classical music, 3–4, 68–69, 105n.13
West Indian residents, 71
Wherewithal Foundation, 36–37
White, Robert, Jr., 126
white ethnonationalism, 170
White House, the, 7–8, 200, 201–2

white men, 38, 40, 47–48, 179
whiteness, 4, 8, 14–15, 20, 26–27, 66, 77
   and appropriation, 14–15, 159–61, 161n.37, 162–64, 165
   and fear, 53–54, 80–81
   and gentrification, 25–26, 53–54, 75–76, 97–98, 127–28
   and local government, 87–88
   and sound, 9–10, 29, 84–85, 86
   and space, 187, 194
white residents, 6–7, 8, 17–18, 22–23, 34n.8, 73, 187–88
   and music, 52–54, 77–79, 86, 138–39
   as newcomers, 67–68, 89–90
   and wealth, 35, 184–85, 187n.25
white spatial imaginary, 194
white supremacy, 3–5, 33n.5, 38–39, 170, 188, 194, 200, 207
white women, 90, 185–86, 186n.22
Whole Foods, 2, 15–16
whoops, 78, 96–97
Wildlife Acoustics Song Meter SM4 recorders, 115–16, 115n.23
Williams, Anthony, 178
Williams, Brett, 9–10
Wilson, Avery, 78
Wilson, Makiyah, 171–72
Wilson, Olly, 83
Wilson Building, 17–18, 190–91
Winehouse, Amy, 54
women and gender studies, 15
Wong, Deborah, 26–27
working class, 2–3, 6–7, 65, 77
   Black, 2n.5, 2–3, 3n.8, 30, 44–46, 74–75, 104, 158–59, 198, 204–5
worship practices, 69, 78, 179, 183–84

XIB, 134–35

Yaddiya, 126–27
younger generations, 133–36, 138, 180–81, 197–98, 205
   See also Black youth
YouTube, 139–40

zoning issues, 77, 91–92
Zukin, Sharon, 183–84